The Oral Tradition of the American West

Adventure, courtship, family, and place
in traditional recitation

Edited by Keith Cunningham
Introduction by W.K. McNeil

CW00953450

August House Publishers, Inc.
LITTLE ROCK

Printed in the United States of America

10 9 8 7 6 5 4 3 2 1

LIBRARY OF CONGRESS CATALOGING-IN-PUBLICATION DATA

Cunningham, Keith
The oral tradition of the American West :
adventure, courtship, family, and place in traditional recitation /
Keith Cunningham.—1st ed
.p   .cm.
(American folklore series)
Includes index.
ISBN 0-87483-150-4 (alk. paper) : $23.95
ISBN 0-87483-124-5 (pbk. : alk. paper) : $11.951
Oral tradition—West (U.S.). 2. Folklore—West (U.S.) 3.
West (U.S.)—Social life and customs.
I. Title.   II. Series.

GR109.C86 1990
398'.0978—dc20   90-43180

First Edition, 1990

Executive in charge: Ted Parkhurst
Project editor: Judith Faust
Design director: Ted Parkhurst
Cover design: Byron Taylor
Typography: Heritage Publishing Company

This book is printed on archival-quality paper which meets the
guidelines for performance and durability of the Committee on
Production Guidelines for Book Longevity of the
Council on Library Resources.

AUGUST HOUSE, INC.   PUBLISHERS   LITTLE ROCK

The Oral Tradition of the American West

AMERICAN FOLKLORE SERIES

This title is part of the
American Folklore Series,
which also includes the
following works:

For Kathy, "my partner…"

Acknowledgments

The twenty-eight reciters who shared their lives and art with me—Carolyn C. Nielsen, my guide to oral performance in the St. Johns, Arizona, area; Clyde and Chris Holyoak, guides to oral performance in the Clay Springs, Arizona, area in 1987 and 1988; and Van N. Holyoak, who fulfilled the same role throughout the 1970s—are responsible for the performances and comments included in this book. The Center for Colorado Plateau Studies, the Northern Arizona University Organized Research Committee, and the Digital Corporation of America helped support fieldwork, transcriptions, editing, and actual writing. While the first group made the book a possibility and the second group helped it become a reality, the responsibility for inferences, theories, analyses, wild guesses, and any errors in transcription is mine, and mine alone.

Keith Cunningham
NORTHERN ARIZONA UNIVERSITY
FLAGSTAFF, ARIZONA

Contents

Introduction

Recitations have received scant attention from folklorists. While there have been occasional collectanea, notes, and even conference papers, the scholarly investigation of American folk recitations dates only from the post-World War II era. To be sure, the existence of such a folk tradition had been noted earlier.

Possibly the first American collector to give more than passing attention to poetic recitations in oral currency was Henry W. Shoemaker. A local enthusiast and chairman of the Pennsylvania Historical Commission during a seven-year period in the nineteen twenties, Shoemaker published a collection of songs and recitations gathered primarily as a result of a newspaper column. In 1919 his *North Pennsylvania Minstrelsy* appeared, followed four years later by a second edition under the same title. In 1931 Shoemaker produced a third edition, this time under the title *Mountain Minstrelsy of Pennsylvania.*[1] This latter edition consists of one hundred four texts and fragments of ballads, folksongs, and local poetry arranged in no discernible order. Although the material is broad ranging, it is unclear what standard was used for inclusion. There is great inconsistency in Shoemaker's notes; indeed it is often unclear whether the comments offered are his own or those of his informants. For most texts some remarks are attached. Sometimes these include source and provenance, but just as often, much less information is given. These comments are filled with such judgments as "this is about right," or "the above is filled with many errors," or "nearly right," assessments that suggest, among other things, collection from memory culture rather than from a living tradition.

It is evident throughout that several of the texts are recitations, although it is not always obvious where and how they were used. Such items as "Friendship on Indian Run," "Song of Old Potter," and "Gilder Roy" may very well have been recited, for they seem more like poems than songs. About some texts, though, there is no doubt that they are recitations, for the accompanying commentary identifies them as such. Thus, the following tantalizing information is appended to the lyric "The Atlantic Cable":

> In lumber camps, where hundreds of men lived together, with few books, such historical poems were chanted, with endless variations and additions, and many learned most of them. I write these from memory of camp chants in 1881-1882, although they were sung in several ways, yet telling the essential facts--John C. French.[2]

Unfortunately, such data is usually missing from Shoemaker's work. That and other weaknesses, such as correspondents admittedly changing words to make rhymes, make Shoemaker's book much less valuable than it otherwise would be. Today, Shoemaker's star has fallen considerably, and for many, he is regarded as "inventive" rather than scholarly. Even so, there can be little doubt that his descriptions of folk recitations are accurate and valuable, albeit limited in both quantity and quality.

Shortly after Shoemaker's collection was published, another, and more prominent, name in Pennsylvania folklore studies began recovering folk recitations in the Keystone State. Shoemaker's material came mainly from woodsmen and lumber workers, but George Gershon Korson's texts were recorded over a period of three decades from miners. Beginning in 1924 Korson started collecting various genres of folklore from Pennsylvania coal miners, eventually publishing his finds in five books and numerous articles. While he commented at great length on several genres, Korson said little about the recitations he collected. Only occasional brief remarks reveal that he was aware of the tradition and had seen it at firsthand. Typical are the following remarks suggesting that recitations often were used to voice protest themes:

> In St. Gabriel's Cemetery, Hazleton, a pioneer anthracite miner's tombstone bears the following epitaph:
>
> > Fourty years I worked with pick and drill
> > Down in the mines against my will,
> > The Coal Kings slave, but now it's passed;
> > Thanks be to God I am free at last.
>
> Interesting is the fact that these stray verses were often memorized by miners and recited in saloons and other places. Thus they entered into oral circulation to become folklore. Invariably, they were the work of Irish or British miners.[3]

At the same time Shoemaker and Korson were active, George Milburn was also recording recitations from hobos. Milburn, a native of Oklahoma, was a short-story writer and collector of folklore who spent some time gathering material in hobo "jungles" and on boxcars. Much of his collection was published in *The Hobo's Handbook* (1930), a book that has correctly been characterized as the source of most "of our knowledge of the American tramp and hobo muse."[4] Mainly a compilation of songs, there are also a number of poems said to be prominent in hobo repertoires. Thus, Milburn documents the existence of the tradition, but like both Shoemaker and Korson, he doesn't go much further. The occasions prompting such recitals, why some items appeal to the folk group and others don't, what makes a good recitationist, and other similar questions are usually not even asked, much less answered. In short, Milburn, like other early collectors of folk recitations, provides little more than texts.

Most of the few studies of folk recitations that exist concentrate on the tradition as it is found among white Americans. There is a vibrant recitation tradition in African-American folklore known as "toasts" that can hardly be characterized as overstudied, but it is the most frequently considered form of black American folk recitation. Toasts are extended narrative poetic recitations that borrow much of their rhyming, rhythmic schemes, and imagery from the traditional ritualized insults called "dozens." In 1970 Roger D. Abrahams, one of the first scholars to study toasts, stated that the bibliography on the topic consisted of only four items—his own article, that of one of his students, one collection of a few texts, and a folktale collection containing a reference to toasts and some texts similar to toasts.[5] The situation has changed in the past two decades so that there is now a more extensive list of studies that can be cited. Many of these publications, however, are like William Labov, Paul Cohen, Clarence Robins, and John Lewis's article "Toasts" in that the approach used is not that of the folklorist.[6]

Roger D. Abrahams' *Deep Down in the Jungle* (1964) is among the most extensive collection of toasts and still one of the most valuable studies of the form. Abrahams recorded his texts in the early nineteen sixties while living in a black neighborhood in South Philadelphia. *Deep Down in the Jungle* is a noteworthy book not only for its extensive collection of texts but for other reasons as well. It was among the first folklore books to concentrate on urban rather than rural lore. It was a pioneering study of ghetto Negro folklore. And, finally, it was an honest, scholarly, unbowdlerized treatment of materials regarded by many as obscene.[7] Abrahams' discussion of toasts is in two respects similar to that of most subsequent commentators on the topic. He tends to overlook the connections of these poems to southern life, preferring to think of them as revelatory of urban ghetto values. Also, although he is aware that white informants relate similar poetry, Abrahams considers toasts essentially a form of Afro-American folklore. Indeed, he even refers to toasts as "the greatest flowering of Negro verbal talent."[8]

With *"Get Your Ass in the Water and Swim Like Me": Narrative Poetry from Black Oral Tradition* (1974), Bruce Jackson produced the second major collection of toasts. Jackson, who has produced several important works on black prison lore, collected his texts primarily from prisoners in Texas and Missouri.

Whereas Abrahams sees toasts providing insights into urban ghetto life, Jackson considers them links to the life of the underworld. The two also differ in their conclusions about the origins of toasts. Abrahams notes that the tradition "is strongly paralleled in the professional medium of the blackface minstrel stage. It is impossible to say with our present knowledge of early Negro lore whether such narrative recitations existed among the Negro before the beginning of the minstrel show and were borrowed by white performers for the minstrel stage, or whether they were an invention of the whites, later borrowed by the Negro and recast. At any rate, we know that in the later history of the blackface show, recitations, often comic ones, became a part of the show."[9]

Jackson, however, suggests that the toast tradition is derived from prison and hobo life. Both men make good points, but too little is known about the tradition's history to enable anyone to make anything more than speculative conclusions about its origins.

As has generally been the case historically with traditions shared by both blacks and whites, both sides of the tradition have not received equal treatment. Except for a number of unanalytical collections on well-known items like "Change the Name of Arkansas" and an excellent treatment of "Lady Lil," there are almost no works on white recitations similar to toasts.[10] It is not difficult to ascertain why toasts and similar recitations found among whites have received little scholarly consideration. The texts are usually what many people consider obscene, and folklorists, as well as most other scholars, have historically been uncomfortable working with such material. The settings are often in barrooms and similar places; the characters are often outlaws, prostitutes, pimps, and others generally regarded as undesirables; and the recitations often deal with drugs, alcohol, and guns. In short, toasts, and related material, are concerned with lifestyles and a class of people that many academics find discomfiting. Most folklorists have been white and have found it easier to deal with such traditions when found among people of a different racial or cultural group, such as Afro-Americans.

With the exception of toasts, there was no significant work on folk recitations until the 1970s. Then, for whatever reason, there was a sudden flowering of interest in the form. The first evidence of this blossoming attention was a 1972 note by Keith Cunningham discussing a recitation he collected from seventy-eight year old Pinedale, Arizona, rancher Horace Crandell.[11] A year later, I published a note on material collected in Stanford, Indiana, from Mrs. Frances Petmecky Smith, an informant of German-English descent. Despite her dual ethnic background, Mrs. Smith's folk traditions all seemed to come from her mother's—the English—side of the family. In her comments Mrs. Smith provided texts and contexts as well, and although she was describing activities of a past era, her remarks are useful because they indicate how and why many folk recitations were and are used.

Mrs. Smith's family frequently had "get-togethers" that required each person present to perform in some manner. Most people offered songs, riddles, games, or tongue-twisters, but some people preferred doing recitations. These were usually nonsensical pieces, spoken as fast as possible in order to heighten the humor.

Mrs. Smith recalled several items her mother performed at these gatherings. One was a song Mrs. Smith called "Bo Ranger," a number of ancient lineage that is believed by some to date to medieval tales about Raynard the Fox.[12] She also remembered a number of recitations, of which the following is the longest:

Finest to a fraction, old Mother Jackson,
Round top and two-toed britches...
Whack, smack, dead pig, dead horse kicked a blind man's eyes
    out.
I saddled up my old Sour Buttermilk
And rode him nineteen miles down the road
Beyond where nobody lived and never will be.
You know the road as well as I do...
There I met old Tom Winkle. I asked him
(which he wouldn't, which he couldn't),
To grind me nineteen rods of steel
Nineteen times as fine as bolted-wheat flour.
He bolted me up to my shins,
Run me back across the barn floor,
Threw me over the barn door,
And broke my neck over the back of the moonshine.
Now all who don't believe this
Has to drink a pint of Pigeon's milk,
Stewed in an old cow's horn
And stirred with a cat's feather![13]

It is of interest that Mrs. Smith said none of her mother's recitations had titles, meaning that her mother referred to them all merely as recitations. That is noteworthy because most published collections give titles for every text as though informants supplied the titles. Mrs. Smith's instance suggests that such titles were not necessarily the rule.

Far more important than these two notes was a session held at the 1974 American Folklore Society meeting in Portland, Oregon. Papers and remarks were delivered by Kenneth S. Goldstein, Robert D. Bethke, Karen Baldwin, and Roger deV. Renwick, making this what still remains as the most elaborate formal discussion of recitations by folklorists. Goldstein and Renwick treated aspects of the tradition in England while Baldwin and Bethke considered American traditional performers of recitations. This panel produced a great deal of interest and floor discussion, some of it quite lively, as a result of which it was decided to compile revised versions of the papers for publication. Ultimately the Portland articles, and four others, were published in *Southern Folklore Quarterly* as "Monologues and Folk Recitations," the first issue of a folklore journal devoted to the topic.

Like the American Folklore Society panel, much of the *Southern Folklore Quarterly* special issue is devoted to British rather than American recitations, but one can't honestly say that the non-American oriented essays are irrelevant to scholars studying the tradition in the United States. For example, Edward Hirsch's essay, "A Structural Analysis of Robert Service's Yukon Ballads," deals with the work of a Canadian poet whose poems are commonly found in the repertoires of recitation performers throughout North America.[14] Goldstein's lead essay, "Monologue Performance in Great Britain," includes important definitions and explanations of why recitations have been generally overlooked by folklorists. He also illustrates how recitations create numerous expectations and responses that are shared between the performer and the audience, a theme echoed in some of the other essays.[15] The eight essays display two basic approaches. The first four are surveys of various aspects of the genre while the last four emphasize the human element by providing field studies of living recitation performers.

Goldstein suggests the term *monologue* be used for a form of oral recitation, defining the latter as "a solo spoken performance of any passage, or selected piece, of prose or poetry." The monologue is "a solo, stylized, theatrically-mannered oral performance from memory of a self-contained dramatic narrative in either poetic or prose form."[16] While most of those commenting on folk recitations would likely agree with the first definition, there is less universal acceptance of the second, mainly because it is a more academic term little used by traditional reciters. Goldstein's essay is, however, a model of the performance-centered approach to the study of folk recitations, focusing as it does on performance style, terminology, performance contexts, performers, repertory sources, acquisition of performance styles, dialect use, and themes. Uncharacteristically for a folklorist committed to the performance school of scholarship, Goldstein argues for the validity of the item-oriented, variant distribution approach in determining the traditional nature of performed texts. He adds a qualifier, though, namely that "we must employ the same theoretical concepts in collecting procedures and comparative textual analysis as we do in traditional ballad and folktale scholarship." Unfortunately, few recitations have been regarded on a par with ballads and folk narratives probably, as Goldstein suggests, because of "preconceptions about their nature."[17] Consequently, few recitations have been accorded the same treatment reserved for ballads and folktales.

All of the essays are important, but especially noteworthy for present purposes are those papers dealing specifically with American recitation performers and performances. Robert D. Bethke's perceptive examination of the repertoire of seventy-one year old Hamilton "Ham" Ferry of Childwold, New York, is an intriguing discussion showing links between popular poetry presentations and traditional ballad singing. For Ferry, recitations are an alternative to singing, and Bethke notes that when he is free of the melodic constraints of the ballad form "and commitment to the Northeast norm for 'tragic songs' of the type he knows, Ham slips easily and confidently into the role of interpretative barroom entertainer."[18] A number of field collectors have called attention to informants who recited ballad texts rather than sang them, but to date only Bethke has discussed at length those traditional artists who utilize recitations in the same manner as ballads.[19]

Karen Baldwin's "Rhyming Pieces and Piecing Rhymes: Recitation Verse and Family Poem-Making" is a pioneering work in two areas.[20] First, it is among the first extended studies of folk recitations, and second, it is an early essay on family folklore, a field that has received more subsequent scholarly attention than recitations. Her paper reveals the sort of

14

useful data that can often be gathered from intensive examination of one's own family traditions. Over a period of at least four generations, her mother's family, the Solleys of Clearfield County, Pennsylvania, maintained an active tradition of "making" and "speaking" recitation poetry. Baldwin demonstrates that these poems served many functions in addition to providing entertainment. Most notably, the recitations served to develop and strengthen bonds among various family members.

Baldwin illustrates that the tradition was far more complex than it might initially appear. For example, not all family members created the same types of poems and they did not all use them in the same manner. Generally, the men made poems "on the spot" and first used them "where they were made for the enjoyment or embarrassment of those whose actions and interactions occasioned the verses and were recorded in them."[21] In contrast, most of the women's compositions were reflective and reminiscent rather than first-person, on-the-scene reports.

Baldwin ends her story on what many readers will consider a sad note. Although the Solley recitation tradition lasted for about a century, it is now defunct. It didn't die without a valiant effort on the part of the youngest generation, many of whom made some attempts at producing poems. Unfortunately, these proved to be false starts, and now the Solleys have "expert polka and championship clog dancers, baton twirlers, roller skaters, trumpet and poker players, and practical jokers—but no more family poets."[22]

By far the longest article in the *Southern Folklore Quarterly* special issue, Gershon Legman's "Bawdy Monologues and Rhymed Recitations," is not specifically devoted to American material but includes a number of items that are in American repertoires.[23] Legman offers three broad categories—dramatic monologues, mock speeches and complaints, and rhymed recitations—and gives numerous examples complete with his usual extensive bibliographic and historical notes. Several of the texts are from British informants or sources, but there are two unusual versions of well-known American bawdy recitations. One, "The Ballad of Chambers Street," is regarded by many as the most aggressive and most anti-woman of all recitations, bawdy or otherwise. The second, "Our Lil," is a folk version of a poem by Eugene Field (1850-1895) that may well be the most popular erotic rhymed recitation in America during the last half century.

While the *Southern Folklore Quarterly* special issue is important, it should not be considered a definitive work; in fact, the editors do not claim it is anything more than a preliminary collection of studies. Indeed, they even point out important potential areas of inquiry that the issue slights. These include analyses of recitations on commercial recordings or in minstrel shows, patent medicine shows, variety entertainment extravaganzas that have widespread appeal, and rural schoolroom elocutionary recitations. The latter activity, now mostly a thing of the past, was an important influence in shaping the repertoires of traditional reciters. On the plus side, *Monologues and Folk Recitation* provided the earliest extended documentation of the tradition, and with its several suggestions of fruitful avenues of investigation, it should have stimulated further studies of folk recitations. Unfortunately, it has had little influence, for until the present book, only two subsequent publications on recitations have appeared; both, however, are valuable works.

As a bonus offering for subscribers to *Southwest Folklore*, Keith Cunningham produced a record, "Uncle Horace's Recitations," that included a sixty-three page issue of *Southwest Folklore* as the liner notes. Among the contents are transcriptions of the twelve texts by Horace Crandell, his comments on each item, a biography of Crandell, the texts of seven other recitations in the Arizona Friends of Folklore Archive, a bibliodiscography of recitations in that archive, and a fourteen-page essay, "On the Recitation."

Taking the *Southern Folklore Quarterly* special issue as both a point of reference and of departure, Cunningham's essay includes a discussion of the recitation as a folk form, nomenclature, definition, sources, textual variation, and interaction with other forms. He disagrees with Goldstein about the use of the term "monologue," preferring "recitation" for two reasons. First, it is the term preferred by most American performers; second, "monologue" has a specialized and widely accepted meaning in literary criticism that differs slightly from Goldstein's usage. Thus, Cunningham argues, the usage of "recitation" to refer to the subject matter is ultimately less confusing.

Cunningham further criticizes Goldstein's work on other counts, notably for providing a definition that is somewhat confusing because it involves both what is performed and the performance style. He also suggests that Goldstein is too quick to characterize British pub performances as typical of folk recitation styles of English speaking performers in general. Based on his own fieldwork, Cunningham concludes that some of the "typical characteristics" outlined by Goldstein do not apply to Anglo-American performances. In other words, his argument is that a performance aesthetic applies in the United States that is different from that found in the British Isles. Despite these quibbles, Cunningham concurs with Goldstein's conclusions. In fact, the remainder of his essay is an expansion and refinement of several points made by Goldstein.

Cunningham concludes that the recitation is an item of folklore subject to the same forms of variation as ballads and folktales. Furthermore, it is "part of a larger tropism in culture emphasizing verbal performance, constantly interacted and interchanged with ballad, and [it has] affected the development and dissemination not only of popular poetry but also of belletristic verse."[24] These points are illustrated not only with numerous printed texts but by the items heard on "Uncle Horace's Recitations."

Since Cunningham's 1978 record and special issue, only one significant publication on folk recitations has appeared. Ronald L. Baker's "Lady Lil and Pisspot Pete" is an extended discussion of the folk dissemination of Eugene Field's 1888 poem. Basing his comments on twenty-five field-collected versions and texts in printed sources that probably came from oral tradition, Baker seeks to explain why this poem is so popular. He argues persuasively that the story of an insatiable schoolmarm, Lil, who is killed in a fornication contest by the unpromising half-breed, Pete, often serves as a means of reducing male fears and anxieties about sex. He also contends that versions with "the schoolmarm as antagonist may also serve to reduce male hostilities toward the oppressive moral authority of adults, since an authority figure, the schoolmarm, is presented as not so very moral—thus relieving young males from the pressure of a too ideal model."[25]

Why have so few folklorists concerned themselves with the study of folk recitations? That is a question with a complex answer that cannot be adequately answered in a few sentences, so the following comments are nothing more than a mention of a few possibilities, some of which have been hinted at earlier in this essay. Probably one reason recitations have not received greater attention from folklorists is that most scholars have been extremely narrow in their focus. Most genre studies have been concerned with folk narratives and balladry, so much so that they have in part helped create the popular misconception that "folklore means folksongs, plus Paul Bunyan."[26] Because recitations are not folk narratives of the same kind as say, Cinderella, or the Vanishing Hitchhiker, and they are not ballads in any sense, they have for the most part been ignored.

A second probability is that folklorists have misunderstood the nature of the recitation tradition. Some scholars have assumed that recitations belong solely to the area of children's folklore, a field in which they had no particular interest. As the present book amply demonstrates, this assumption is false, for adults participate in the tradition just as much as kids.

A third likelihood is that recitations have been generally ignored because some of the texts recited by some performers in folk tradition are obscene. Historically, bawdy materials have received the least attention from scholars, and although the study of such items has increased in recent years, serious consideration of this aspect of folklore is still in its infancy.

Two final possibilities deserve mention, and they may be the most important of the several discussed here. One is the longstanding preference of folklorists for texts that are of anonymous origin and are not taken directly from printed sources. As Goldstein and Bethke note, this inclination is compounded when the recitationist "is found to be the author of his or her recitation materials."[27] In truth, the ideal is simply that—an ideal rather than a reflection of reality. Many of the items found in folk repertoires are of known authorship and are directly derived from printed sources. For example, the original authorship of many ballads in folk tradition is known, as several editors of ballad collections have demonstrated.[28] This disinclination to deal with texts of known authorship taken from printed sources has meant folklorists have been slow to accept material known to come from popular culture, the point of origin for many recitations. Typically, popular culture is regarded as existing on a different level from folklore, with no interaction between the two levels. Actually, though, popular culture and folklore, and other forms of culture, are on the same level and constantly interact.[29] Most folklorists probably agree with that characterization and with the idea that all people have

17

folklore. At the same time, most folklorists conduct studies suggesting that neither viewpoint is correct.

Whatever the reasons why most earlier folklorists have ignored folk recitations, it is hoped that the present volume by Keith Cunningham will point out the value of studying this topic. By calling attention to the numerous possibilities for important work in this generally neglected area of folklore, Cunningham's book should stimulate extensive subsequent investigations of folk recitations. Whether it does or not is, of course, up to other folklorists.

William K. McNeil
OZARK FOLK CENTER
MOUNTAIN VIEW, ARKANSAS

NOTES

1. The first two editions were published in Altoona, Pennsylvania, by the Times Tribune Company. The third edition, the one quoted here, was published in Philadelphia by Newman F. McGirr.
2. *Ibid.*, p. 68.
3. George Korson, *Black Rock: Mining Folklore of the Pennsylvania Dutch* (Baltimore: The Johns Hopkins Press, 1960), p. 349.
4. D. K. Wilgus, *Anglo-American Folksong Scholarship Since 1898* (New Brunswick, New Jersey: Rutgers University Press, 1959), p. 183.
5. Roger D. Abrahams, *Deep Down in the Jungle: Negro Narrative Folklore from the Streets of Philadelphia* (Chicago: Aldine Publishing Company, 1970), p. 97.
6. The Labov, Cohen, Robins, and Lewis article originally appeared in *A Study of the Non-Standard English of Negro and Puerto Rican Speakers in New York,* volume II, "The Use of Language in the Speech Community," Cooperative Research Project Number 3288 (New York: Columbia University Press, 1968), pp. 55-57, and was reprinted in Alan Dundes, *Mother Wit from the Laughing Barrel: Readings in the Interpretation of Afro-American Folklore* (Englewood Cliffs, New Jersey: Prentice-Hall, Inc., 1973), pp. 329-347. It is worthy of note that there are some unpublished collections of toasts. For references to these see Charles Reagan Wilson and William Ferris, editors, *Encyclopedia of Southern Culture* (Chapel Hill: The University of North Carolina Press, 1989), p. 523.
7. Abrahams revised his book in 1970 and this second edition is the one quoted here.
8. Abrahams, p. 97.
9. *Ibid.*, pp. 107-108.
10. For example, see Vance Randolph, *Pissing in the Snow and Other Ozark Folktales* (Urbana: University of Illinois Press, 1976), pp. 103-105, and the article by Ronald L. Baker, "Lady Lil and Pisspot Pete," discussed later in this essay.
11. Keith Cunningham, "Notes and Queries," *AFFWord* 2:3 (Fall, 1972): 38-39.
12. See Mary O. Eddy, *Ballads and Songs from Ohio* (Hatboro, Pennsylvania:

Folklore Associates, Inc., 1964; reprint of a work originally issued in 1939), p. 204.

13. W. K. McNeil, "Recitations," *Journal of American Folklore* 86:340 (April-June, 1973): 177-178.

14. Hirsch's article appears on pp. 125-140.

15. Goldstein's essay appears on pp. 7-29.

16. *Ibid.*, p. 8.

17. *Ibid.*, p. 22.

18. Bethke's article appears on pp. 141-168, the quoted remarks appear on p. 165.

19. See, for example, W. Roy Mackenzie, *Ballads and Sea Songs from Nova Scotia* (Cambridge, Massachusetts: Harvard University Press, 1928); Phillips Barry, Fannie Hardy Eckstorm, and Mary Winslow Smyth, *British Ballads from Maine* (New Haven, Connecticut: Yale University Press, 1929); and Maud Karpeles, *Folk Songs from Newfoundland* (Hamden, Connecticut: Shoe String Press, 1971).

20. Baldwin's essay appears on pp. 209-238.

21. *Ibid.*, p. 229.

22. *Ibid.*, p. 238.

23. Legman's article appears on pp. 59-123.

24. Keith Cunningham, "On the Recitation," *Southwest Folklore* 2:4 (Fall 1978): 51.

25. Ronald L. Baker, "Lady Lil and Pisspot Pete," *Journal of American Folklore* 100:396 (April-June, 1987): 199.

26. Jan Harold Brunvand, *The Study of American Folklore: An Introduction* (New York: W. W. Norton & Company, Inc., 1968), p. 129. Brunvand points out that most of the stories told about Paul Bunyan are not part of any folk tradition, instead they belong to a literary tradition.

27. Kenneth S. Goldstein and Robert D. Bethke, "Introduction" to *Monologues and Folk Recitation, Southern Folklore Quarterly* 40:1 & 2 (March-June 1976): 4.

28. See, for example, Vance Randolph, *Ozark Folksongs* (Columbia: The State Historical Society of Missouri, 1946-1950); Norm Cohen, *Long Steel Rail: The Railroad in American Folksong* (Champaign: University of Illinois Press, 1981); and my own *Southern Folk Ballads* (Little Rock: August House, Inc., 1987-1988).

29. For further discussion of this point see Richard M. Dorson's article "Folklore in Relation to American Studies" in Ray B. Browne, Richard H. Crowder, Virgil L. Lokke, and William T. Stafford, eds., *Frontiers of American Culture* (Lafayette, Indiana: Purdue Research Foundation, 1968), p. 190.

CHAPTER ONE

Oh, I'll Tell You a Story

DURING THE SUMMER OF 1971, I scheduled a recording session for the second documentary album I was going to produce of Western traditional music. The recording session was held in the Northern Arizona University Music Department practice room because they had the equipment and, most importantly, they were willing to help. Among the people we recorded that day were Horace Crandell and Van Holyoak.

Uncle Horace, as everyone called him, went first. I had interviewed him at his home and had a pretty good idea of his repertoire of fiddle tunes, so I knew in general what to expect. The recording session was structured by my suggesting the titles of fiddle tunes and his playing them. After we recorded the items I was considering using on the record, Uncle Horace said that he would like to record his recitation of "Lasca" because it meant a great deal to him. I had met Uncle Horace through Van, and Van had described his performance of this poem with awe and admiration, so I of course agreed and sat back in my chair as he began. Uncle Horace grasped his fiddle firmly in his left hand and his bow in his right hand, drew himself erect to his full height, and by his presence and projection instantly commanded the rapt attention of those at the session who were familiar with his performance and those who had little idea of what was to come.

1 Lasca

Horace Crandell: I first saw "Lasca" shortly after I was married the first time. I heard it on a record, and then I found a book with it in it, and so I learned it from the book. That would have been approximately 1921 or 1922. It was a history book. I don't know where it came from, and my wife burned it up, and I don't know why. If she burned it, it was done by mistake, 'cause she liked the book, but I've never been able to find it since she died. I've hunted for it. It had some more that I wanted to get.

I want free life, and I want fresh air;
And I long for the canter after the cattle,
The crack of the whip like a shot in battle,
The medley of horns and hoofs and heads
That wars and wrangles and scatters and spreads;
The green beneath, the blue above,
Dash and danger, life and love.
And Lasca!

      Lasca used to ride
On a mouse-gray mustang close to my side,
With loosed robe and bright-belled spur;
Oh, I laughed with joy as I looked at her!
Little cared she, save to be by my side,
To ride with me, and ever to ride,
From San Saba's shore to the blackest tide
      In Texas, down by the Rio Grande.

She was bold as the billows that beat,
She was wild as the breezes that blow;
From her little head to her little feet
She would sway in her suppleness to and fro
By each gust of passion; the sapling pine,
That stands on the edge of the Kansas Bluff,
And wars with the wind when the weather is rough,
Is like this Lasca, this love of mine.
She would hunger that I might eat,
Would take the bitter and leave me the sweet;
But once, when I made her jealous for fun,
O'er something I whispered, or said, or done,
She drew from her bosom a queer little dagger,
Like the sting of wasp!—it made me stagger;
An inch to the left, or an inch to the right,
And I wouldn't be wandering here tonight;
But she sobbed, and sobbing, so quickly bound
Her torn rebozo about the wound,
I quite forgave her. Scratches don't count
      In Texas, down by the Rio Grande.

The air was heavy, the night was hot,
I sat by her side, and forgot—forgot;
Forgot the herd that was taking its rest,
Forgot that the air was a close oppressed,
That the Texas northern comes sudden and soon,
In the dead of night or the blaze of noon;
And once let that herd in a breath take fright,
There's nothing on earth can stop their flight;
And woe to the rider, and woe to the steed,
That falls in front of their mad stampede!
What was that? Thunder? No.
I sprang to the saddle, she clung behind.
Then away on a hot race down the wind!
And never was harsh road half so hard
For we rode for our lives. And you shall hear how we fared
        In Texas, down by the Rio Grande.

The mustang flew, and we urged him on;
There is one chance left, and you have but one;
Halt, jump to earth, shoot your horse;
Crouch under his carcass, and take your chance;
And, if those steers in their frantic storm
Don't beat you both to pieces at once,
You may thank your stars; if not, goodbye
With a quickening kiss, a long-drawn sigh,
In the open air, and the open sky
        In Texas, down by the Rio Grande.

The cattle gaining, and, just as I felt
For my good six-shooter behind my belt,
Down came the mustang, and down came we,
Clinging together—what was the rest?—
A body that spread itself on my breast.
Two arms that shielded my dizzy head,
Two lips that hard against my lips were pressed;
Then came thunder in my ears,
As over us swept that sea of steers,
Blows that beat black in my eyes.
When I could rise—
Lasca was dead!

I gouged out a grave a few feet deep,
There in Earth's arms I laid her to sleep;
There she is lying, and no one knows,
The summer shines and the winter blows;
For many a day the flowers have spread
A pall of petals over her head;
And the little gray hawk hangs aloft in the air,
The sly coyote trots here and there,
And the black snake slides and glitters and glides
Into a rift in a cottonwood tree;
And the buzzard sails on,
And is come and is gone,
Stately and still like a ship at sea;
And I wonder why I do not care
For the things that are like the things that were.
Does a half my heart lie buried there
      In Texas, down by the Rio Grande?

"Lasca" is my first recitation, and it used to be what people would most like to have me recite, but they don't like that so well anymore. I don't know why. They would rather have short ones mostly.

I will never forget my amazement at Uncle Horace's performance. He used his voice like a musical instrument. From the very first line, "I want free life and I want fresh air," with his strong emphasis on the word "want," rapid tempo, and almost strident delivery to the soft, slow, near-whisper he employed for the final question, "Does a half my heart lie buried there in Texas down by the Rio Grande?" his performance was a tour de force which as usual left his audience (in this case me) near tears.

Imagine if you will a great Shakespearean actor of the mid-nineteenth century declaiming "Lasca" (or better yet read the poem aloud as dramatically as you can possibly imagine) and you are on your way to understanding Horace's performance. He thundered, he whispered, he spoke rapidly, he spoke slowly, he *recited*. Boy, did he recite! At one dramatic point in the poem he paused for what seemed to be a long time, and then asked in a sad, conversational tone, "What was the rest?" My first feeling was that he had forgotten his lines, and I was filled with a sense of panic and guilt that I didn't know the lines that came next. I was just about to blurt out the suggestion that we stop the recording so he could relax for a moment and then begin again when he dropped his voice and slowed his tempo so his words sounded like a funeral dirge and answered with arresting emotion what had obviously been a rhetorical question, "A body that spread itself on my breast." I was, all in all, enthralled by his performance. It had the feeling of something once known but now half forgotten, and thus I began an eighteen-year-and-still-counting quest for recitations and reciters.

After Uncle Horace had finished, I recorded several other singers and musicians who were to become a part of the record, and then it was Van Holyoak's turn. I had interviewed Van at his home, too, and we recorded a number of his traditional cowboy ballads that I thought I might use on the record. Van had the largest repertoire of Western songs of any traditional performer I ever knew and cared passionately about their preservation. No performer ever felt the challenge of pleasing an audience, be it of one or one thousand, more than Van, and he was a traditional performer with an impeccable sense of timing. The anticipation of an audience, however, made him physically ill, and this recording session was his very first. His wife, his sons, and his daughters all continue to tell stories of how nervous he was about this session and about how much he wanted to do it.

He also in later years told a wonderful story about one incident contributing to his nervousness during the recording. One of his friends heard about the scheduled session and came to warn him. The friend said, ''Now don't you let that guy swindle you out of any money. That little fee he gave you is obviously just a come-on. Next thing you know, he will tell you that you have to put up some cash. I've heard you sing, and there has got to be something that's not on the up and up if somebody pays you money to record.''

Van was so tense at the recording session that his singing was not at its best; his performances on his later recordings were much better. When we had finished recording his ballads, he seemed to relax somewhat, however, and said, ''You know, the only reason I let you talk me into doing this was because of my dad, Joe W. Holyoak. He was your real cowboy, one of the last, and I wanted to record those old cowboy songs so they wouldn't get lost, in honor of him and to his memory. Now I want to finish up by telling some stories about my dad and read a poem I wrote for him.'' I, of course, remembering Uncle Horace's ''Lasca'' agreed (frankly wondering what was coming next), and Van began his performance.

2   Rodeo Judge

Van N. Holyoak: Well, my dad was quite a practical joker. He was always pulling pranks on people. And at a dance in Hubbard one night, the people used to take all the babies in in carriages. So him and two other boys thought it'd be quite a practical joke to take and switch the babies while they were back on the stage outside of the dance. Then they swapped them babies around, and everybody left and drove ten, fifteen miles to go home. And they was three days a-getting all the babies turned back. It was probably about 1895 or 1896.

Another time—oh, after my dad got pretty old—they was sitting there in church one day, and my uncle was awful bad to go to sleep. And church had just barely got started, and Dad reached over and nudged him, says, "Hey, Ed, they want you to get up and dismiss church." And he did.

Well, another time Dad was going into town. He was punching cows for a ranch. When he was going in, a fellow was plowing out there in the field—and, like I say, Dad was quite a noted liar—so he hollered at him and said, "Hey, Joe. Stop and tell me a lie."

Well, Dad said, "I haven't got time. Your dad was shingling the roof of his granary, and he fell off and broke his leg, and I'm on my way into town after a doctor."

The old boy unhooked his plow horse and whipped over and under to get in to help his dad. When he got there, there his dad was—still laying shingles on the granary.

Now, that's the kind of a character my Dad was. He was a real oldtime cowboy. His quirt is in the Cowboy Hall of Fame. He was laid up for a long time when he broke his hip. In fact, the doctor said he would never walk again. He was just used to being outside and doing whatever he wanted to do, and so I started writing poems for him to try and keep him down, and this is one I wrote for him.

There's a man you see in the summertime.
He helps to make the show.
He's booed by all the spectators,
The judge at the rodeo.

He's a crying post for the cowboys,
Like, "They blew the whistle late,"
Or, "Sir, can I have a re-ride?
The bull caught my leg on the gate."

They say, "Judge, you're a phony.
This show must have a fix.
I rode that bull in Flagstaff.
Uncle Charlie marked me 46."

Then the hollow-chested cowboy,
With his spasmodic cough,
Who says, "Can I have a re-ride?
That bull just bucked me off."

Then there is the cowboy
Who grabs the riggin' and spurs the dees,
Humps up like a camel
Till his chin rests on his knees.

He hollers, "Can I have a re-ride?
That horse is dead as a log.
If you didn't see me spur him,
You need a seeing-eye dog."

Then you have the cowboy
Who is always on the make.
Says, "Judge, mark me in first place;
I'll give you half the take."

26

There's no man in the world
Who's rated half as low
In the losing cowboy's opinion
As the judge at the rodeo.

Van's performance was as understated and non-theatrical as Horace's was dramatic. The stories Van obviously told from memory, and the transitions from one to the other were extremely polished and effective. The poem he read from a piece of paper he had folded up in his shirt pocket. He delivered the stories with a very natural conversation-like tone, but it was a performance in the form of conversation rather than conversation itself just as the stories were stories *about* stories rather than stories themselves. There were no conversational interactions with the audience; Van's stories about his father were Western oral performance, and Van was as clearly performing as Uncle Horace had been. The poetry, too, Van delivered in a non-theatrical style, yet he emphasized the basic rhythm and rhyme of the poem so that it was a pulse—basic, elemental, just beyond consciousness. I knew what to do with Van's excellent, well told stories about his father—I published them as Western examples of the local character tradition. I published the poem, too, but I had no idea what to make of it; it fit no category. Poems (as I discovered to be true of "Lasca") which had known authors, were learned by their performers from records or books, and only *then* became recitations "bulged out" the currently accepted definitions of tradition quite a bit. Poems written by their performers and read from pieces of paper pulled out of shirt pockets also simply didn't fit the definitions of folklore I had learned.

A few years after the recording session, I took Bill Leverton, an Arizona television personality who produces human interest features in the style of Charles Kuralt, to interview and film Van. His feature was, in my very prejudiced opinion, a masterpiece. I had told Bill that Van, like his father, was known—among other things—as a teller of tall tales, commonly called "lies," and that was the performance form Bill decided to pursue in his interview. He introduced his feature by explaining he had begun his interview with telling Van he had heard of his reputation for telling lies. The camera shows Bill saying to Van, "Tell me a lie." The camera shifts to a close-up of Van, who says simply and directly, "I don't know any." The camera shifts immediately to Bill, who looks puzzled and a little disappointed, and then back to Van, who shrugs his shoulders after the awkward silence and begins to tell a series of less subtle lies. Bill reported that he was half-way back to Phoenix before he realized Van had told him the biggest lie of all right then and there at the beginning of the interview.

All I can say is I was a little slower than Bill, and I was more than half-way home before I realized the lesson Van had tried to teach: he had shown me oral tradition as it is in the American West, and that "book" definitions need to be changed if they don't fit the reality of field experience. This slowly dawning revelation was assisted by my discoveries that Van regularly told the same three stories about his dad in almost exactly the same words and in the same order, and that many traditional oral performers wrote their own poems and read or recited them with the same archetypal intonation. Thus began another quest for traditional oral poems and oral poets.

I discovered that all across the American West there are individuals, families, and communities for whom oral performance of poems and stories—variously called readings, recitations, or pieces—is as natural as speaking, and that their performances—called reciting, giving a piece, or doing a reading—involve stories and poems from a variety of sources. This book is a reporting of my quest. It presents transcriptions, made according to performer's pauses and oral emphases, of one hundred fifty-three field-recorded recitation performances and their performers' introductions, conclusions, and comments grouped into thematically related chapters so that the reader may experience both the performances and the performers.

In a very real sense, this book is a mystery that asks not only "Who done it?" but also "What is it that they done?" and "Why did they do it?" As is true of any good mystery, the cast of characters is important.

Cast of Characters

JOSEPH C. BOLANDER, born 1907, is the unofficial oral historian of Orderville, Utah, and the Mormon United Order which flourished there in the last century. He worked for many years at Pipe Springs National Monument and regularly recited poems in the park's interpretative programs. He uses pseudo-dialects, different voices, and his customary beautiful elfin smile as parts of his comic prose recitation performance. He taps his feet and rocks his rocking chair to the rhythm of his poetry recitations.

REINHOLD "TEX" BONNET, born 1912, was for many years a buckaroo on Nevada, Oregon, and Utah ranches. He also ran a bar in Paradise Valley, Nevada, where he entertained his customers with cowboy songs and recitations. His performances involve a certain amount of drama but are closer to Van's delivery than they are to Horace's. There is about Tex a childlike enthusiasm, an easy ability to express his innermost feelings, and a trust in the goodness of the world.

ELDA BROWN, born 1896, is a venerated, nearly legendary oral performer from St. Johns, Arizona. Her father was a producer of plays and theatrical events, and she often starred in his productions because, as he always said, he picked only the best actors. Her portrayal of Oliver in *Oliver Twist* is recollected with the same awe and appreciation that lovers of another theatre tradition reserve for Charles Kingsley's Hamlet. As she modestly says, "I've done a lot of readings in my time and played many parts."

GRANT E. BROWN, born 1925, is a retired school teacher who now lives in Eagar, Arizona. He is noted for his humorous readings and occasionally uses costumes as a part of his performances. The hat and wig and funny nose he describes using say a great deal about his performance. There is a long American tradition of comic skits reflected in his readings and a great deal of artfulness and drama in his "act"; he obviously dearly loves performing.

MADELINE COLLINS, born 1908, was an active member of the Flagstaff Senior Citizens Club. She performed "Lady Yardley's Guest," from memory at a Christmas meeting of the club. She stood to perform it, and the other club members were seated in a loose circle. As she performed the lines, "And spake with a queenly gesture / Her hand on the chief's brown breast," she made a sweeping gesture with her right hand which culminated in her hand resting on the breast of the Hopi lady sitting next to her. The Hopi lady had been following Madeline's performance with rapt attention, and she reached up and patted Madeline's hand. They twinkled at each other, and Madeline continued her performance without missing a beat. Through the years she has contributed a number of other texts and information about oral performance. Her reciting is studied and quiet but highly dramatic and always includes a carefully planned series of gestures.

ALIDA CONNOLLY, born 1913, is a folk poet who has written hundreds of poems and performs them with great enthusiasm and skill. Alida has an irrepressible joy which makes her extremely animated and dramatic performances of her humorous poems and her serious poems alike highly successful. Her lifelong love of dancing is reflected in her emphasis on rhythm in her oral performance.

HORACE CRANDELL, deceased, held basically the same unofficial position in Clay Springs, Arizona, that Elda Brown holds in St. Johns; he was recognized as the leading old time reciter in the area and had a wide repertoire of both serious and humorous recitations which he performed. His "Lasca" was widely regarded by several generations in the Clay Springs area as the supreme example of the reciter's art.

LaVELLE WHITING DeSPAIN, born 1921, is one of the recognized poets and writers of prose readings in St. Johns. Her first husband, killed in an airplane crash in 1961, was Elda Brown's nephew, and her magnificent version of "Little Klaus and Big Klaus" comes from the same Grandpa Whiting (Edward Marion) from whom Elda learned "Willy and the Giants." LaVelle is a master of a conversational performance style that involves the audience in the performance. Her delivery of the line, "Dead grandmothers for sale! Dead grandmothers for sale!" as a peddler's cry would make a stone lion laugh.

ADA HOLYOAK FOWLER, born 1954, is Van Holyoak's daughter and shares both his love of poetry and his skill at joshing. She has written a number of poems and reads them to her family and friends. As was also true of her father, her poetry is largely a private, solitary activity; her style of reading it aloud to family and friends is also very similar to his. Her poetry is, she explains, her way of dealing with life.

ANONA HEAP, born 1905, is Alida Connolly's sister. She is an independent, forceful older sister who performs numerous poems and recitations written by others and powerful prose accounts of her life which she has written.

KRISTI HODGE, born 1974, is Van Holyoak's first grandchild and shares with him and her mother Ada Holyoak Fowler the practice of writing poetry and reading it to family and friends. In addition, she has memorized and recites a number of poems her grandfather wrote and one that he performed for her as a bedtime story. Her performance is remarkably similar to her grandfather's except that, at this point in her career, her tempo is noticeably more rapid than his. Her grandfather's death is a major factor in her life.

JOE S. HOLYOAK, born 1955, is Van Holyoak's older son. He, like his father and grandfather before him, is a master teller of tall tales and, like them, loves to joke and jokes to love. He wrote this poetry after his father's death and reads it to his wife, his children, and friends. He, like his sister Ada and his niece Kristi, is extremely articulate about the process of writing poetry and its place in his life. His oral performance, like theirs, is clearly based on his father's example.

The Holyoak children who feature in the book are VANDEE, born 1980, SARA, born 1982, VAN A., born 1983, and DEEDRA, born 1985. They learned a recitation, which they perform in unison with exaggerated emphasis on its rhythm and rhyme, and tape-recorded it. They, along with their sister DEEANA and their brother JOSEPH JAMES, are the next generation, and if the past indicates the future, some of them will become reciters, and some of them will write poetry they perform.

VAN N. HOLYOAK, deceased, is the reciter, singer, and poet who opened Clay Springs, Arizona, to the world by helping the many traditional artists he knew in the area record their art. He was featured on a number of records and appeared at most of the major American folk festivals. He was noted as much for his dry wit as for his poems and performances.

DON JACKSON, born 1908, describes himself as an old-time Clay Springs cowboy, and his self description is extremely apt. He was a close friend of Joe W. Holyoak, Van's father, and the two of them performed for each other. He is a singer as well as a reciter, and he performs his memorized poems in a very conversational, matter-of-fact manner. He said of "Lasca," "Did you ever ride in a stampede? Well, I have, and that poem gives the real feeling of what it's like, and that's why I like it."

DELBERT D. LAMBSON, born 1923, is another poet and performer of the St. Johns, Arizona, area. He is extremely intense about his poetry and very dramatic in his performance, particularly when he is reciting something that he did not write but has learned from someone else. His passions for his country and his religion are the core of his performance and his life.

LEON LAMBSON, born 1921, lives in Ramah, New Mexico. He is Delbert's brother and is noted over a wide area as a superb musician who for years led a local band that enjoyed a great deal of popularity. He has undoubtedly written as many songs as his brother has written poems. His performance of "Touch of the Master's Hand" with his band reflects his long professional experience. He is a professional performer, but his performance is traditional. Because of his health, he no longer performs in public except when he is asked to do so for a funeral, but he receives many such requests because he and his many years of performance are widely remembered with respect and love across the cultures in the Ramah, New Mexico, area.

KATY LEE, born 1920, is LaVelle Whiting DeSpain's sister. She is famous for her singing of a family song and her telling of traditionalized but conversational stories about her family in days past. She also is one of the area's unofficial playwrights and regularly produces plays and skits for family, church, and community events.

EDWARD Z. NIELSEN, born 1912, is widely known to family and friends by his nickname of "E. Z." Nielsen. He is also widely known for his performance of comic prose recitations. He lives in St. Johns, Arizona. His introductions and the monologues he performs are very theatrical, and he is a superb comic actor who enjoys acting. He is an entertaining entertainer.

RALPH ROGERS, born 1904, is another old-time Clay Springs cowboy. He was a noted rodeo bronc rider throughout Northern Arizona and has only recently given up the sport because of a serious injury. Joe S. Holyoak remembers that Ralph used to like to play horse with kids but was so familiar with bronc riding from his long rodeo experience that he almost always bucked them off. Joe said, "If you could ride Ralph, you were ready for the real thing." He is best known as a performer for his very deep voice and wide repertoire of cowboy ballads, but he also occasionally recites in a melodic, sonorous tone.

STANLEY SHUMWAY, born 1911, is a retired school teacher who has written a series of poems as a part of his autobiography. He also operated a sawmill business. His usual audience for his poetry is his family. His poems are highly sophisticated and thoroughly traditional, and he reads them straightforwardly. His performance is very much like that of Joe S. Holyoak or Ada Holyoak Fowler, and his poems are particularly effective and well crafted examples of Western traditional verse.

WILFORD J. SHUMWAY, born 1909, is Stanley Shumway's brother. He is a consummate dramatic performer who is accustomed to reciting before large audiences and seems to enjoy it thoroughly. As he indicates, reciting is his talent, and his "Casey at the Bat" needs to be heard to be believed.

The images and characters he creates by his performance are extremely vivid and heroic.

BILLY SIMON, deceased, was one of the grand old performers of Prescott, Arizona. In addition to being known as a powerful singer, he was also the person who created the melodies for several cowboy ballads that passed into tradition all across the American West. He, like Horace Crandell and Van Holyoak, volunteered his recitations at a recording session that concentrated on ballads and music. There was a romantic core to Billy that he communicated clearly by his performance. Many of his recitations concerned ultimate questions and created poignant feelings of longing and loss; these were balanced by the broad humor he employed in others.

ALICE GENE TRIPP, born 1946, of Austin, Texas, is a typical modern day Texan who just happens to have a rare treasure—three of her grandmother's oral performances that she has memorized and reproduces in an unbelievably delightful and playful fashion. In her recitations she acts the part of her grandmother acting the parts of the narrators of the performances.

MARGARET WITT, born 1906, is Don Jackson's sister. She also lives in Clay Springs and recites. She has items from the West's past and performs them, comic and serious, with great skill. She has a number of recitations performed from the point of view of children who, like those Shakespeare created, speak profound truths in childish language.

And now my story's begun.

CHAPTER TWO

Mostly for Entertainment

ENTERTAINMENT IS A MAJOR function of most recitation performances. Oral performance in the American West usually involves humor and pathos or both together, chills and thrills, laughter and tears, but the recitations in this chapter are ones in which entertainment seems to be the dominant purpose.

3 *The Revival Meeting at Punkin Center*

Joseph C. Bolander: This one I picked up when I was growing up. I think I was a junior in high school, to be right sure, but we had a course in English literature that year taught by Roberta McGregor who was an awful good teacher, by the way. She gave us an assignment at the very beginning of the school year: ''At the end of this school year, well, first I'm going to make you an assignment to prepare a well told story, a reading, or something like that. I'm not going to say another thing about it the rest of the year. You'll have the whole year to work on it, and I expect something pretty good, and your whole year's credit will depend on what you come up with.''

Well, that was eight or nine months away, so I didn't give much attention to that for a long time. Finally, along in May, why Miss McGregor dropped the bomb; she says, ''Tomorrow we start on the readings you were assigned the beginning of the year.'' Well, I was kinda let down a little bit. I hadn't prepared a thing on that, just plumb forgot all about it, but when I went home, I done quite a bit of thinking. I knew I had to come up with something or lose a whole year's credit in English literature. Anyway, we had an old Edison phonograph, you know, the kind with the horn on and those cylinder records, and among these records was two or three of the experiences of Uncle Josh in Punkin Center, so I played two or three of them and decided I'd try and memorize one of them. I wanted to do one, ''The Husking Bee at Punkin Center,'' but that was a little bit involved. I'da had to play several parts and besides that, I'da had to sing ''The Little Brown Jug,'' so that

definitely left me out of that, so I settled on "The Revival Meeting at Punkin Center," and this is it. *(Laughs long and heartily)*

Last winter we had a revival meeting in Punkin Center, and purt nigh the whole dern town got religion. Some of them have got it yet, and some of them have shed it just like a cat shedding its hair. Well, we needed it. Things had got so bad in our church we had to have a one-armed brother take up the collection.

We had some interesting things at our revival. We had a choir consisting of Hank Slocum, first bass *(spoken in a low voice);* Dave Crosby, second bass *(spoken in a lower voice);* and Lige Wells, pitcher *(spoken in falsetto);* and he pitched the tunes so high that nobody but him could reach them, and he couldn't carry a tune in a suitcase, so Samatha Hoskins had to do most of the singing, and I don't think Samatha's voice converted anybody much, but Samatha just had to sing. Gosh, you couldn't stop her with a red lantern.

Well, we had the preacher from Crab Tree Corners come to our revival, and I don't believe I ever will forget his sermon. He said, *(spoken slowly in a solemn voice),* "Brothers and Sisters, hell is full of beautiful women, automobiles, fast horses, and champagne."

And old Jim Lawson stood up and said, "Oh, death, where is thy sting?" We all expected to see old Jim get religion because a couple of weeks before he'd had a pretty bad scare. He was coming home from the saloon with his jug under his arm, and he ran his old peg leg through a knothole in the sidewalk, and he stayed right there and walked around and around that wooden leg for about three hours, and the parson asked him if he wasn't going to mend his ways, and he said no, he reckoned not. There was only one knot hole in that sidewalk, and he knew where that was now. Golly, that busted up the revival meeting.

Well, I don't know how I done, but I got my credit. Easiest grade I ever earned.

4   *A Son of the Beach*

Elda Brown: I'm 92 years old, and I've given lots and lots of readings and played many parts in my time. I know right where a copy of this one is, so I'll do it for you.

I sell-a da fish,
And I sell-a da crab;
I'm-a not-a so good,
But I'm-a not-a so bad.

I live-a in a shack
Where the sea gulls dey screech.
I'm Tony Diego,
A son of da beach.

I guess maybe you tink
I pretty big fool
'Cause I never go
To an American school,

And I don't know so good
The American speech.
I joost Tony Diego,
A son of the beach.

They say to me,
"Tony, what for you stay here?
You'll make-a more money
If you sell-a da beer."

I said, I don't care
If I never been rich.
I rather joost be
A poor son of the beach.

Last week I hear people,
They talk on the sand
About a fella named Roosevelt,
Big-a chief man.

I don't hear so good
What they say in the speech,
But it sounds like he, too,
Is a son of da beach.

Now, I don't tink
They mean he's a fella like me
'Cause he don't even live here
On the beach by the sea.

So I don't understand,
Maybe him and me each
Is two different kinds
Of the son of da beach.

Well, I'm joost Tony Diego
And damn glad I am
That I'm-a not what they call
That big chief man.

'Cause someday I die,
And when heaven I reach,
They will say "Hi, Tony,
Come on in, you son of da beach."

Now, I want to tell you about my quilting.

5   *The Blue Hen Chicken*

Joseph C. Bolander: Now, this is the only one of the fifteen or so that I used to do quite regularly that I remember really well without effort because it's the one I have used the most recently. I remember an old man Si Chamberlain that lived here used to give this when I was a kid, and I was interested in it. Then when I was a missionary down in Florida about 1930 or '31, there was an old man came out; he was about seventy years old. He was from northern Utah, and he was quite an entertainer, too, and he had this, and he used to entertain with it, you know, so I decided I wanted to learn that, so I did.

You know, well, if you don't know, then I will tell you, for a long time ago we keep some hen chickens, and one day Katerina, that is mine frau, she say to me, "Jacob Woggenhousen Roggenfelt," that is me, "why don't you put some eggs under that old blue hen chicken? I think she want to set."

"Well," I say, "I guess I will." So I get a dozen of the nicest eggs, and I take them out to the barn for the old hen. She make her nest in the hay mound, oh, about five or six feet up. Now, you see, I never was very big up and down—I pretty big all the way around the middle—and so to reach that nest, I gets me a barrel for to stand on, and I climbed up on the barrel, and when my head come up even with that nest, that old hen, she gives me such a peck mine nose runs all over mine face mid blood, and then the head of that barrel braken down, and I go ker-slam. By jingo, I never knew I could get in a barrel before, but there I was tight stuck. No way I tried could I get out, so I calls to mine frau, "Katerina, Katerina, come and pull me mid the barrel out."

Well, by and by, Katerina, she come, and when she see me, she laugh and she laugh seeing me there in that barrel my face all covered with blood and eggs, and she say, "Jacob Woggenhousen Roggenfelt, why don't you whip off your face off and pull down your face down?" And she laugh, and she laugh till I think she would die.

Now, you see Katerina, she speak English pretty good, but I say with my greatest dignitude, "Katerina, are you going to stop laughing and pull me mid this barrel out?"

"Oh, yes, Jacob," she says, "I will pull you with the barrel out." So she puts me and the barrel down on our side, and she gets hold of the barrel, and I gets hold of the post, and the first pull, I yells, "Donner and Blitzen, stop it! There's nails in the barrel!"

See, when I go down, the nails, they bent down. When I come out, oh, they sticken all the way around. So she go get neighbor Hansen to come mid the saw. When he see me, he laugh, and he laugh, and Katerina, she laugh, and she laugh till I get all red in the face. Then neighbor Hansen, he go to work with his saw, and pretty soon I get up with half a barrel around my face.

Katerina, she say, "Now wait a minute. I want to get a pattern of that new overshirt you are wearing." But I didn't wait. I pull that thing off, and I threw it in the woodpile.

Now, when we get to the house, Katerina, she say soft like, "Jacob Woggenhousen Roggenfelt, when are you going to set that old blue hen chicken?"

"Katerina," I say, "you never mention that old blue hen chicken to me again, you get a pill from me." I tink she no say that no more. Now when I get on a barrel, I don't get on a barrel, I get on a box.

I don't recite much anymore, but I always have to give "The Blue Hen Chicken" when the family gets together. I used to do quite a bit, but that's about all I do now.

6 *Trapper Bill*

Horace Crandell: This was composed by the late Milo Wiltbank. I got it out of his book. I never heard anybody say it. I just said it over and over until I got it the best that it was possible for me to say it, and then I'm ready.

I met a friend the other day,
My good neighbor, Trapper Bill,
And we sat down to chat a while
As good neighbors often will.

Said I to Bill, "What's that
You got a-carrying on your back?"
Says Trapper Bill, "That's a baby skunk
I got in that there gunnysack."

"What! A baby skunk
And haven't you killed it yet?"
Says Trapper Bill, "I'm gonna take it home
And raise it for a pet."

"But baby skunks are tender, Bill,
At least so I've been told.
He's apt to freeze some night.
The howling wind is cold."

Then Bill bit off another chew
And slowly scratched his head.
"This baby skunk won't freeze at night;
He's going to sleep with me in bed."

Says I to Bill,
"I think your notion's swell.
But tell me, please, what will you do about
That awful smell?"

You think that worried him?
Not a dog-gone bit.
"That baby skunk," said Trapper Bill,
"Will soon get used to it."

7 Let Us Spray

Joseph C. Bolander: This man and woman had a flat tire in their automobile, and while he was fixing it, he tried to entertain her by telling her some stories.

There was a mama skunk and some little baby skunks going through the woods, and they met a bear, and the little baby skunks says, "Well, Mama, Mama, what'll we do?"
She said, "Let us spray. Let us spray."

8 Uncle Josh Gets a Letter from Home

Edward Z. Nielsen: I have one I've said a time or two about Uncle Josh getting a letter from home. It's a real old one.

I just got a letter from home, and I had the gol-darnest time a-getting it. They sent me up to Post Office A, then Post Office B, then Post Office C. Well, finally I got to the right post office. I had the gol-darnest time a-getting into it. Where the door ought to be, they had a little merry-go-round, and you had to get into that thing and go play merry-go-round for a while, and I got into it, and it started to going round, and before I could get out of it, I's back on the sidewalk. Before I could get out on the sidewalk, I's back in the post office. I came darn near bein' a dead letter right there in the post office.
Well, I got in finally, and I got my letter. I guess I'll read it now. I didn't have very much time to read while I's in that windmill. Well now, let me see, they had a 'lection down home. Yes sir, the whole dern town went Republic. They had nine majority. The election

would have been unanimous except for Ezra Hopkins, and he's cross-eyed, and he marked in the wrong column, so his vote went Democratic. *(Laughs.)* I'll bet they cut old Ezra off at church for doing that.

Let's see now what the letter says. Poor old Aunt Eliza Hopkins is dead. Yes sir, the poor old critter, she died, and they didn't bury her. They cremated her a while, and now she can't have no tombstone.

Hold on, let's see what that letter says. Oh yeah, she got her tombstone all right. They sprinkled her ashes over the top of the lawn, and then they put up a sign:

> Poor old Aunt Eliza
> Walks through this grass
> And we can prove it.

That's off a record, one of those 78s. My sister had that about 1920 or somewhere along in there.

9   *My Last Request*

Horace Crandell: It was several years ago, and we put on a minstrel show—a bunch of us folks up there in Clay Springs. And a school teacher, he got this piece. It was a pianologue. He played the piano with it, and he and his wife gave it, so that's where I got it. I got it from him.

My last will hain't been made out yet.
I ain't got much to leave,
And I know that all my gamblin' friends
Am surely going to grieve

'Cause I don't pay no gamblin' debts
That's made by crooked dice.
I ain't never been accused of cheating
'Cept just once or twice,

But here I is. I's almost dead.
My last hand's to be played.
I'm going where dice ain't never seen.
They ain't allowed, I'm afraid.

My last request am not for flowers
And buds to grow on me.
No monuments with name and age
For weeping friends to see.

But oh! I'll open my mouth and smile
And send my thanks to you,
If you'll plant a watermelon on my grave
And let the juice soak through.

39

Don't waste a single melon seed,
But plant dem in the ground
And let the roots grow down to me
And hold me all around.

Even throw dem juicy rinds
On my restin' place,
And my ghost will see that luscious melon
Laid right above my face.

Den my mouth will taste that fruit
I'm satisfied to say.
I'll be in nigger hebben shore,
If you'll do as I say.

My last request am not for flowers
And buds to grow on me.
No monuments with name and age
For weeping friends to see.

But oh! I'll open my mouth and smile
And send my thanks to you,
If you'll plant a watermelon on my grave
And let the juice soak through.

10 *Coonskin Huntin' Down in Moonshine Holler*

Edward Z. Nielsen: One of my readings is "Coonskin Huntin' Down in Moonshine Holler." I used to eat this stuff up, but no more. I forget quicker than I
remember. I got this off of a 78 record Dad used to have. The story was on
both sides of the record. I don't know how long Dad had the record, but when
I heard it and learned it first was about 1932, '33, or maybe '34.

Me and my pa, we live down here in Moonshine Holler 'bout a
mile, a mile and a half, or two mile. One morning I got up, and I seys
to Pa, I seys, let's go laugh and talk and coonskin hunting if he cared.
He asked me he didn't care, so I went outside, and I called up all
them dogs—all but Old Shorty. Then I called up Old Shorty, too. We
went strollin' on down the mountain till we got on top of the hill, and
then all of a sudden all them dogs, they treed one—all but Old Shorty.
Then Old Shorty treed him, too, up a long, straight sapling black gum
spruce. It was about ten feet above the top on an old, dead chestnut
snag. Now, I told Pa I'd climb up there and twist that thing out if he
cared. And he asked me he didn't care, so I climbed up, and I shook,

and I shook, and I shook till finally I heard something hit the ground, and I looked around, and it was me, by gosh, and all them gal-blamed dogs was right on top of me—all but Old Shorty. Then Old Shorty got on top of me, too. So I told Pa to knock them dogs off if he cared. He asked me he didn't care. So Pa picked up a pine knot and knocked all them dogs off—all but Old Shorty. Then he knocked Old Shorty off, too.

So I got up (kind of 'peared to Pa like I weren't hurt), and we went strollin' on down the mountain, and all of a sudden all them dogs, they treed another in an old dead huckleberry log. It was about three foot through on the small end. So I told Pa we could chop that thing out to save time if he cared. He asked me he didn't care, so Pa picked up the ax, and the first lick he cut Old Shorty's long, smooth, slender tail off right close up behind his ears. Just like to ruint my dog, by gosh. So we decided that was enough of ruints for one day, so we decided to go home.

Now when we got about home, Pa spied the whole darn pig patch clear full of pumpkins. Now we went down there and chased those pumpkins around among those pigs till finally I got mad, and I picked up a pumpkin by the tail and slammed its brains out 'cross a pig. Then Pa he got mad at me and cussed me just like I was a red-headed stepchild, by gosh. Then Pa told me to hush and shell them a bucket of slop.

Then I got up to fixin' the fence, and then I decided to go down to Sal's house. Now Sal, she lives down here in Moonshine Holler on Tough Street—the further up the street you go, the tougher they get, and Sal, she lives in the last house. Sal, she lives in a great big white house painted green with two big front doors on the backside. Now I told Pa beings it was sort of sunny-like I'd take a ride if he cared. He asked me he didn't care, so I went out to the lot, put the bridle on the barn, the horse on the saddle, laid the fence up to the side of the gate, and the horse got on. Now we went strollin' on down the road sort of studyin' like till finally the stump over in the corner of the horse got scared at the fence, and the fence reared up and throwed me off right face full in the middle of the road in a gully 'bout ten foot deep right smack in a brier patch and tore the left sleeve outa my Sunday britches. So I got up, brushed the dirt off of the horse, got back on, and went leading him on down the road.

Now when we got to Sal's house, I knew Sal was glad to see me 'cause she had both front doors shut wide open and all the windows nailed down. So I got off, I hitched the fence to my horse, I walked in, I spit on the bed, throwed my hat in the fireplace, and down I sat right in a big armchair on a stool. We got to talkin' 'bout ticks and politics, and all the other ticks till finally Sal loosed, ''Bud, let's go down to the peach orchard, and I'll get some pears, and I'll make a huckleberry pie for dinner.'' So I asked her I didn't care, so we went strollin' on down toward the peach orchard. Now I was walkin' just as close as I could get to Sal, her on one side of the road and me on the t'other. Now when we got to that peach orchard, I told her I'd climb up there and shake her down some apples if she cared. She asked me she didn't care, so I climbed up, and I shook, and I shook, and I shook till finally the limb what I was a-standin' on broke off, and I fell down straddle of the fence, both legs on the same side (skinned my right shins right above my left elbow) and I told Sal right then and there that's the last time I was goin'a be in Moonshine Holler, and I ain't been back since, by gosh.

11   *When Melindy Sings*

Horace Crandell: We used to have P.T.A. meetings, and we'd go to them all the time, and they'd have programs. My late wife, you never could get her to sing. This time they wanted her to sing, and she decided she would. I run across that piece just at that time, and her name was Melinda, and I thought that would be a good one to top off her song. She didn't know anything about it, and she got up and sang, and I gave this piece, and it made her mad. So I never did dare say that again, and this is the first time I'd tried to say it since that time.

Go away. Stop that noise, Miss Lucy.
Throw that music book away.
What's the use to keep on trying.
If you practice till you're gray,

You can't make dem notes come flying
Like the ones dat rants and rings
From the kitchen to da big woods
When Melindy sings.

You ain't got dem natural organs
To make dat sound come right.
You ain't got da turns and twistin's
To make it seem so sweet and light.

And I'm telling you now, Miss Lucy,
And I'm telling ya for true,
When it comes to real right singing,
'Tain't no easy thing ta do.

Easy 'nough for folks to holler,
Lookin' at dem lines and dots.
When there's no one round to sense it
And the tune comes out in spots.

42

Ain't you ever heared Melindy?
Blessed soul, take up the cross.
Honest angel. Ain't you joking, honey?
Well, you don't know what ya lost.

Ought to hear that gal a-warblin'.
Robin, larks and all dem things,
Dey hush dey mouths and hide dey faces
When Melindy sings.

Man a-playing on da fiddle
Puts his fiddle on the shelf.
Mockingbird, he jus won't try to whistle
'Cause he so ashamed himself.

Man a-playing on da banjo
Drops his fingers on da strings.
Bless my soul, forgets ta move 'em
When Melindy sings.

She jus opens her mouth and hollers
"Come to Jesus, you all hear."
Sinners' trembling steps and voices,
Timid-like have drawn near.

Then she turns to "Rock of Ages,"
Simply to the cross she clings.
And ya find your tears a-droppin'
When Melindy sings.

It's sweeter den da music
Of an educated band.
It's dearer den da battle song
Of triumph in de land.

It's holier den de evening
When the solemn church bells ring.
As you sit and listen with me
When Melindy sings.

Mandy, stop that baking, hear me?
Susie, make that child keep still.
Don't ya hear dem echoes rolling
From de valley to de hill?

Let me listen. I can hear dem
T'rough the brush of angel wings.
Sweet and low. "Swing low, sweet chariot."
As Melindy sings.

12 *That Wedding Scaremony*

Edward Z. Nielsen: One of the recitations I know is called "The Wedding Scaremony." I haven't said it for a long time. I hope I can remember it.

Well now, I just come from a vedding, and ah, such a vedding you never did see the like ofs. The groom, he was mine brother and the woman, she was no relations by me before the vedding scaremony. Now, she is mine sister-in-law. You know, it's a funny business; when a vedding is, you get mothers-in-law, sisters-in-law, brothers-in-law, fathers-in-law; and half of the times most of them are nothings but outlaws.

Oh, but I did have a vonderful time at that vedding—even if I did spill some soup in mine vest pocket. Nice new vest too, almost paid for. It was oyster soup. Something happened between my soup plate and mine lip as what William Shookaspook would say. Somebodies bumped mine elbow, or maybe the spoon leak, I don't know. But anyway, the soup all landed in mine vest pocket. Soup anyway is a poor thing to invest. It was oyster soup. You know, one of them fish what lives in a pocketbook built like a nut. Anyway, it was oyster soup. Now, I don't know who the lucky one was what got the oyster, but whoever he was, he kept it a secret; he did not let it slip out. Oh, it was good soup though; you could tell everybodies like it by the noise. It sounded just like the ocean waves dashed high on the ironbound coast. It was what you call quick soup. You know, just so quick, why, the soup was all on the inside or on the bibs what everybody stuck down in their necks.

Then vaiters, they took away the soup bowls, and they bring in a cooked turkey with no dress or anything on it—joost a-naked, that's all. And my, my, such a grabbing there was, and vhen the grabbing game was over, all I had was the piece where the ax chopped the head off. I got it in the neck the same just like the turkey did. And when the white meat, and the black, and the blue meat was all gone, Levy Lavemiska, he's the man what runs the junk yard, he bid seven cents for the bones, but right away he quit bidding when old Abby Cohen bid nine cents. They did not get my bone though, no sir. I stuck my neck right down in mine vest pocket with the soup. My little boy, he's just tickled to death when he gets a bone to chew.

The last thing what them waiters bring around was a whole bunch of nuts. We are a bunch of squirrels, I guess they think. Anyway, everbodies get a different kind of nuts. One man, he got a coconuts. Another man, he got the peanuts. Another man he got the walnuts, but the ones what I got come off from an automobile truck.

Then the last thing those waiters brought around was a little bowl filled with water, and mine brother (I never was so disembarrassed in my life) such an ignoramus, such a know-nothings, such a head full of emptiness, that dumbenbell, he wash his hands in his. Why, I put sugar in mine and drunk it. It was good, too.

And then when all the eats stuff was all gone, we decided to go into the deception room to dance. Now, I don't know a thing about the dance, but a fat woman what looks like the models to a battleship, she comed over. She said to me she did not like for to see me be a walnut. That don't sound like the word she used; anyhow it had a wall in it: walnut, wallflower, poison ivy, or something. Anyway, she said she did not like for to see me be a wallflower—that was it. So she told me, "Would you like to dance?"

I told her, "Sure I would like to dance. That's one thing about me, by golly; I am a game sports model. I don't stop for nothings. "Now, like I said, I don't know a thing about the dance, but I don't even know what part to hang onto, but she do, and just the minute that that jazz-a-hound music begins to start, she gets a strangle hold on my neck and an uppercut on mine chin, and away we go—down.

Now I'm on the bottom in the first round, and she's on the top, and I wait without a breath for the referee to blow his whistle and a taker offer. But he don't not a-do it for about five hours, seems to me. I can hear the faint tinkle, tinkle of that jazz-a-hound music far, far away. But I cannot see nothings, joost the stars, and pretty soon a big load is lifted from mine mind. They drew her off, and then I tried to stood up, but like two pancakes my legs feel, and when I did stood up, I find that mine pants don't even come to the tops of mine shoes—now I'm rolled out so much I am six inches taller.

Then I am ready to went home. I am sick in the head. She broke every bone in mine vest pocket. So I look all around for mine brother. I want to went down and shook his hands and offer him mine granulations and mine sympathies, so pretty soon I find him. He's up in his room. He's a-packin' his trunk. He's a-puttin' in a-both his shirts (one of them is clean) vhen I walk in. "Where you a-going?" I asked of him.

"To the honeymoon," he tells me.

"Where is this honeymoon?" I asked of him.

"Niagara Falls," he tells me.

And right away I tell him if he falls like I did, he won't last long. Then mine brother explains to me Niagara Falls is the place where everybodies go when they are vedded.

"That is not where I went when I was wedded," I tell mine brother.

"And where did you go when you was vedded?" he asked of me.

I told mine brother, "When I was vedded, I vent to the dogs."

"That was your own fault," mine brother tells me. "You should have bought a wedding license in place of a dog license." And then mine brother, he laughs at me.

He thinks that's a good joke, but even if he is my full brother on both of mine sides, I have got just as much of a smart as he, so I told mine brother, "The reason I bought a dog license instead of a wedding license was because everybodies told us our love was puppy love."

Then I am ready to vent home. Now, I don't want to went by the front way out because when that battleship sits on me the nice crease what was in mine pants slipped a way over on one side, so I am no longer a game sports model or stylish. So I want to go by the back way out. So I grabs my hat, and I slips out by the kitchen door.

My sister-in-law over to Farmington sent it to me about twenty to twenty-seven years ago, so I could say it at a wedding, and I've said it all over since.

13 *Are You Growing Older?*

Alida Connolly: One morning we were going to Springerville; in between the sink and the dishwasher I wrote this.

Are you growing older?
Watch for these signs:

When people start to call you grandma,
And you can't kneel down for prayer,
And your teeth repose in a glass,
And you wash away the gray from your hair,

When a stranger gives you his place
In a theater or on a crowded bus,
And people take your arm
As you cross the street with a lot of fuss,

Or reach down to help you rise
From that very low, soft overstuffed chair,
And there's lines of character on your brow
And a prolonged hurting in your feet,

When nine o'clock seems a right likely time
To drag your weary self to bed,
And there's more romance in going out to dinner
Than ever goes on in your head,

When driving after dark that center line seems very dim,
And you take a chance,
And it seems more fun to stay home and read
Than attend the much-advertised dance,

When the eye of the needle seems to shrink
And get smaller every year,
And that handsome man on the street
Treats you with respect and calls you "Mother Dear,"

When you get an inch or two shorter
'Cause your shoulders tiredly droop,
And it's just too much work to eat the beefsteak,
So you settle for the soup,

When the muscles in your legs and underarms
All wiggle and squiggle and turn to flap,
And it seems another person's hiding
In the back of your lap,

When it's very hard to keep awake,
And you keep dozing off in church and drop your books,
And you shudder as you look in the glass and mutter,
"My gal, you've lost your looks."

When you've lost all your ambition and your enthusiasm,
And it's no fun to go.
When you chew your food carefully. (It's those new teeth.)
And your reflexes are very slow.

When you reach out for your glasses
Soon as you open up your eyes,
And your figure's all soft and lumpy
And about twice its size,

And you seem to have a lot of grandchildren
In stages from large to small,
Then you find the salt in the refrigerator,
And you can't remember names at all,

When you lose the desire to go on that long dreamed-of trip
Or climb that big, high hill,
And you finally learn to accept changes
And hold your temper and sit quiet and still,

And you do enjoy rocking in that rocking chair
Pulled ever so close to the fire
With your fuzzy house slippers and housecoat and a book—
It seems your heart's desire,

47

When you wake up in the morning
And feel that life has just passed you by,
But there isn't time for you to worry,
And it's just too late to cry,

When crack filler for those wrinkles
Seems to work out very neat,
When there's bunions on every toe
And calluses on your feet,

When your old true love is in a rest home,
And the rest of them are dead,
And another one's shoulders have shifted,
And he's bald where his hair was curly and red,

When you worry about blood pressure and arthritis,
And the change of life is long past,
And looking at your snoozing mate,
You wonder, "Where is that romance that was supposed to last?"

When those darling babies you used to cherish and cuddle
Are grown women now and gray-haired men,
And they're always in a hurry,
And you can never talk to them,

When folks just don't speak loud enough
For you to ever hear,
And you walk ever so carefully on the ice
Where you used to skate without fear,

When the frost is on the pumpkin,
And the body weighs on the cane,
And the expression on the face that once was young and radiant
Is now just one of pain,

When money doesn't matter,
Or all the lovely things that it can buy,
And your thoughts dwell on that great hereafter
In that great land waiting beyond the sky,

And you think of all the foolish sins that you've committed,
And you wish they'd just go away,
So you might not be really old, my dear friend,
But you're fast becoming that way.

So better straighten up your life and repent
And do it mighty fast,
For all the signs point out that life is short,
And yours is slipping mighty fast.

So gather all your blossoms while you may
And don't forget to make out that will
'Cause you're soon going to be going on a long awaited journey,
And if the Lord don't want you, then the devil will.

I read that to my sister Anona, and she said. "That's too close to home. That's not funny!"

14 *The Jewish Wedding*

Horace Crandell: Most everything I recite is poems, but I have one that isn't. It's a story, "The Jewish Wedding."

Hello, everybody. I'm so glad to have the privilege of standing up before a me and saying a few words unta me.

I'm so glad that we are all scattered so close together here among these valleys. You know, when I first come to this country I had nothing. Now with the help of de Lord, I'm now five hundred dollars in debt.

Seems to me like everybody wants to get married nowadays. Even me, I vant to get married, but every time I find a girl I vant to marry for love, I always find out she ain't got no money.

The other day there's a fella who vorks for me decide he vant to get married. So I give him half a day off. Sometime it takes longer. Then in a few days I got an invitation to de vedding, and it says, "Mr. Davinski, your presence is requested right away fer the weddin'." Now why can't they wait till I get to da vedden before they get their presents? Stingy people.

Vell, I decided to go, and ven I get there everybody in polite society was there. Mr. and Mrs. Lavinski, and Mr. and Mrs. Abinsteen, and everybody vas there. And then there was a nigger there or er' an Irishman there. Nobody asked him to come, and nobody had a nerve to ask him to leave so he jus stayed.

But was everybody dressed up. Um hum! The men all had on brand new Texaco suits, with stand-up collars that their wives had fixed 'em so they couldn't turn right or left. They did it on purpose so they could tell what young lady they was lookin' at. And de women, dey don't have nothing on at all hardly, and dey think they was dressed up.

And den de bride and groom come marching down de aisle and vas dey dressed up. Um hum! The bride's hair was all upholstered in the latest style. Pompy-doodle style, with its white feather sticking up. All done up in exquisite knot with a high white feather sticking out. And her teeth, they were a beautiful. Both of them. And if

49

wouldn't have been for that pimple on her left nose, she would have been a so nice lookin'.

She had on a brand new calico dress with a great long trail behind, and two little girls went along and held up the trail. And two little girls walk along in front throwing flowers in front of dem. Paper flowers, two pounds for a nickel.

And the groom, was he dressed up! He had on a brand new suit, double buster. It was made for his brother when he got married. And it fit him too, all except the coat and pants. 'Twas all right when he stood up, but when he sat down, he jus stood up again.

And den they go marching back up the aisle, and de preacher, he say de most beautiful things. He says, "You two take hold each other's right hands." And he says, "There are three things in this life that people have ta do. First you're borned, today you are married, and now there's nothing left to do but die." And then everybody want to cry. And I want to cry, too, but I didn't have no handkerchiefs. And then, purty quick, he says, "And now I pronounce you husband and wife." And then everyone wants to kiss da wife. Even me, I vant to kiss her, too, so I got jus as close as I can, and when she wasn't lookin' I make a jab ta kiss her. And she saw me jus in time, and she ducked, and I kissed dat Irishman right square in front of da face. An dis make him mad, and he wanted to fight everybody. But shucks, dat Irishman, he can't fight. Me and my brother and two cousins almost whip him one day.

And den somebody said we all go down to da recreation hall, and we'll have a few parts. So I vant to get as close to dis bride as I can. So I got walkin' pretty close, and I got a little too close, and I stepped on her trail, and her skirt come off. And she turned around and give me an awful look, and then she fainted. And they had to throw water in her face, and then her complexion come off.

And then we get down to de recreation hall, and there are two sisters there, Rachael and Rebecca. And one of dem sang a beautiful song, "Ye Sleep in de Ditch" by Hellen Squealer Pillbox. You know, three weeks ago that women couldn't sing a note. And he took her down to de doctor, and he cut her utensils out. Now, she sings beautifully. And he's going to send her to Italy to have her voice calcimined. The other one, she sang a beautiful ballad. And when she got through, I turned to Lavinski and said, "What do you think of her execution."

"By golly, I'm in favor of it."

And then there was Lavinski's wife. All the time, that women don't feel good. She got an absence in the brain, and the doctors say if she don't have dat operation she'll be fiddle-minded. And she got exclamatory rheumetis. She hollers all the time. Three weeks ago she ate a sick fish, and it give her toenail poisoning, and the doctor says if you won't have it, you better have her life insured. So I had her life insured, and now it don't make no difference how much medicine I give that women, she always gets better.

And den someone says dinner is now served. So they all rush down to de mess hall, just like a mess a pigs. Dey run and dey jump and knock each other down, and dey fall all over each other. Dey had an awful time. I know, I was the first one down to da dinner, and I saw it all happen.

And den dey pass da menu around. The first thing dat was on it was menu. Well, I didn't try any of dat. Then they had macaroni and tomatoes, macaroni and cheese, and sweet chili and lobster. And then they had a chicken there, too. And they passed this chicken around. They said the one that gets the vishbone, all he had to do is shut his eyes and make a vish and the vish vill be granted. Vell, I got the vishbone, but I didn't have time to shut my eyes and make a vish right at dinner time. And I looked over and saw Mr. Lavinski and says, "Say, that is a beautiful tie you've got on."

He says, "That ain't my tie; that's macaroni and tomatoes."

Then purty quick they started throwing rice and old shoes at the bride and groom, and they hit him, too. And purty quick somebody threw an old shoe at me and hit me right where I was gonna sit down. I turned around and looked, and it was that Irishman, and he had his foot in it. Then he kicked me again, and he kicked me twice more. Promised me anothern, but he couldn't reach me; I was too far under the table. And den when I got out, I picked up a tomato, and I threw it at dat Irishman and hit him right square between da face.

It was a cowardly tomato, one of dem kinds dat hits and den runs. Den dat Irishman, he take after me. I run for the back door and never stopped till I got home. And believe it or not, dat's the last time I'm ever going to a Jewish vedding unless they pay me fare both ways.

Goodbye, everybody.

15 *The Joke*

Katy G. Lee: Oh, golly, the only reading I can remember, it's really not... I'm sure it must have been published, was something my daddy used to say. He'd say, let's see:

Once upon a time,
Or so it is averred,
That in the awful depths of hell
A merry laugh was heard.

Up rose the prince with darkling brow
And pointing with his staff,
"Stand forth, bad one,
And tell us how in hell you came to laugh."

There came a voice from out the throng,
It had an English accent strong,
"I had to laugh," he cried,
"I caught the point of a joke
I heard twenty years before I died."

I really don't know any others. My treasure, everybody knows, is a song that's been in the family, and that's what I usually do is sing it.

16   *A Preacher Preaching About the Bible*

Grant E. Brown: My mother used to give a reading. Well, actually I found it and sent it to her. She gave it, and it was called "A Preacher Preaching About the Bible." And he wasn't quite right on it. She added to it, and when she passed away, I thought, "I hate to see that go with her." So I've been giving it a little bit since then. I'll close by giving that one. It says:

Lo, The Queen of Sheba, she went down unto Jerusalem riding on a mule, and the mule flung her, and she fell among thieves who passed her by on the other side. By and by, she got back on that mule, and she could see them a-comin' from afar off. And five of them was wise and five was foolish, and they came away with palm leaf fans crying in a loud voice, "Hosanna to Susanna of Ephesians!"

And she rode on down that road, and they waved those palm leaf fans in that woman's face, and she looked up in the second story window, and she said in a loud voice, "Fling down Jezebel!"

And the answer came back, "We're not a-gonna fling down Jezebel."

She said unto them again, "Fling down Jezebel!"

And the answer came back again, "We ain't a-gonna fling down Jezebel."

And she said unto them yet a third time, "Fling down Jezebel."

And they changed their minds, and they flung her down seventy times seven. And she broke in so many pieces they could not be numbered, and they fed the multitude, and there was five fishes and three loaves left over, and there was weepin' and wailin' and snatchin' out of teeth, and they passed over the river Jordan, and when they got on the other side, they set down at the Feast of the Passover.

And there was a man who had two sons, and he divided his money, and one took his and went into a far country and wasted it all on righteous living, and when it was all gone, he comes sneaking back home and killed his brother's fatted calf, and the rains fell, and the winds blew, and the floods came, and everybody on the earth was drowned except Adam and Eve.

So, Brothers and Sisters, here we is, but there's one question I'd like to ask. Just one question, and that is: "On the Day of Judgment, whose wife is Jezebel gonna be?"

17   *The Christmas Villain*

LaVelle Whiting DeSpain: This one, "The Christmas Villain," is kind of like, oh you know, the old one where the bank president is trying to beat the orphans, and we did this one, and we got a lot of laughs, and it was fun to do, and we do it every Christmas Eve. I guess you could just say it's a kind of a reading.

'Twas the night before Christmas,
And all through the house,
No one was happy
Because of a louse.

It's not stockings hanging
He'd like to see.
He'd like the necks
Of these unfortunate three.

And at this point all three of them put their hands around their necks.

It's not visions of sugarplums
Dancing through their heads,
But where would they sleep
Because they had no beds.

Mom in her rags,
Too worried to nap,
Oh, where would she get the money
To pay off this sap?

The mortgage was due
At midnight, you see.
Oh, what would happen
To this unfortunate three?

And at the door
They heard such a clatter
They sprang to the window
To see what was the matter.

And what to their wondering
Eyes should appear
But this horrible man.
How their hearts raced with fear!

He sprang to the door
So lively and quick
They thought for a moment
It might be St. Nick.

The mortgage money he demanded
For he had no shame,
As he ranted and raved
Calling each one a bad name.

Their plight was desperate
On this cold Christmas night,
For the weather was freezing,
And the wind it did bite.

We had the wind come in here.

His eyes how they twinkled.
His nose like a cherry.
It was plain to see
He'd had too much sherry.

Then the villain burps real loud.

He went right to work
As busy as he could be,
For he was determined
To evict this unfortunate three.

They pled and they cried
For just one more chance,
But the villain said no
And started to dance.

But hark! What was this?
They heard another clatter.
The villain was wise.
He knew what was the matter.

He was furious and frantic.
He failed at his trick,
For there in the doorway
Stood dear old St. Nick.

What a welcome sight
In his little suit of red.
It soon gave them to know
They had nothing to dread.

He wrote out his check
For the amount that was due
And let the villain know
His skullduggery was through.

The villain was defeated.
In anger he rose,
And putting his finger
Aside his nose.

We heard him explain
Ere he went out of sight,
"I never believed in Santa,
But I do after tonight."

18 *Setting a Hen*

Grant E. Brown: I've also given just non-rhyme type readings through the years. I've got an old hat I put on, false hair underneath it, and a nose. If I don't say anything funny, people get a kick out of how it looks anyway, but one that's typical of that is called "Setting a Hen," and its from the old country. I don't know what old country. It really isn't any one, but a lot of people don't know that. He says:

Mr. Varris, I see that almost everybody writes something for the chicken papers now days, and I thought perhaps maybe I could do that, too. I could write all about what took place mid me last summer. You know, whether if you don't know, then I tell you. Katrina, that was my frau, and me, we keep some chickens for a long time ago. One day she says to me, "Socrey," that's my name, "why don't you put some eggs under that old blue hen chicken. I think she wants to set."

"Well," I say, "maybe I guess I will." So I take some of the best eggs out to the barn. Where the old hen hide her nest is the side of the hay mound five or six feet up, and you see, I never was very big up and down but always pretty big all the way around in the middle that I couldn't reach the nest till I found a barrel to stand on. When I stand up on the barrel and when my head come up by the side of that nest, that blasted old hen gave me such a peck that my nose ran all over my face mid blood, and when I dodged back, that blasted barrel, he break, and I come tumbling down ker-slam wham! *(Laughs.)* I never thought I could go inside a barrel before, but there I was tight stuck mid my face all bloody and eggs, and my vest pulled all up under my arm holes, and when I saw I was tight stuck, I holler, "Katrina! Katrina!" Then she come and see me mid my face all bloody and eggs, my vest way up under my arm holes, she just lay down on the hay, laugh and laugh. I say, "What you lay there and laugh like old blue for? Why don't you pull me mid the barrel out?"

And she says, "Oh wipe off your face and pull down your vest." Then she lay back like she split herself more as ever.

Mad as I was, I say, "Katrina, don't you gonna come and pull me the barrel out?"

And she says, "Of course, I will, Socrey." And she roll me over, and I take a-hold of the door knob, and she pull on the barrel.

But the first pull she made, I holler, "Donner and Splitzen, stop that! There's nails in the barrel!" You see, when I went down, the nails went down, but when I come out, they stick me all the way around. Well, to make a short story long, I says, "Why don't you go get neighbor Hoffman to come and saw me the barrel off?" And he come; he like to split himself with laugh, too, but he rolled me over, sawed the barrel all the way around off, and I still have half a barrel around my face.

Katrina, she says so softly, "Wait a minute while I get a pattern of that new hopper shirt you have on." Mad as I was, I pulled a knife out of my pocket and whittled the confounded hoops off that barrel for the woodpile. I'll burn that one again. And Katrina, she says, "Socrey, don't you gonna put some eggs under that old blue hen?"

Mad as I was I says, "Katrina!" She speaks pretty good English. "Katrina, if you ever say dat to me again, I get a bill of writing of you from the lawyer." And I tell you, she don't say that no more.

And now, Mr. Varris, now when I stand up on a barrel, I don't stand on it. I get a box.

19 *Good Morning, Dr. Martin*

LaVelle Whiting DeSpain: Both of my daughters were in the Miss Arizona Pageant. When my one daughter, the youngest one, was chosen, I was just really put out. My brother-in-law was dying of cancer, and I was staying at the hospital, and she came and said, "Mother, I've got to have a reading."

And I said, "Claudia, that's just impossible." But I did it. I guess death

was just so much on my mind. It's about a young mother who is dying of cancer, and it's quite dramatic, and she gave that reading, and I thought it was quite nice.

"Good morning, Dr. Martin, I'm sorry I'm late. Oh, I feel just wonderful and disgustingly healthy. Really, I never felt better. I have such a busy day. But I promised Bob I'd stop by for the lab report. It seems silly when we both know that this report will be negative. I'm almost embarrassed now as I think how I rushed in here last week so sure that something was radically wrong. Sickness is a luxury I just can't afford. Maybe I should come back later. I have so many little errands to take care of today. This is a special day at our house, Dr. Martin. Our twins are four years old today. Just four years ago today, Dr. Martin, you handed me my babies so beautiful and bright and healthy. And they were mine—mine and Bob's. Four wonderful happy years so full of love and happiness that at times it almost frightens me. God, I know, sent us twins to make up for those long years of waiting and longing."

"You know, Mary, we don't always know God's plan for us. We become impatient with Him. God hadn't forgotten you, nor will He ever. I especially want you to remember this, Mary, when I tell you what I must tell you today."

"Oh, yes, Dr. Martin. God has been good to me and has given me a healthy body, and no one appreciates this blessing more than I. Now, I really must run along. I have so much to do and so little time to do it."

"Yes, Mary, so little time, but how did you know?"

"Know? Know what, Dr. Martin? That I'm always running out of time? That there aren't enough hours in the day to accomplish all that I want to? Dr. Martin, you seem in a serious mood today. Is something wrong? Are you trying to tell me something? You... you look so grave, Dr. Martin, so serious. This isn't like you. No, Dr. Martin, don't... don't look at me like that. I'm well! I'm well! Do you hear? I don't want to hear that lab report now or ever. Why? Why are you standing there glaring at me like a judge who's just condemned his prisoner to death?"

"Oh, Mary, Mary, don't make it so difficult. It's... it's incurable. You have six weeks, maybe a month."

"No! No! I won't accept it. I'm alive! I'm going to go on living. How can you tell me I've only six weeks to live? Who do you think you are, Dr. Martin? God? God and only God has the power over life and death, and no mortal—not even you, Dr. Martin—has that power. I love life. It's all I know. You can't take it from me. Do you hear, Dr. Martin? Do you hear?"

"Yes, Mary, I hear. I would do anything... anything...."

"Then tell me it isn't true. Tell me it's just a bad dream. You seem to forget, Dr. Martin, I have two precious children who need a mother. And Bob, my Bob, who can't ever find a pair of socks without my help, do you realize what this will do to him? To them? How can I give him enough love in six weeks to last a lifetime?"

"We all must die, Mary. An early death just means one lives in eternity a little longer."

"Yes, Dr. Martin, you have your medical books, your lab reports, your x-ray, but you have overlooked one very important factor, and that is faith. Even death can't destroy that. Faith, hope, and determination, they gave me my babies. Can't these important factors give me my life? You know all the answers, Dr. Martin. You answer that one."

"No, Mary, I don't know all the answers. If I did I would be God. You see, I too have my doubts. I... I lost my wife."

"Oh, Dr. Martin, I'm so sorry, so sorry. God, dear God, help me, help me. Strengthen me for I can't do it alone. Give me the strength to live and the courage to die."

CHAPTER THREE

Mostly for Children

RECITATIONS AND RECITING are dependent on children. Children are a primary audience in families and communities where recitation thrives because of the mutually appreciative, highly satisfactory audience-performer relationship. To recite for children and share their wonder and delight or to be a child and "go to bed on" a poem someone dear performs for you is to share a moment not soon forgotten.

It is in childhood that the reciter of the future is introduced to the craft. There are recitations that are taught to children within the family, and it is through childhood exposure to recitation that the child sees oral performance as a valued skill to be developed and enjoyed and is acquainted with its techniques and forms.

20   *Oh, I'll Tell You a Story*

LaVelle Whiting DeSpain: Grandma Hatch was a great storyteller, and we'd say to Grandpa Hatch, "Now, you tell us a story, Grandpa." And he'd say:

Oh, I'll tell you a story
About Old Mother Morrey,
And now my story's begun.
And I'll tell you another
About Jack and his brother,
And now my story's done."

We'd say, "Oh, Grandpa!" And he'd say it again. That was his talent.

21   *The Sugar-Plum Tree*

Horace Crandell: I learned this one not too long ago. I found a book some-where, and I'd heard Van N. Holyoak say it several times, and then I ran

across this book that had it, and I learned it. I don't remember when. It's not too long ago. Must have been in the '60s.

Have you ever heard of a Sugar-Plum Tree?
It's a marvel of great renown.
It blooms on the shores of the Lollipop Sea
In the garden of Shut-Eye Town;

The fruit that it bears is wondrously sweet
(So the people who've tasted it say)
And good little children have only to eat
Of that fruit to be happy next day.

When you get to that tree, you'll have quite a time
To capture the treasures I sing;
That tree is so tall no person can climb
To the boughs where the sugar-plums cling!

But there high up in that tree is a chocolate cat,
And a gingerbread dog prowls below—
And this is the means you contrive to get at
Those sugar-plums tempting you so:

You just have to speak to that gingerbread dog,
And he barks with such terrible zest
That chocolate cat at once is agog,
As his swelling proportions attest.

Then that chocolate cat goes cavorting around
From this leafy branch unto that,
And the sugar-plums tumble, of course, to the ground.
Hurrah for that chocolate cat!

There are sugar-plums, gumdrops, and peppermint canes
With stripings of crimson and gold,
And you carry away from that treasure that rains,
As much as your apron can hold!

Come, little child, cuddle closer to me
In your dainty white nightcap and gown,
And I'll rock you away to that Sugar-Plum Tree
In the garden of Shut-Eye Town.

22   *Put My Little Shoes Away*

Madeline Collins: This song "Put My Little Shoes Away" was sung to rock me to sleep when I was two and three years old in Florida. We came up to Ohio a

year later, and I don't know when I first memorized it and started to recite it.

Mama dear, come bathe my forehead,
For I'm growing very weak.
Just one little drop of water
Pour upon my burning cheek.

Mama dear, I'll be an angel
By perhaps another day.
Say you'll do it, won't you, Mother?
Put my little shoes away.

Santy Claus, he brought them to me
With a lot of other things,
And among them was an angel
With a pair of golden wings.

Mama dear, I'll be an angel
By perhaps another day.
Say you'll do it, won't you, Mother?
Put my little shoes away.

Soon the baby will be walking.
Then they'll fit his little feet.
He will look so neat and cunning
As he walks along the street.

Tell my darling little playmates
That I never more will play.
Give them all my toys, but Mother,
Put my little shoes away.

23 *Big Wicked Bill*

Kristi Hodge: ''Big Wicked Bill'' is one Grandpa didn't write, but he told it to us a lot when we were kids, and I learned it because he always used to say it to us. It's the one we would go to bed on.

Sometimes in the hush of evening
When the winds grow tired and still,
By my fire I sit dozing and dreaming,
Let memories bring back what they will.

I hear a cry of ''Mush!''
As the whip flicks out and cracks like the shot of a gun.
There's a malamute team coming straight toward me,
Eight dogs, they're all on the run.

61

That leader is big, and he comes running low,
Pulling that sleigh with a will.
I've never condensed my memory of him,
My lead dog, Big Wicked Bill.

That driver seems worried as he hurries that team,
And in fear he keeps looking back.
As night closes in, he hears it again.
It's the cry of a killer wolf pack,

And then the northern lights come out to play,
Like fingers they feel for the sky.
That driver yells, "Mush!" to that weary team.
It's "Mush!" or we've all got to die.

The moon looks down on that race of death,
That wolf pack closing in.
That driver knows if his lead dog falls,
The battle's over for him.

Till his rifle is empty, he holds them off,
Then unafraid they close in for the kill.
The driver knows his life depends
On the fangs of Big Wicked Bill.

But still pulling strongly Bill fights them off
Right up to cabin door.
While getting inside, I soon realize
Big Bill won't fight anymore.

"Wicked?" Yes, that's what I named him when he's a pup.
"Wicked" 'cause he loved so to fight.
But because he stood off that killer wolf pack,
I lived through a horrible night.

Now, if you've never owned a big malamute,
Then perhaps you just don't understand
This longing I get especially at night
Just to feel his big head in my hand.

So now in the hush of the evening
When the winds grow tired and are still,
By my fire I sit waiting for memories to call
Hoping they bring Big Wicked Bill.

24 *Little Orphan Annie*

Alice Gene Tripp: I was born in Paintsville, Kentucky, and lived there for six weeks, and then my family moved to Dayton, Ohio, and we lived there till I was between four and five, then we moved to Texas. I have lived the biggest part of my life between Dallas and Fort Worth, but my recitations come from my maternal grandmother. She was from Lexington, Kentucky, and I just learned her recitations from her by repetition. Because I was the oldest of four, I heard them four times longer than the youngest child would have. They were strictly for the kids. She would sit and knit and tell stories and do poems. One of them was "Little Orphan Annie." I like "Little Orphan Annie."

Little Orphan Annie's come to our house to stay,
To wash the cups and saucers up, and brush the crumbs away,
An' shoo the chickens off the porch, an' dust the hearth an' sweep,
An' make the fire, an' bake the bread, an' earn her board-an'-keep;
An' all us little children, when the supper things are done,
We set around the kitchen fire an' have the mostest fun
A-list'nin' to the witch-tales that Annie tells about,
An' the goblins will get you
      If you
           Don't
                Watch
                    Out!

And once they was a little boy who didn't say his prayers—
An' at night way up stairs,
His mammy heard him holler, an' his daddy heared him bawl,
An' when they turn't the kivvers down, he wasn't there at all!
They seeked him in the rafter-room, the cubbyhole, the chest,
They seeked him up the chimbly flue, an' ever'where, I guess;
But all they ever found was jist his pants an' roundabout!
An' the goblins will get you
      If you
           Don't
                Watch
                    Out!

An' once there was a little girl who laughed an' grinned,
An' make fun of ever' one, an' all her blood-an'-kin;
An' onc't when they was "company," an' ole folks were there,
She mocked 'em an' she shocked 'em, an' said she didn't care!
An' just as she kicked her heels, to turn and run an' hide,
They was two big Black Things a-standin' by her side,
An' they snatched her through the ceilin' 'fore she knowed what
    she's about!
An' the goblins'll get you
        If you
              Don't
                    Watch
                        Out!

So you better mind yer parents, and yer teachers fond and dear,
An' churish them 'at loves you an' dry the orphan's tear,
An' help the pore an' needy ones that gather all about,
Or the goblins'll get you
        If you
              Don't
                    Watch
                        Out!

25   *The Irish Washer Woman*

Ralph Rogers: Now, there's a tune I play on my harmonica that's a fast tune that they used to quadrille by when I was a kid, and they call it "The Irish Washer Woman," and we used to call it:

There was an old hen;
That had a white foot.
She built her nest
In a mulberry root.

She muffled her feathers
To keep her eggs warm;
If you'd leave her alone,
She'd do you no harm.

And here's the tune. *(Plays harmonica.)* **Could you step to that?**

26 *Willy and the Giants*

Elda Brown: These stories have stayed with our families all our lives. My children have wanted me to put some of these stories down. I don't think our grandchildren could possibly realize what these stories meant in our lives. We had no television. We had no radios. We had no picture shows. We had very, very few books to read. We'd read them over and over, all that we did have, and so these stories were one of the great influences on our lives.

Once there was a little boy who lived across the ocean with his mother in a small country that had a king for a ruler. Willy and his mother and his little brother and sister were poor. Their father had died, and Willy wanted to go away to work, but his mother didn't want him to. He was too little.

One day he heard that the king had offered to give a large sum of money for anyone who would come in to the village and kill a big wild hog that was bothering them until they couldn't gather their gardens and their produce there, and so if anyone would come and kill this pig, they'd give him a large sum of money. Willy begged and begged his mother until finally she consented for him to go even though she was very afraid. He went in to the king, and when the king saw him, he laughed and said, "What could you do? All of my men haven't been able to kill that big pig. How could you do it?"

And Willy said, "Yes, but you said anyone could come that wanted to and try, and I want to try."

So finally the king said, "Well, all right, but I'm sure afraid to let you go out there. Go out east of town there where our gardens are, and you'll see in that big fence, and all around there that big pig will come after you."

So Willy went out there, and he was kind of afraid, but he thought, "I'll think of something. I know I can think of something." So he was walking along, and he looked around, and he saw that big old pig coming, and oh, he was so big, and his teeth were so big, sticking out the side of his mouth. And he was scared, but he couldn't think what to do, and all of a sudden he saw an old schoolhouse over there, and so he ran for that schoolhouse. By the time he got there, the old pig was so close to him that he couldn't even shut the door to keep him out, but he got down to the other door, and he got out and shut that door, and then he ran around where the pig had come in behind him, and he shut that door, so he had the old pig locked in the schoolhouse. Oh, he was happy!

So he went back to the king, and he said, "Well, I've got your old pig locked up down there in the schoolhouse. Go get him."

And the king just couldn't believe it, and the men rushed down there, and sure enough, he did have. And so the king gave him a big sack of money, and he went home, and oh, his mother was so happy, and they bought a lot of things that they needed, and they were living so good, and they fixed up their house and everything.

And then one day Willy heard that the king had said anybody that would come and kill a big old bull that was destroying so much of their crops and was killing some of the men, and they were all afraid to go out in the woods or any place to get their cattle and things. Anyone that would kill this big bull, he would give him part of his kingdom. Oh, Willy wanted that so bad, and so he begged and begged his mother until finally she consented for him to go. And when he came to the king, the king said, "I can't let a young boy like you go out and fight against that big bull."

But Willy said, "Please, you told me that I—anybody that could kill him—and I know I can kill him."

And so the king finally said, "Well, all right. I'll let you, but I hate to."

And so Willy went way out in the woods where they told him that he'd find the bull, and he had his slingshot, and he thought that's what he'd use 'cause he didn't have a gun or anything like that. So he was walkin' along, and all of a sudden he heard that big old bull coming, and he saw him, and he had the longest horns that Willy had ever seen, and oh, he was so scared he didn't know what to do. All he could think of was to climb up a tree, so he climbed up a tree just as fast as he could, and oh, that bull was so mad he just hit against that tree and bumped it as hard as he could, and he was so mad that he started to try to climb up that tree and put his front feet up in there, and do you know? He caught his horns between two limbs, and he couldn't move. He was caught right there, and he couldn't move. All he could do was just beller.

And so Willy, he jumped down out of the tree and took his knife and cut the old bull's throat, and then he went back to the king and said, "Well, your old bull's a-hangin' back there. You can go and get him if you want to." And the men ran to see, and sure enough, the old bull was hangin' up in the tree.

Well, then the king gave Willy part of his country, and so Willy went home, and oh, his mother and his brother and sister, they were so happy, and they lived quietly and nice for awhile.

And then another time the king said, "Anyone that can come and kill three old giants that are so wicked and so mean to us that we cannot keep on living here if someone doesn't kill them for us, anyone who can do that, that can kill these giants, they can marry my beautiful daughter."

Oh, Willy had seen this beautiful daughter, and he wanted to marry her, and so he hurried and got ready, and he went to kill the giants, and when he came to the king's place, the king said, "Oh, this is so much worse than the other, I hate to have you go."

But Willy said, "Well, I'm a-goin' anyway." And so the men went and showed Willy where the old giants came down off of the mountain, and they thought he'd find them there. And so Willy went way out that way. He didn't see any giants, but pretty soon he heard them, and when they came, they were so big that even their footsteps made the earth kind of shake. And they stomped along, and they came, and oh, they were so big. Willy had never seen anything that big, and so he hurried and climbed up a tree and decided he'd wait and see what he could do and what they would do, so he climbed up that tree, and he just sat there and waited, and those three old giants came, and they talked, and they talked. They talked so loud they just would make everything shake. They laid down under the tree that Willy was up in, and they went to sleep.

Well, Willy, just think what he did! He threw a little rock and hit the old giant—the old middle giant, the one that was the big captain of them all—he hit him right on the forehead just hard with a rock 'cause Willy had all those rocks in his pocket, little round rocks that he threw in his slingshot, and that old giant, he jumped up, and he was so mad that he hit one of the giants that was beside him and said, "What did you hit me like that for?" And he hit him and killed him, and then he laid back down, and Willy threw another rock, and that one hit him harder than ever right on his forehead. Oh, he jumped up, and he was so mad, and he said, "It wasn't that other one that did it. It was you!" And so he hit the other giant and killed him, and then he laid back down again, "Now, I'll get to sleep." And he went to sleep, and Willy threw another rock and hit him so hard that he jumped up, and he looked up that tree, and he said, "Why, you little mean boy! Get down from there as fast as you can." And he shook the tree, and he shook Willy right down out of the tree, and when he got down there, the giant looked at him, and he laughed, and he said, "Now, you could do all of that, a little old boy like you! Well, you come with me. I'm going up to my cave, and you come and go up there with me, and then we'll decide what we'll do with you. I know what I'm going to do with you."

So they went up to the old giant's cave, and oh, Willy was worried, and he kept thinking what could he do, what could he do. And so finally the old giant said, "We've got our dinner all ready, so I guess we'd just as well eat a little while (some of it) now 'cause my friends are gone, so you just as well eat a little with me." And so they sat down, and that giant took the biggest bowl of soup Willy had ever seen in his life, and he gave Willy a bowl.

And all of a sudden Willy had an idea, and he said to that giant,

"I'll bet I can eat more soup than you can."

Oh, the old giant just laughed, and he hawed; he said, "You eat more than me?"

And he said, "Yes, sir, I'll bet you that I can."

And so the old giant said, "All right, let's go ahead." And you know what Willy did? He stuck a plastic sack down in front of his shirt, and instead of eating the soup, he'd pour the big bowl of soup down in there when the giant wasn't looking, and pretty soon that big old bag was just full of soup.

And the giant had eaten all that he could eat. He couldn't eat anymore, and he finally said, "Well, I didn't believe you could eat that much, but you sure have."

And so Willy said to the giant, "I know something else that I can do. I'll bet you that I can cut my stomach and let that soup all out, and I'll bet you can't."

And that giant said, "Well, I can do anything you can. Let's see you do it." So Willy took a knife and cut that plastic bag. Out went all the soup!

And the old giant said, "Well, if you can do that, so can I, and I'm too full, so I will." So he cut his stomach... and then he died.

And so then Willy, he laughed and went back to the king, and he said, "Well, your giants are all dead up there if you want to go see them." At first the men were just afraid to go and to look and to see, but finally they went up there, and there were the three old giants dead.

So Willy married the beautiful daughter of the queen and lived happy ever after over there.

I learned that story from my father.

27   *Companion Poems*

Grant E. Brown: I've been called on quite a lot to be master of ceremonies at wedding receptions and things like this. The reason they asked me was because they knew I'd be willing to make a fool out of myself which I always did, and they enjoyed that, so I have a lot of little crazy things that has no redeeming value whatsoever.

My mother taught me not to smoke;
I don't;
Nor listen to a dirty joke;
I don't.
She made it clear
I must not wink
At pretty girls
Or even think
About intoxicating drink;
I don't.

A lot of you
Chase women, wine, song;
I don't.
I don't even know
How it is done.
You'd think I
Wouldn't have much fun.
I don't.

And then its companion:

I never kiss; I never neck;
I never say darn; I never say heck;
I'm always good; I'm always nice;
I play no poker, shake no dice;
I have no line of funny tricks,
But give me time. I'm only six.

28   *The Bee Sting*

Alida Connolly: Okay, I'll do ''The Bee Sting'' now. We lived on a ranch on Oak Creek, and we were waiting for electricity. In the meantime, we had this old john that sat down by the creek. The water snakes loved to have a nest in it, and there were always black widows, but the worst thing of all was one day in a hurry, we were going to St. Johns, I ran down there, and I sat on this bee, and we were starting to St. Johns, and it just got funny. I didn't have any paper in the car, so I just pulled a little scrap here off of this and a little scrap off of that and the back of a book, and by the time I got to St. Johns, I had this poem about the bee sting.

My head is real hard.
I don't doubt it one bit,
But there's one thing I've learned, brother,
And that's look before you sit.

We live in the country,
And when we go to the rest room to rest,
We go a mile to the east
With a turn to the west.

One day when I finally reached it,
I was too exhausted to see
That the seat was already occupied
By a cantankerous bee.

A bee whose main purpose there
Was gathering honey,
Though I wouldn't touch it
For any man's money.

He pulls out his little weapon,
I'll swear it was red hot,
And he applied that little dagger
To a most vulnerable spot.

A spot where for sympathy
Even my best friends can't see,
But like that old familiar song,
Ouch! There's been a change in me.

Next morning in Sunday school
My intentions were the best,
But that spot just started itching,
And it gave me no rest.

And I wiggled, and I squiggled,
And I squirmed in my chair.
The people around me
All turned to stare.

So if I never get to heaven,
Just please don't blame me,
But put all the blame
On that troublesome bee.

And now when I enter,
I gaze all around
At the walls and the ceiling
And the floor and the ground.

'Cause I aim to spot him
'Fore he nips me.
I ain't furnishing no more honey
For a red hot bee!

My mother always said, "Lida, that's vulgar!" But kids just love it. Whenever a bunch of us get together and there's some children, they ask me to do "The Bee Sting."

29   *Raggedy Man*

Alice Gene Tripp: My maternal grandmother's stories and poems were ones you didn't find in books, and it was important to commit them to memory like "Raggedy Man."

Oh, the Raggedy Man, he works for Pa,
And he's the nicest man ever you saw.
He comes to our house most every day,
And he waters the horses, and he feeds them hay.
And then if our hired girl says he can,
He milks the cow for Elizabeth Ann.
Ain't he a nice old Raggedy Man?
A Raggedy, Raggedy, Raggedy Man.

And the Raggedy Man, he tells most rhymes,
And he tells me, too, if I'm good sometimes.
He knows about brownies, and fairies, and elves,
And squeaky-come-squeeze that swallers themselves,
And out by the stump in our pasture lot
He showed me a hole that the wonks has got
Way down deep in the ground,
And they can turn into you or Elizabeth Ann.
Ain't he a funny old Raggedy Man?
A Raggedy, Raggedy, Raggedy Man.

And one day the Raggedy Man says to me says,
"What you gwanna be when you grows up?
Is you gwanna be a rich merchant like your pa is
And wear fine clothes,
Or what are you gwanna be, goodness knows?"
And then he just laughs with Elizabeth Ann
When I says, "I wants to be a fine Raggedy Man."
A Raggedy, Raggedy, Raggedy Man.

I know when my children were growing, they would request the stories, and it was like, "Two 'Raggedy Mans' and one 'Little Orphan Annie,' and I'll go to sleep."

30   *Essay on a Frog*

Margaret Witt: Let me tell you the "Essay on a Frog." I learned it years ago. I haven't learned any new ones for a number of years. I'm getting too dense. It come out in the paper, and I learned it from that.

What a wonderful bird the frog are.
When he stands, he sits almost.
When he hops, he flies almost.

He ain't got no sense hardly.
He ain't got no tail hardly either,
And when he sits, he sits on what he ain't got almost.

31   *Big Klaus and Little Klaus*

LaVelle Whiting DeSpain: I have "Little Klaus and Big Klaus." It's a family story. There are several stories that we always have to have at family reunions and such—that and make taffy candy—and "Big Klaus and Little Klaus" is one.

There is two men...

Would you like to hear this? Okay, this is a family story.

There is two men. One was Little Klaus and one was Big Klaus. And Little Klaus only had one white horse, but Big Klaus had six big white horses. One day Big Klaus said to Little Klaus, said, "Little Klaus, I'll make an agreement with you." He said, "I'll let you take my six white horses on Sunday and use them. If you'll let me take yours six days of the week, you can take mine one day of the week."

So they had this agreement, and so they thought that was fine. One day, it was on a Sunday, and all the people were coming from church, Little Klaus was so proud of these horses, and so he decided to do a little bragging. As they got closer, he said, "Get up, my seven white horses."

Big Klaus heard him, and he reprimanded him. He said, "Little Klaus, you know better than that. Only one of those horses belongs to you. The other six are mine, and I don't want to hear you ever say that again."

He said, "Okay, I won't." He did pretty well for a while, and then he was tempted again. They were having a big celebration, and again he said, "Get up, my seven white horses."

Big Klaus heard him, and he said, "Little Klaus, I gave you fair warning, and so I'm going to kill your horse."

Poor Little Klaus was just so sad because he knew Big Klaus really meant what he said, and he did kill his horse. Little Klaus was so sad he took and skinned the horse and tanned the horsehide, and every place he went, he took his horsehide with him. At night when he was out and not at home, he'd sleep on his horsehide. One time he was traveling, and it was getting late, and he knew this farmer lived quite close, and so he walked to the farm. He asked if he could sleep in the loft, and the woman said yes, so he climbed in the loft. He prepared for night. He could see from the loft. He could see into the farmer's house, and he could see the farmer's wife was having a nice dinner with a minister.

He watched for a while. Oh, he was so hungry looking over at them. They had roast. They had potatoes. They had nice rolls. They had cake and punch. He kept watching, and pretty soon he could hear the farmer coming home, and the farmer's wife heard the farmer coming home. Little Klaus watched as the farmer's wife hid the food in the oven, and she hid the minister in the window seat because her husband didn't like ministers.

The farmer came, and he was putting up his horse, and he saw Little Klaus. He said, "Come down, my good man. What are you doing up there?"

He said, "Well, your wife said I could sleep in your loft."

He said, "Oh, come on in. Let's have some supper." So they went in, and the farmer said, "Little Klaus is going to have supper with us."

The woman said, "All right." And she got some bread, milk, and cheese, and onions and started putting them on the table.

Little Klaus was sitting in the corner on his horsehide, and he started crinkling it.

He said, "What's that?"

He said, "That's my magic horsehide."

He said, "Why do you call it magic?"

And he said, "Well, it can discern many things."

He said, "What do you mean?"

And he said, "Why are we eating bread and milk when in the oven is a lovely roast, and cake, and nice food?"

He said, "Really?"

He said, "Yeah, just look and see."

So he opened the oven door, and all this nice food was there. The farmer was just amazed, and they sat down and enjoyed a nice meal.

When they finished the meal, again Little Klaus crinkled the horsehide.

And he said, "What did it say this time?"

He said, "There's a minister in the window seat."

He said, "A minister in my home?"

"Yeah," he said, "there's a minister in your home."

He said, "I don't believe it." He went over and opened the window seat, and he said, "There sure is. Little Klaus, I have to have that horse's hide." He said, "I'll give you a bushel of money if you'll sell me that horse's hide, and I'll give you another bushel of money if you'll get rid of this minister."

He said, "Well, I hate to part with my horsehide, but... well, I guess I will. I'll sell it to you." So he sold it to him, and he put the money in a wheelbarrow, and he went down the road, and he put the minister on top.

The minister said, "Oh, Little Klaus, don't drown me. I have a life's mission ahead of me. Please don't drown me."

And he said, "What will you give me?"

And he said, "Well, I'll give you another bushel of money."

Well, that sounded like a fair deal, so he said, "Okay." So he gave him another bushel of money, and Little Klaus let the minister go his way. He went down the street with all this money, and he saw Big Klaus coming.

Big Klaus couldn't believe his eyes, and he said, "Little Klaus, where did you get all that money?"

And he said, "Well, you know you killed my horse, and I took the hide, and I tanned it, and I sold it."

And he said, "You got that much money for one horsehide?"

And he said, "Yes."

And he said, "Oh, boy, I'll see you later," and he went home, and he killed his six horses. He tanned their hides, and he went down the street calling, "Horsehides for sale. Horsehides for sale," but nobody would buy his horsehides. Well, he was really upset with Little Klaus, and he was searching for him.

In the meantime, Little Klaus decided to pay his grandmother a visit. He had bought a fine buggy and some nice clothes, so he wanted to show off to his grandmother. He went to her house, and he called, "Grandmother," and he went through the house calling for her, and he couldn't find her. He went to her bedroom, and there she was in her bed. She had just passed away. So he decided he'd take Grandmother. He put her fine Sunday clothes on her, and he propped her up in the buggy and went down the street. He passed an inn, and he became thirsty, and so he thought, "I'll go in and get something to drink." So he propped Grandmother up in the buggy, and he went in.

He said to the innkeeper, "I'd like a drink, and why don't you take a lemonade out to my grandmother? She's sitting out in the carriage. Why don't you see what my grandmother wants to drink?"

So he went out to the carriage, and he said, "What do you want to drink?" And she didn't say anything. He asked her two or three times, and she didn't say anything. So he bumped her and said, "What do you want to drink?" She fell off of the carriage seat onto the ground, and he said, "Oh!" He ran over, and he said, "Oh! I've killed Little Klaus's grandmother. Oh, Little Klaus will never forgive me." And he just agonized, "Oh, what will I tell Little Klaus?" Finally, he said, "Little Klaus, I'm so sorry, but I've killed your grandmother."

"You've killed my grandmother?"

"Oh, yes," he said, "I didn't mean it." He said, "I'm so sorry. Little Klaus, if you won't do anything to me, I'll give you a bushel of money, and I'll give her the finest burial ever a person could have."

Little Klaus said, "Well, I'm really heartbroken about my grandmother, but we can't do anything, so, okay, I'll take the money." So he had more money, and he went down the street, and he had even more money than last time.

He met Big Klaus, of course, and Big Klaus said, "Little Klaus, where did you get all that money?"

And he said, "Well, I sold my dead grandmother."

"You sold your dead grandmother?"

He said, "Yes."

"Oh, and you got that much money?"

He said, "Yes."

He said, "Well, I'll... I'll see ya." So he went to make a visit to his grandmother's house. He took a little poison along and a nice lemonade, and he went in and had lemonade with his grandmother, and she toppled over dead. He took and dressed her in her fine clothes, and he went down the street yelling, "Dead grandmothers for sale. Dead grandmothers for sale." Oh, the people started throwing eggs and tomatoes at him, and oh, they just gave him such a bad time, and he said, "Little Klaus has tricked me again. This is it. I'm gonna find Little Klaus, and I'm going to drown him." So he got a big gunnysack, and he went looking for Little Klaus. It didn't take him too long. (They lived in a little town.) And he saw Little Klaus, and he said, "Little Klaus, I've had it. I've killed my grandmother. I've killed my horses, and you have lied to me the last time. I'm going to drown you." So he put Little Klaus in his gunnysack, and he tied it tight with a big knot in the top of the gunnysack, and he went towards the river.

As he passed the church, he could hear them singing, and he

thought, "This is not a nice thing I'm doing. Maybe I should go in and say a prayer before I drown Little Klaus."

So he went into the church, and while he was in the church, an old man came along, and he had all these cattle, and he said, "O-o-oh, I'm so old. I wish I didn't have to have these cattle. I just wish I could die."

Little Klaus yelled from the gunnysack. He said, "Sir, if you wish you could die," he said, "we could arrange it real soon." He said, "Come close." So the old man came close, and he said, "Just untie the sack, and pretty soon your dream will be realized."

And he said, "Really?"

And he said, "Yes, it will be an easy death."

He said, "Okay." So he untied the sack, and he said, "Now, there's one request. I want you to take care of my cattle."

And he said, "I will, don't worry." So he put the little man in the gunnysack, tied the knot, and went down the street with all those cattle.

Big Klaus came out, and he started pulling the sack, and he said, "Gee, Little Klaus got lighter." He said, "That paid me to go in there and pray. My burden is lighter." And he pulled his sack and went towards the river and dropped the sack in the river. Then later he saw Little Klaus coming with all his cattle and said, "I can't believe my eyes. I just drowned Little Klaus. What has happened?" He said, "Little Klaus, what happened?"

He said, "Well, you know when you drowned me," he said, "down at the bottom of the river," he said, "there's an old man. He had all these sea cattle, and he asked me if I'd take care of them," and he said, "so I promised him I would."

And Big Klaus said, "This is astounding! I can't believe it." He said, "Would you do me a favor, Little Klaus?"

And he said, "I sure will."

And he said, "Would you just put me in a gunnysack and drown me? I've got to have some of the sea cattle. These are the finest cattle I've ever seen."

He said, "I'll be glad to." So he got the sack, and he tied the knot, and he drug Big Klaus over to the bridge, and he dumped him in, and that was the end of Big Klaus.

One time when I was teaching a Sunday school class, I said, "Now, if you'll be good, afterwards I'm going to tell you a real good story." It had some things in it that I thought if the Superintendent walks in, he'd wonder why I was telling these children this story. My kids just loved it. You start to tell it in Sunday school and you think it's quite a nice story, but then it's quite morbid. All the time I was telling it, I worried about three things: that the Superintendent would come in, that someone would hear the children laugh

when I said, "Dead grandmothers for sale," and that they might go home and tell their parents about the story.

32   *The Good Old Days*

Joseph C. Bolander: Now, here's one I learned in more recent years by Ruth Shook. Just notice and think about here how many of these things from the good old days you can remember in your lifetime.

When we were living the good old days,
They really weren't so good.
You read by the light of a kerosene lamp,
And you heated your homes with wood.

You carried water up the hill
To wash with and cook and scrub.
You took your bath behind the stove
In a galvanized laundry tub.

I still can smell that old lye soap
And feel the sting and the hurt
When some of the stuff got in your eyes,
But it really got the dirt.

We slept on corn husk mattresses
Sometimes three in a bed.
If you were late, you got the foot,
'Cause early birds had taken the head.

We trudged through snow, and ice, and mud
To get to the seat of learning
Where there was a potbelly stove
Which froze your back while your front was really burning.

We drank from a cup by a water pail
On the bench where the teachers had set it,
And any ailment any kid had
The rest were sure to get it.

The cows were milked in a drafty barn
While the wind whistled through the cracks,
And the drifting snow while you were inside
Filled up your fresh-made tracks.

A little house at the foot of the hill
Half hidden with brush and weeds
Through summer's heat and winter's cold
Filled other family needs.

Now you may look with envying eyes
On these days if you're twenty,
But I've been through the good old days,
And once, my friends, is plenty.

How many of you kids remember all those things?

33 *A Teacher's Tools*

Grant E. Brown: I taught for several years, and when I substitute teach sometimes, I like to get their attention and entertain them a little bit, so I go through:

I ask them if they know the difference between a duck, and I tell them, "There's no difference at all. They're both the same, and the reason you can tell that is because it's the same distance between his legs."

And I ask them if they've heard about Herman, Thurman, and Vermin. They were twins. All except Elmer, and Elmer had hair about this color, and he had to go to bed before the others because he slept slower.

And they are interested sometimes in knowing about the guy who was real curious about what happened to the sun when it went down, and he sat up all one night wondering what happened to it, and it finally dawned on him.

And then the guy crossed a crocodile with an abalone, and he came up with four little abadiles and a crock of bologna.

Things like that.

34 *Mary Had a Little Lamb*

Van N. Holyoak: Now, this is about the first thing I ever learned to recite. Somebody taught it to me, and I was about half grown before I figured out why my dad liked it and why he had me recite it for people and why they reacted the way they did.

Mary had a little lamb.
Its fleece was soft and silky,
And every time it wagged its tail,
There was Wendell Willkie.

Grandpa's Recitations (35-44)   Kristi Hodge: When I was little, grandpa taught me recitations, and whenever we would go anywhere, he would ask me to say them. I've known them as long as I can remember.

35   Ooey Gooey Was a Worm

Ooey Gooey was a worm,
A little worm was he.
He crawled up on a railroad track,
And the train he didn't see.
Ooey! Gooey!

He taught me to say the last line like that and to make a face and wrinkle my nose when I said it.

36   There Were Two Bums

There were two bums,
Two jolly chums,
We lived like royal Turk.
If we had luck and fun and chuck,
The hell with a man who'll work.

37   Mary, Mary, Quite Contrary

''Mary, Mary, quite contrary,
How does your garden grow?''
''With silver bells and cockle shells
And one damn petunia.''

38 *Mary Had a Little Lamb*

Mary had a little lamb.
It was only worth a quarter,
And every time it wagged its tail,
There was Jimmy Carter.

39 *I'm A Cute Little Girl*

I'm a cute little girl
With a cute little figure.
Stay back, boys,
Till I get a little bigger.

40 *I Love Myself*

I love myself.
I think I'm grand.
I go to the movie,
I hold my hand,
I put my arms
Around my waist,
And when I get fresh,
I slap my face.

41 *Fuzzy Wuzzy*

Fuzzy Wuzzy was a bear.
Fuzzy Wuzzy had no hair.
Fuzzy Wuzzy wasn't
Fuzzy, was he?

42 *Where's the World's Best Grandpa?*

Some of the ones he taught us he had a part in, too. Once my other grandpa
and grandma came all the way from Oregon visiting, and he came in and he
did one. He says, "Where's the world's best grandpa?" and he had taught us
to point at him whenever he said that and yell, "Right there!" So we did, and

our other grandparents looked like kinda shocked, and he just shrugged and said, "Well, you can't argue with a kid, can you?"

43   *Questions and Answers*

He always asked me a set of questions, and I gave the answers he had taught to me.

Question: Who loves ya?
Answer: Nobody.
Question: Who whips ya?
Answer: Everybody.
Question: What do they whip you for?
Answer: For nothing.
And then he would whisper: Except me.

44   *Everybody Hates Me*

Everybody hates me.
Nobody likes me.
I think I'll go eat worms,
Big, fat, juicy ones,
Long, skinny, slimy ones.
Ah, how they tickle when they squirm.

I want to teach these recitations to my cousins because there's only a few of us kids who ever got to know Grandpa, and I'm kind of sad they never got to know him, so I feel like teaching them these recitations, so they'll give them a part of him.

45   *Garbage Truck Monster*

Vandee, Sara, Van A., and Deedra Holyoak: *(As the oldest child, Vandee served as spokesperson for the group and introduced their performance.)* **Vandee, Sara, Van and Deedra will be recitaling "The Garbage Truck Monster," and here we go:**

The garbage truck monster
Roars up the street,
Looking for garbage
To pick up and eat.

He stops at a can
And gulps down his dinner.
The foul-smelling mixture
Goes into his "inner."

Bottles and boxes
And cans disappear
As he gnashes and smashes
And grinds into gear.

He growls and he howls,
And I guess I know why—
If I ate what he ate,
I'm sure I would die!

46 *If I Was a Blossom*

Joe S. Holyoak: I've always just wanted to sit down and write a children's book, but I never have done it, but I wrote this one for my kids.

If I was a blossom,
I'd live up in a tree.
If Jack Frost didn't bite,
Do you know what I might be?

I'd become a little green apple,
And the birds would nurture me.
They know that I'm the prize fruit
That's in that apple tree.

The children, they would dream of me
When tucked down in their beds,
But none of them will bother me.
I'm too high over their heads.

I think in a beat. I really don't know. Most of the time anyone says something, I got a pun or a rhyme or something I can throw in. I try to outgrow it, but it keeps me in trouble out to work most of the time.

47 *A Smile*

Ralph Rogers: One night we got a bunch of people together during a bunch of songs and recitations and the like, and this one man Andrew gave three of them that night that was really good, and I tried to get him to write one of them out for me. "No," he said, "you do all right with your singing. You don't need my recitations." So I stayed mostly a singer, but my mother taught me a

song when I was around about just between six or seven years old, and it's a good recitation.

The thing that goes the farthest
Toward making life worthwhile
That costs the least and does the most
Is just a pleasant smile.

A smile that bubbles from the heart,
That loves its fellow men,
Will drive away a cloud of gloom
And coax the sun again.

It's full of worth and goodness, too,
With manly kindness blent;
It's worth a million dollars,
But it doesn't cost one cent.

48   *A Lime Tong, Tong Ago*

Grant E. Brown: I don't know how long it took me to learn this thing, but I know it's taken me a long time to forget it.

Once upon a lime tong, tong ago, a fungry hox met a bunch of grybrid hapes vanging from a hine. Now the fungry hox wanted those grybrid hapes, so he mried with all his tight by junning and rumping as kigh as he hould. But he saw it was abso-usely luteless, so he went along with a shoulder of his shrug a-saying, ''I thought those rapes were gripe, but I nee sow they're seally rouer.'' Now the storal to the mory is if you see some rapes on the ground, you better buy them on the vine.

49   *The Day Mother Saved Our Bacon*

LaVelle Whiting DeSpain: Every year we had a pig, and that was our winter's meat, and that pig got sick one time. Oh, Mother came down to the house (we had an old tamarack hedge, and the pigpen was on the other side), and she said, ''Jack, come here and have the other children stay there.''
''Mother, what's the matter?''
''None of your business; just none of your business.''
And, of course, we got up there and hid in the tamarack hedge, and we could see that Roscoe was really, really sick, and Mother had Jack help her give the old pig an enema. She saved our bacon, and we held a little prayer circle before they did it.
Anyhow, I did this thing up for our reunion. You know, the old... you've seen how they... DA da Da da DA da DA-A. That's how we did it.

The first character enters, and they all keep moving with the speaking, bobbing up and down by bending their knees. This little boy says:

This story is true
That we now tell.

And the little girl says:

It's a story that was written
By our Grandma Bell.

Enter Melody saying:

'Twas the day Grandma and Jack
Saved our bacon.

Enter then another little girl with a package of bacon, and Eddy says:

Oh, Mama, come quick.
Our pig's not well.

Mother says:

The pig's not well?
Well, how can you tell?

Eddy:

She's grunting and groaning,
And her eyes are glazed.
Her color's not good,
And her hair has raised.

Mother:

She's sick all right.
Those symptoms tell it all.
An aspirin won't help her,
Not even Hadacol.

Eddy:

It's our winter's meat.
We can't let her die.
Oh, Mama, save our bacon!
Just try, try, try.

Mother:

With Jack by my side
I know just what to do.
Now back to the house
With all of you.

Then Nanette comes in, and Nanette says:
>Oh, Mama, let us go.
>We won't be in the way.
>To the tamarack hedge
>We promise we will stay.

Enter Ken wearing a sign saying he's Uncle Jack:
>Well, don't give us problems.
>We've a fight ahead,
>And if we don't win,
>Old Roscoe will be dead.

And then Nanette:
>With syringe in hand,
>Jack looked just like a pro
>As up to the pigpen
>The anxious few did go.

Ken:
>With Mother assisting
>Relief is now in sight and
>With prayers from the children,
>Old Roscoe won her fight.

Enter Karma:
>Then Dad fattened her up
>And prepared for the killing.
>The thoughts of her death
>Were really quite chilling.
>
>But with visions of pork chops
>Dancing through our heads
>And winter approaching,
>We children would be fed.

Then Mel comes in:
>Old Roscoe would forgive us.
>This we all knew.
>It was one of those jobs
>That we just had to do.

Karma:
>It's the end of our story.
>Oh, please don't cry.
>It's a fact of life
>That each must die.

Then Mother:
>We tell you this story
>Because it is true,
>Because there's a moral
>For each one of you.

Now, all together they say:
>Faith without works
>Can't be had.
>It's a lesson that was taught us
>By our mom and dad.

That really happened, and this went over really big at our reunion.

50   *The Tree Deedle*

Alice Gene Tripp: Grandma only had the two rhyming recitations I remember, but she always did "Willy and the Tree Deedle," and it was told... it was always told with the same sound effects. When Willy knocked on the door, you know, she knocked, and there always was this little squeaky voice that said, "Come in."

Once upon a time there was a little boy named Willy, and Willy went to visit his gaga, and in his gaga's back yard was a great big oak tree, and he was out playing in the back yard, and he noticed a little bitty door in that tree that he had never seen before.

So he went over to the door, and he went knock, knock, knock, knock *(knocks on the table),* and a little squeaky voice said, "Come in." And he opened the door, and there were some steps, and the steps went up, up, up into the tree, and Willy went up, up, up the steps, and when he got to the top of the steps, there was another little door, so Willy went knock, knock, knock, knock *(knocks on the table),* and a little squeaky voice went, "Come in." And there sat the great, yeller-eyed Tree Deedle, and Willy said, "Well, hello! My name is Willy."

And the Tree Deedle said, "Well, hello. My name's the Tree Deedle." And the Tree Deedle said, "Well, I'm very glad to meet you. Are you very glad to meet me?"

And Willy said, "Yes."

And the Tree Deedle said, "Well, I's just setting down to supper. Would you like something to eat?"

And Willy said, "Don't mind if I do."

So the Tree Deedle said, "Have some pie."

And Willy said, "Oh, I love pie." But the pie was made out of old, empty spools, and Willy said, "P.U! I don't like pie made out of old, empty spools."

And the Tree Deedle said, "You don't? Why, I am very fond of pie made out of old, empty spools. Have some cake."

But the cake was made with tacks in it instead of raisins, and Willy said, "P.U! I don't like cake made with tacks in it instead of raisins."

And the Tree Deedle said, "Why, you don't? Why, I am very fond of cake made with tacks in it instead of raisins." So the Tree Deedle said, "Well, let's go see the Man in the Moon."

And Willy said, "Okay, but how do we get there?"

And the Tree Deedle said, "Well, you follow me." And they went out on a limb of the tree, and they caught hold of the tail of a comet. (A comet is a star that has a long tail, and it goes *foo-o-o-o-o* through the night skies.) And they landed on the moon, and there was the Man in the Moon, and he was just setting down to supper, but all he had for supper was green cheese, and Willy said he didn't like green cheese either. So they all got through, and the Man in the Moon said, "They're having a dance down on the earth tonight, and they're giving a prize to the one that can dance the longest."

So they decided to go. So they went over to the edge of the moon, and Willy said, "How do we get down?"

And the Man in the Moon said, "Why, you jump."

And Willy said, "I'm afraid to jump. I want my mama."

And the Man in the Moon said, "Well, sit down. I'll push you."

And they thought that was a fine idea, so Willy sat down on the edge of the moon, hung his little legs over, and the Man in the Moon pushed him, and he went *woo-o-osh* through the night sky and *pouf!* landed on a stack of black cats, and the cats went, "Meow! Pht, pht, pht, pht."

And Willy jumped up, brushed the cat hair off his clothes, wiped it out of his eyes, sneezed it out of his nose, and he was ready to go to the dance.

Well, the Tree Deedle, he was afraid to jump, too, so he sat down on the edge of the moon, and the Man in the Moon pushed him, and he went *woo-o-osh* through the might sky, and he landed on a stack of black cats, and the cats went, "Meow! Pht, pht, pht, pht."

So the Tree Deedle stood up, and he wiped the cat hair out of his eyes, and sneezed it out of his nose, brushed it off his clothes, and the Man in the Moon, he jumped, and of course, of course, he landed on a stack of black cats. They went, "Meow! Pht, pht, pht, pht." So he got up and wiped it out of his eyes, sneezed it out of his nose, and they all went off to the dance.

When they got to the dance, the music was playing, and everybody was dancing, and they danced, and they danced, and they danced, and they danced. And after a while Willy, who was little and short like me, had to sit down 'cause his little legs got tired.

Everyone else danced and danced, but after a while the Man in the Moon, who was really short and really fat, he got tired, and he had to sit down.

And everybody danced and danced and danced and danced, and after a very long time there was nobody but Tree Deedle, who was tall and thin like my Uncle Gene, and there was nobody left on the floor but Tree Deedle. Everyone said, "Three cheers for the Tree Deedle. The Tree Deedle has won the prize!"

At the last part of the dance when they got tired and sat down, she would say, "because he had little short legs like Alice Gene," and she always said, "The Tree Deedle danced the longest because he was tall and skinny like Uncle Gene." So they were given characters in the family, but the order of it, the tree where the door was, and the sound effects where they went *woo-o-osh* **through the night and** *pht!* **landed on a stack of black cats, all of it, it was pretty much always the same.**

CHAPTER FOUR

About Adventure

"WESTWARD, EVER WESTWARD," direct the words of a well-known recitation text. Steinbeck called it "Westering," but by whatever name it is called, there is in the Western psyche a love of and fascination with adventure and adversity, the distant and unknown, and the supernatural and the unknowable. If Europe was settled by peoples who drifted ever westward from India, the American Westerner has gone about as far as he can go without starting around the globe again. Recitations that glorify and romanticize adventure—or parody it, which is another way of acknowledging its power and attraction—are common in Western oral performance.

51   *High Chin Bob*

Joseph C. Bolander: Now, this is one I picked up out of *Arizona Highways* **over the years of the magazine. This is one about the West titled "High Chin Bob." It's the story of a cocky, over-confident, glory-hunting cowboy who attempts to rope a mountain lion, evidently with the intention of dragging it to death. Now, it's quite a ballad evidently, but I only saw the first and last verses, and that's all I know, so you have to use your imagination of what went on between the first and last verse. Anyhow, this is laid in the high Mogollon Rim country of east-central Arizona.**

Way up high in the Mogollons
Among the mountain tops
A lion cleaned a yearling's bones
And licked his thankful chops.
When on the picture who should ride
A-trippin' down the slope
But high chin Bob with sinful pride
And a maverick-hungry rope.
"Oh glory be to me," said he,
"And fame's unfading flowers.
All meddling hands are far away,
I'm riding a top horse today,
And I'm top rope at the Lazy J.
Hi, kitty cat, you're ours."

That's the first verse, so you have to use your imagination as to what went on from then on. The cowboy evidently got his loop on the lion all right, but the lion proved to be a whole lot more than he bargained for. It's said that Bob's ghost is still riding up in those peaks, riding a pale horse and always followed by a shadowy mountain lion. Well, this is the last verse:

Way up high in the Mogollons
A prospect man did swear
That moon streams melted down his bones
And heisted up his hair.
A reedy cow horse thundered by.
A lion trailed along.
A rider gaunt but chin on high
Yelled out this crazy song.
"Oh glory be to me," said he,
"And to my noble noose.
Oh, stranger, tell my pards below
I took a rampin' and dream in tow
And if I never lay him low,
I'll never turn him loose."

52 *Lasca*

Van N. Holyoak: Now, you said in that book you wrote to go with the record of Uncle Horace that no one says the original words to "Lasca." Well, I do the original words, I think. And if I don't, it's your fault 'cause I got them out of that thing you wrote.

It's all very well to write reviews,
And carry umbrellas, and keep dry shoes,
And say what everyone's saying here,
And wear what everyone else must wear;
But tonight I'm sick of the whole affair,
I want free life, and I want fresh air;
And I sigh for the canter after the cattle,
The crack of the whips like shots in a battle,
The mellay of hoofs and horns and heads
That wars and wrangles and scatters and spreads;
The green beneath, and the blue above,
And dash and danger, and life and love—
And Lasca!

      Lasca used to ride
On a mouse-gray mustang close to my side,
With blue serape and bright-belled spur;
I laughed with joy as I looked at her!
Little knew she of books or creeds;
An *Ave Maria* sufficed her needs;
Little she cared, save to be at my side,
To ride with me, and ever to ride,
From San Saba's shore to Lavaca's tide.
She was as bold as the billows that beat,
She was as wild as the breezes that blow;
From her little head to her little feet,
She was swayed in her suppleness to and fro
By each gust of passion; a sapling pine,
That grows on the edge of a Kansas bluff,
And wars with the wind when the weather is rough,
Is like this Lasca, this love of mine.

She would hunger that I might eat,
Would take the bitter and leave me the sweet;
But once, when I made her jealous for fun,
At something I'd whispered, or looked, or done,
One Sunday, in San Antonio,
To a glorious girl on the Alamo,
She drew from her garter a dear little dagger,
And—sting of a wasp!—it made me stagger!
An inch to the left, or an inch to the right,
And I shouldn't be maundering here to-night;
But she sobbed, and, sobbing, so swiftly bound
Her torn rebozo about the wound,
That I quickly forgave her. Scratches don't count
      In Texas, down by the Rio Grande.

Her eye was brown—a deep, deep brown;
Her hair was darker than her eye;
And something in her smile and frown,
Curled crimson lip and instep high,
Showed that there ran in each blue vein,
Mixed with the milder Aztec strain,
The vigorous vintage of Old Spain.
She was alive in every limb
With feeling, to the finger-tips;
And when the sun is like a fire,
And sky one shining, soft sapphire,
One does not drink in little sips.

Why did I leave the fresh and the free,
That suited her and suited me?
Listen awhile, and you will see;
But this be sure—in earth or air,
God and God's laws are everywhere,
And Nemesis comes with a foot as fleet
On the Texas trail as in Regent Street.

The air was heavy, the night was hot,
I sat by her side and forgot—forgot;
Forgot the herd that were taking their rest,
Forgot that the air was close oppressed,
That the Texas northern comes sudden and soon,
In the dead of night, or the blaze of noon;
That once let the herd at its breath take fright,
Nothing on earth can stop their flight;
And woe to the rider, and woe to the steed,
Who fall in front of their mad stampede!

Was that thunder? No, by the Lord!
I sprang to my saddle without a word.
One foot on mine, and she clung behind.
Away! on a wild chase down the wind!
But never was fox-hunt half so hard,
And never was steed so little spared;
For we rode for our lives. You shall hear how we fared
        In Texas, down by the Rio Grande.

The mustang flew, and we urged him on;
There was one chance left, and you have but one;
Halt! jump to the ground, and shoot your horse;
Crouch under his carcass, and take your chance;
And if the steers in their frantic course
Don't batter you both to pieces at once,
You may thank your star; if not goodbye
To the quickening kiss and the long-drawn sigh,
And the open air and the open sky,
      In Texas, down by the Rio Grande.

The cattle gained on us, and, just as I felt
For my old six-shooter behind in my belt,
Down came the mustang, and down came we,
Clinging together, and—what was the rest?
A body that spread itself on my breast,
Two arms that shielded my dizzy head,
Two lips that hard to my lips were pressed;
Then came thunder in my ears,
As over us surged the sea of steers,
Blows that beat blood into my eyes;
And when I could rise-
      Lasca was dead!

I hollowed a grave a few feet deep,
And there in Earth's arms I laid her to sleep;
And there she is lying, and no one knows;
And the summer shines, and the winter snows;
For many a day the flowers have spread
A pall of petals over her head;
And the little gray hawk hangs aloft in the air,
And the sly coyote trots here and there,
And the black-snake glides and glitters and slides
Into a rift in a cottonwood tree;
And the buzzard sails on,
And comes and is gone,
Stately and still, like a ship at sea;
And I wonder why I do not care
For the things that are, like the things that were.
Does half my heart lie buried there
      In Texas, down by the Rio Grande?

53 Coffee

Kristi Hodge: After Grandpa died, I looked through his book of poems, and I read this one, and I liked it, so I learned it. I don't remember him saying it to me, but it was his, and I liked it, so I learned it.

I've tasted finest nectars,
From the lands across the sea.
I have sipped the milk and honey
From contented cows and bees.

I've drank the finest liquors
From the wineries of Spain.
And I've been in cocktail lounges
Where they serve the pink champagne.

Now, I'll tell you about a liquid
That will perk a fellow up
When it's served hot and steaming,
Ah—coffee from a cup.

You can smell its soft aroma
As it floats along the breeze,
As it boils in a campfire
In a grove of aspen trees.

There's been bad men apprehended,
Wild horses chased and caught
As men sipped the amber liquid
From a granite coffee pot.

To a cold and hungry cowboy
In the land our fathers trod,
The juices from a coffee bean
Were like nectars from the gods.

Now, when I get to heaven,
If that should be my lot,
I hope St. Peter greets me
With a steaming coffee pot.

54 Lazy Horse

Kristi Hodge: The reason I memorized some of Grandpa's poems that he wrote was because he never did them much outside the family, and I figured

if I didn't do them, they would never get done. I just want people to know what he wrote.

Did you ever ride a lazy horse
When you had somewhere to go?

Now, I don't mean a sluggish horse
Nor one that's sort of slow.
I mean that stupid, lazy beast,
One that you can't make go.

You start to hit a canter.
He'll kick up and wring his tail,
So you start to take it easy.
He moves slower than a snail.

So you take down half your lasso.
You whip him good and hard.
He humps up and travels sideways.
You haven't gained a yard.

So you spur him in the belly
Till you think his ribs will break.
His hide is thick; it's tougher
Than the rind on a dollar steak.

So you finally lose your temper,
And you whip him in the eye.
He lifts his leg up to his belly
To brush away a fly.

Your heart is broke, your patience gone,
You don't know what to do.
So you tie up by a cedar
And start to loafing, too.

You spend the day a-cursin' him,
But he don't care, of course.
The finest kind of cowboy
Is no better than his horse.

55   *Airtights*

Billy Simon: Lots of folks these days think that cowboys must of had lots of milk. Hoowee! There was no way you could have milked one of them cows unless you shot it first, and the boss wouldn't have liked that, but along somewhere in there they started making and selling canned stuff which, of

course, we called "airtights," and one of the most popular was the canned milk 'cause most of that camp coffee (Arbuckle, we called it, 'cause that was the most popular brand) would float a horseshoe, and something to cut that acid was appreciated, and I remember one evening in camp this old cowboy picked up a can of Carnation milk, held her up, and offered a toast.

Here's to Carnation,
Best in the land,
Comes to the table
In a little red can.

No tits to squeeze,
No hay to pitch,
Just punch a hole
In the son-of-a-bitch.

56   *Jake Neal*

Delbert D. Lambson: Now, let me stand up. It always feels better to stand up when you recite poetry.

I wrote this poem to Jake Neal. Jake was a trapper, and he paid for his farm with trapping, and he was well-known around the country. They came to him for advice and instruction on trapping 'cause this was a trapping area at the time, and coyotes had to be kept down. This is what I wrote in memory of my dear, dear friend and father-in-law Jake Neal. He lived in one house— built it, lived in it, and died in it.

I want to talk about a man
That most of you may know.
Now this is not a eulogy,
Just a timely word or so.

Jake used to be a trapper,
The finest in the West.
By the number of the furs he took,
He must have been the best.

He spent his winters in the country,
Just himself and his old hound,
Cooking on the open fire
And sleeping on the ground.

He could read signs and set a trap
And fix it up just right
And make it so inviting,
He'd have a coyote overnight.

96

Men came to seek his counsel
On how to catch a cat
Or even take a mountain lion
And lots of things like that.

He took the proceeds of his work
And bought a little farm
And built a cozy little house
To keep his family warm.

Jake could take his team of horses
And plow a furrow straight.
His work would start at daylight,
And when he finished, it was late.

He took that fifty acre farm
And worked and made it pay
With corn and oats and barley
And an awful lot of hay.

He kept a barnyard full of hens
And cared for them each day,
And while other men were going broke,
He made his chickens pay.

He took pride in all he did.
That has always been his way.
The care with which he did his work
Was how he lived from day to day.

He knows the value of a dollar.
He has never practiced greed.
He never spent a foolish dime
On what he didn't need.

He never really had a lot of
The riches of the earth.
His life was built on values
Of a far, far greater worth.

He comes closer to pure charity
Than anyone I've ever known
By the service that he rendered
And by the love he has shown.

Now, I do not claim to be a judge,
But I know that God is just,
And if this man doesn't make it,
I feel sorry for the rest of us.

He never speaks in anger.
You never hear him raise his voice.
He speaks no ill of any man.
Kind words have been his choice.

His children and grandchildren
Are blessed by him each day
Because of all the little things
He does along the way.

And so a big bouquet of roses
Is what I want to give
While he is still here with us
For the life that he has lived.

Yes, Jake is in his twilight,
Though his evening glow is bright,
And his love will warm and bless us
Far, far into the night.

God bless you, sir, and keep you.
As you have loved us, we will love.
May God prepare a place for you
In His mansions up above.

For we know you have a family
Waiting for you over there
When you leave this frail existence
And climb the golden stair.

Yes, your darling wife is waiting
To take you by the hand
And walk into eternity
In that quiet peaceful land.

57 *Sweet Freedom*

Delbert D. Lambson: I inherited from my father-in-law the art of trapping coyotes. I know some people frown on that, and I'm beginning to frown on that, too. I don't think I'll ever trap again. I don't think those coyotes are going to take too well to me on the other side. As I grow older, I see things in

a different light than I did before, and I believe that all things are precious in the sight of God, and I wrote this. It's a different kind of a thing, and I don't know whether I can give it the way it ought to be given. It is called "Sweet Freedom," and it's about my relationship with an individual coyote.

As I looked and saw
A wary coyote moving
Quietly through the brush
Out of rifle range
And up a sandy draw,
Then stop and steal
A glance in my direction
As if to say, "I fooled you,"
But what he didn't know
Would cause his dying,
For in his path was lying
A trap he could not see
Was hidden there by me
With such skill that he
Could not avoid its clasp.
I had him in my grasp,
But, woe is me,
My victory was not sweet
As I thought that it might be,
And so I let him free,
As free as he could be,
And I felt
Sweet satisfaction
In my heart.

That's my farewell to the coyote and to coyote trapping.

58 *Sheridan, Twenty Miles Away*

Horace Crandell: This was on the other side of the record of "Lasca," and I just learned it directly from the record. I liked "Lasca" and "Sheridan" very much and possibly tried to imitate them. It just gets into you. It gets right inside of you, that's all, and, of course, when you say them, that expresses your feelings more or less.

Up from the South at the break of day,
Bringing to Winchester fresh dismay,
The affrighted air with their shudder bore,
Like a herald in haste to a chieftain's door,
The terrible grumble and rumble and roar,
Telling a battle was on once more,
And Sheridan, twenty miles away.

Louder still those billows of war
Thundered along the horizon bar;
Wider yet into Winchester rolled
The roar of the Red Sea uncontrolled,
Making the blood of the listener cold,
As he thought of the fate in the fiery fray,
And Sheridan, twenty miles away.

But there is a road in Winchester town,
A good broad highway leading down;
And there through the flush of the morning light,
A steed as black as the steeds of night
Was seen to pass as with eagle flight;
As if he knew the terrible need,
He dashed away with the utmost speed;
Hills rose and fell but his heart was gay,
With Sheridan, fifteen miles away.

From under those swift hooves, thundering south
The dust like smoke from a cannon's mouth;
Or the tail of a comet sweepin' faster and faster,
Foreboding to traitors the doom or disaster,
The heart of the steed and the heart of the master
Were beating like prisoners assaulting their walls,
Impatient to be where the battlefield calls;
Every nerve in the charger was strained full play,
With Sheridan only ten miles away.

From under those spurning hooves the road
Like an arrowy Alpine river flowed,
The landscapes sped away behind,
Like the ocean flying before the wind,
And the steed like a barque fed with furnace ire
Sped on with his wild eyes full of fire.
But lo! he is nearing his heart's desire;
He is sniffing a smoke from the roaring fray,
With Sheridan only five miles away.

The first that the general saw were the groups
Of stragglers then the retreating troops;
What was done? What to do? A glance told him both,
Then striking his spur with a terrible oath,
He dashed away, mid a scene of assaults.
The line of retreat was checked there because
The sight of the master compelled them to pause.
With foam and with dust, the black charger was gray.
With a flash of his eye and red nostrils display,
He seemed to that whole great army to say,
"I have brought you Sheridan all of the way
From Winchester down to save the day!"

"Hurrah! Hurrah for Sheridan!
Hurrah! Hurrah for horse and man!"
And when the statues are placed on high,
Under the dome of the Union sky,
May it be said in letters both bold and bright,
"Here is the steed that saved the day,
By carrying Sheridan into the fight,
From Winchester, twenty miles away!"

59 *Billy the Kid*

Reinhold "Tex" Bonnet: I'll recite you that piece of poetry about Billy the Kid.

There wasn't a man
On the Santa Fe
That'd go to the mat
With Shack Bronshay,

Nor ride a horse,
Nor shoot a gun,
But the devil himself
With the deeds he done.

They put him in jail
For a thousand years
For changing irons
Or rustling steers.

Shack made a mistake one day.
A stranger standing at the Long Horn Bar
Slowly puffed on a mild cigar

As Shay walked in,
And he quickly saw
That stranger end
With a loud guffaw.

Boom! From his hip
He neatly threw.
He shot that stranger's
Cigar in two.

That stranger never
Moved nor spoke
Except to ask
For another smoke,

And then in the stranger's way
A ready match
He made a motion
As though to scratch.

His right arm swung up.
It held a nickel gun,
Boomed twice,
And the game was done.

Shay's body was dead
Before it hit the barroom floor.
Billy the Kid, from Santa Fe
Rode safely on o'er
To Old Mexico.

60   *The Irishman's Lament*

Madeline Collins: My older sisters tell me our dad would recite "The Irish-man's Lament" with great vigor and elocutionary powers. (Our name is Powers.) I cannot say the song is complete as I never heard my dad say it. I was the youngest of the family.

I'm an honest Irish laborer
Both hearty, stout and strong.
To idleness I'll not confess;
To our race it don't belong.

Though I am strong and willing to work
For the wants of life so dear,
Where ere I go to ask for work
There's no Irish wanted here.

They may think it a misfortune
To be christened Pat or Dan.
To me it is a blessing to
Be called an Irishman.

61   *Casey at the Bat*

Wilford J. Shumway: Now, I want to tell you the true story of "Casey at the Bat." I had thought all these years that Casey was a fictitious person, but he was not. He was a real person. And you know what? Okay. Casey struck out that day, but they went on to win the game, Mudville did. Here's what happened. The pitcher threw a spitball. They didn't know what it was in those days, but accidentally (he was wiping his mustache, you know) he threw a ball that he afterwards told Casey, "Casey, no one could have hit that." He said, "I don't know what happened." He said, "I've tried since to duplicate that pitch, and I can't." What he didn't know was that he'd thrown a spitball. They didn't know for fourteen years after that. Then they out- lawed it, you know.

All right, so here's what's happened. He threw it. Casey swung and missed, but so did the catcher, and the ball rolled back toward the backstop. Casey looked around and saw what was happening and bolted for first. The catcher ran over there, grabbed up the ball, dropped it, picked it up again, and threw to first too late. And he overthrew first. Casey saw it, and he went to second, and by that time old Blake and Flynn were already home, so that tied the score right there, you see. Then through a series of errors (I think they overthrew second again), Casey came home to win the game!

It looked extremely rocky for the Mudville nine that day.
The score stood two to four with but an inning left to play.
So when Coony died at second and Burrow did the same,
A pallor wreathed the features of the patrons of the game.

A straggling few got up to go, leaving there the rest
With that hope which springs eternal within the human breast.
For they thought if only Casey could get a whack at that,
They'd put up even money now with Casey at the bat.

But Flynn preceded Casey, and likewise so did Blake.
The former was a puddin', and the latter was a fake.
So on that stricken multitude a death-like silence sat,
For there seemed but little chance of Casey's getting to the bat.

But Flynn let drive a single much to the wonderment of all.
And the much despised Blakey tore the cover off the ball.
And when the dust had lifted, and they saw what had occurred,
There was Blakey safe on second and Flynn ahuggin' third.

Then from that madding multitude there went up a joyous yell,
It rumbled in the mountaintops, it rattled in the dell;
It struck upon the hillside and rebounded in the flat,
For Casey, mighty Casey, was advancing to the bat.

There was ease in Casey's manner as he stepped up to the plate.
There was pride in Casey's bearing and a smile on Casey's face.
And when responding to the cheers he lightly doffed his hat,
No stranger in that crowd could doubt 'twas Casey at the bat.

Ten thousand eyes were on him as he rubbed his hands with dirt.
Five thousand tongues applauded when he wiped them on his shirt.

And then the leather-covered sphere came hurling through the air,
But Casey still ignored it in haughty grandeur there.
Close by the sturdy batsman, the ball unheeded sped.
"That ain't my style," said Casey. "Strike one," the umpire said.

From the benches black with people there went up a muffled roar
Like the beating of storm waves on a stern and distant shore.
"Kill him! Kill the umpire!" shouted someone from the stands,
And it's likely they'da killed him had not Casey raised a hand.

With a smile of Christian charity, great Casey's visage shone.
He stilled the rising tumult; he bade the game go on.
He signaled to Sir Timothy; once more the spheroid flew,
But Casey still ignored it, and the umpire said, "Strike two."

"Fraud!" cried the maddened thousands, and an echo answered,
     "Fraud!"
But one scornful look from Casey, and the audience was awed.
They saw his face grow cold and stern. They saw his muscles strain,
And they knew that Casey wouldn't let that ball go by again.

And now the pitcher holds the ball, and now he lets it go.
And now the air is shattered by the force of Casey's blow.

Oh! Somewhere in this favored land the sun is shining bright.
Somewhere the band is playing, and somewhere hearts are light.
And somewhere men are laughing, and somewhere children shout,
But there is no joy in Mudville. Mighty Casey has struck out.

I learned "Casey" thirty or forty years ago. I have five brothers, and every one of them has a little special thing they do, and every time we have reunions, the uncles have to perform, so I have to do "Casey." Everybody knows what's coming, and they all get out of the way when I spit water like tobacco juice, but I wrote a second ending to that poem once (it's rhymed so it sounds like the rhythm of this other fellow) in which Casey knocked the ball over the fence and into the middle of town. He won! I said, "I'm tired of the guy striking out! This time he's gonna win." The family didn't know... they thought that somehow I had forgotten, and one of them tried to prompt me. Yeah! They were astonished! I can't remember that new ending, though. I just used it that one time.

62   *The Cremation of Sam McGee*

Horace Crandell: Sometimes I change the things I recite from the way I read them. For instance in the "Sam McGee," in the place it says, "God only knows," I changed it to say, "The good Lord only knows," because it sounds better to me.

There are strange things done in the midnight sun
By the men who moil for gold;
Every Arctic trail has its secret tale
That would make your blood run cold;
The Northern Lights have seen queer sights,
But the queerest they ever did see
Was that night on the marge of Lake Lebarge
I cremated Sam McGee.

Now Sam McGee was from Tennessee, where the cotton blooms and
  blows.
Why he left his home in the South to roam 'round the Poles, the good
  Lord only knows.
Sam was always cold, but the land of the gold seemed to hold him like
  a spell;
He'd often say in his homely way, "Man, I'd sooner live in hell."

'Twas on Christmas day we were musing our way over the Dawson
  trail.
Talk about cold! through our parkas' fold it stabbed like a driven nail.
If our eyes we'd close, then the lashes froze till sometimes we
  couldn't see;
It wasn't much fun, but the only one that whimpered was Sam
  McGee.

That very night, as we lay packed tight in our robes beneath the
     snow,
And the dogs were fed, and the stars o'erhead were dancing to and
     fro,
Sam turned to me, and "Cap," says he, "I'll cash in this trip, I guess;
And if I do, I'm asking you that you won't refuse my last request."

He looked so low I couldn't say no; then he said with a sort of a
     moan:
"It's that cursed cold that's got right hold and I'm chilled clean
     through to the bone.
Yet it ain't being dead—it's that awful dread of an icy grave that
     pains;
And I want you to swear, foul or fair, you'll cremate my last remains."

Now a friend's last need is the thing to heed, and I swore I would not
     fail;
We started on at the streak of dawn, but Sam was ghastly pale.
Crouched on the sleigh and raved all day 'bout his home in
     Tennessee;
Before nightfall the corpse was all that was left of Sam McGee.

There wasn't a breath in that land of death, and I hurried,
     horror-driven,
With a corpse half-hid that I couldn't get rid, because of a promise
     given.
Sam was lashed to the sleigh, but he seemed to say: "You may tax
     your brawn and your brains,
But you promised true, and it's up to you to cremate my last
     remains."

Now a promise made is a debt unpaid, and the trail has its own strict
     code.
In the days that come, though my lips were dumb, in my heart how I
     cursed that load.
In the long, long night by the lone firelight, and the huskies all in a
     ring,
Howling out their woes to the homeless snows—Man! how I cursed
     that thing.

Day after day that silent clay seemed to heavy and heavier grow;
But on I went, though the dogs were spent and the grub was a-getting
     low;
The trail was bad, and I felt half mad, but I swore I would not give in;
Sometimes I'd sing to that hateful thing, and he harkened with a grin.

Till we come to the marge of Lake Lebarge, and there a derelict lay;
It was jammed in the ice, and I saw at a trice it was called the "Alice May."
I looked at it, and I thought a bit, and I looked at my frozen chum;
"Now here," said I, with a sudden cry, "is my cre-ma-to-re-um."

Some plank I tore from the cabin floor, and I lit the furnace fire;
Some coal I found that was laying around, and I heaped the fuel higher;
The flames they soared, and the furnace roared—such a blaze you seldom see;
And I burrowed a hole in that glowing coal, and stuffed in Sam McGee.

Then I took a hike, for I didn't like to hear him sizzle so;
And the heavens scowled, and the huskies howled, and the wind began to blow.
'Twas icy cold, but the hot sweat rolled down my face, and I don't know why;
And the greasy smoke with its inky cloak comes streaking down the sky.

How long in the snow I do not know that I wrestled with grisly fear;
But the stars come out and they danced about ere again I ventured near;
I was sick with dread, but I bravely said, "I'll just take a peep inside.
He oughta be cooked, and it's time I looked," so the door I opened wide.

And there sat Sam, cool and calm, in the heart of that furnace roar;
He wore a smile you could see for a mile, and he said, "Please close that door.
It's fine in here, but I greatly fear you'll let in the cold and the storm.
Since I left Plumtree in Tennessee, that's the first time I've been warm."

There are strange things done in the midnight sun
By the men who moil for gold;
Every Arctic trail has its secret tale
That would make your blood run cold;
The Northern Lights have seen queer sights,
But the queerest they ever did see
Was that night on the marge of Lake Lebarge
I cremated Sam McGee.

63   *The Hermit of Shark Tooth Shoals*

Van N. Holyoak: This is based on Service and his style, maybe.

Oh, that north country, it's a hard country,
And it mothers a bloody brood.
Its icy arms holds hidden charms
For the greedy, the sinful, and lewd.

And strong men rust o'er the gold and lust
That sears the northern soul,
But the wickedest born from the Pole to the Horn
Is that Hermit of Shark Tooth Shoals.

Now Jacob Kane was this rascal's name
In the days of his pious youth
Ere he cast a smirch on the Baptist church
By betraying a girl named Ruth.

He was just a boy and a parson's joy
Ere he fell for the gold and the muck,
And he learned to pray with the hogs and hay
On a farm near Keokuk.

But a Service tale of illicit kale
And whiskey and women wild
Drained his morals clean as a soup tureen
Of that poor but honest child.

He longed for the bite of the Yukon night
And northern lights' weird flicker,
For a game of stud in the frozen mud
And the taste of raw red liquor.

He wanted to mush along in the slush
With a team of husky hounds
And to fire his gat at a beaver hat
And knock it out of bounds.

So he left his home for that hell-town Nome
On Alaska's ice-ribbed shore.
There he learned to curse and drink and worse
Till the rum, it dripped from his pores.

When the boys on a spree was drinkin' or free
At the Malamute Saloon,
And Dan McGrew and his reckless crew
Shot craps with a piebald coon,

With a sharp command he'd make them stand
And deliver their hard-earned dust,
Then drink the bar dry of rum and rye
Like a Klondike bully must.

Ah, tough as a steak, this Yukon Jake,
Hard-boiled like a picnic egg,
He washed his shirt in that Klondike dirt
And drank his rum by the keg.

Now in fear of their lives or because of their wives,
He's shunned by his best of pals,
An outcast he of camaraderie
Of all but the wild animals.

So he bought up the whole of that Shark Tooth Shoal,
A reef on the Bering Sea;
There he lived by himself on a sea lion shelf
In lonely iniquity.

But far away in Keokuk, I. A.
Did a ruined maiden fight
To remove the smirch from that Baptist church
And bring them heathens the light.

Now the elders declared that all would be spared
If she carried that holy word
From her Keokuk home to that hell-town Nome
To save them sinful birds.

So six weeks later she took a freighter
To that gold-cursed land by the pole,
But heaven ain't made for a lass betrayed,
And they wrecked on the Shark Tooth Shoal.

The crew was tossed in the sea and lost
All 'cept for the maiden Ruth
Who swam to the edge of that sea lion ledge
Where abode the love of her youth.

Now in search of a seal for his evening meal
'Cause he handled a mean harpoon,
He saw at his feet not something to eat
But a girl in a frozen swoon,

Whom he dragged to his lair by her drippin' hair
And rubbed her knees with gin.
To his great surprise she opened her eyes
And revealed his original sin.

His six-month beard grew stiff and weird
Till it gleamed like a chestnut burr,
And he swore by his gizzard in the arctic blizzard
That he'd do right by her.

The red hair fell like a flame from hell
But on the back of that grateful girl,
And the cold sweat froze to the end of her nose
Till it gleamed like a treacle pearl.

But a hopeless rake, this Yukon Jake,
This Hermit of Shark Tooth Shoal,
This dizzy maid he re-betrayed
And wrecked her immortal soul.

Then he rowed her ashore with a broken oar
And sold her to Dan McGrew
For some husky dogs and hot eggnogs
As villains are wont to do.

Now she sings rough songs to them drunken throngs
That come in on the sailing ships.

For a rude stained kiss from this infamous miss,
They give a seal sleek fur
Or perhaps a sable if they're able.
It is much the same to her.

Ah, that north country, it's a hard country,
And it mothers a bloody brood.
Its icy arms hold hidden charms
For the greedy, the sinful, and lewd.

And strong men rust o'er the gold and lust
That sears the northern soul,
But the wickedest born from the Pole to the Horn
Is that Hermit of Shark Tooth Shoal.

64 *Abdul A-bul-bul A-mir*

Van N. Holyoak: There's one that lots of people recite, and I recite it and I sing it.

Now, the sons of the prophets are gallant and bold,
And quite unaccustomed to fear,
But the bravest by far is a man so I'm told
Called Abdul A-bul-bul A-mir.

When they needed a man to encourage the van
Or harass the fort from the rear,
Storm fort or redoubt, they were sure to call out
For Abdul A-bul-bul A-mir.

Now there's heroes in plenty and well-known to fame
In the legends that fight for the Czar,
But none of such fame as the man by the name
Of Ivan Skavinsky Skavar.

He could imitate Irving, tell fortunes by cards,
And strum on a Spanish guitar,
In fact quite the cream of that Muscovite guard
Was Ivan Skavinsky Skavar.

One day this bold Muscovite shouldered his gun,
Put on his most cynical sneer,
Well, he started downtown when he happened to meet
With Abdul A-bul-bul A-mir.

''Young man,'' says brave Abdul, ''is your existence so dull
That you're anxious to end your career?
What I mean to imply is you're going to die,
Oh, Ivan Skavinsky Skavar!''

''Now, take your last look at the sea, sky, and brook,
Make out your report on the war.
What I mean to imply is you're going to die,
Oh, Ivan Skavinsky Skavar!''

Then that fierce man, he took his trusty skidouk
And murmuring ''Allah Akbar,''
With murder intent he most savagely went
At Ivan Skavinsky Skavar.

Well, they fought all that night in the pale yellow light.
Their cries they were heard from afar.

When the sultan drove up the disturbance to quell
And perhaps give the victor a cheer,
He arrived just in time to bid hasty farewell
To Abdul A-bul-bul A-mir.

Then a loud sounding splash in the Danube was heard,
Resounding over meadows afar.
It came from the sack fitting close to the back
Of Ivan Skavinsky Skavar.

Well, there lieth a stone where the Danube doth roll,
And on it in characters queer
Says, "Stranger, when passing by, pray for the soul
of Abdul A-bul-bul A-mir."

65   *The Green Eye of the Little Yellow God*

Van N. Holyoak: This is my wife's favorite piece, and she's always pestering me to do it.

There's a one-eyed yellow idol to the north of Kathmandu;
There's a little marble cross below the town;
And a brokenhearted woman tends the grave of "Mad" Carew,
While the yellow god forever gazes down.

He was known as "Mad" Carew by the men at Kathmandu,
He had a hotter head than they felt inclined to tell,
But, for all his foolish pranks,
He was worshiped by the ranks,
And the Colonel's daughter smiled on him as well.
He loved her all along,
With the passion of the strong,
That she returned his love was clear to all.
She was nearly twenty-one,
And arrangements were begun
To celebrate her birthday ball.
He wrote to ask what present she would like from "Mad" Carew;
They met next day as he dismissed a squad,
And jestingly she said that nothing else would do
But the green eye of the little yellow god.
On the night before the dance
"Mad" Carew seemed in a trance,
And they joshed him as they puffed at their cigars,
But for once he failed to smile,
And he sat alone awhile,

112

Then went out into the night beneath the stars.
He returned before the dawn
With his shirt and tunic torn
And a gash across his temple.
He was patched up right away,
And he slept the day,
While the Colonel's daughter watched beside his bed.
He woke at last and asked her to get his jacket.
She brought it and he thanked her with a nod.
He bade her search the pocket saying,
"That's from 'Mad' Carew."
And she found the little green eye of the god.
She upbraided poor Carew,
The way women are wont to do,
Although her eyes were wet;
She would not take the stone,
Carew was left alone
With the jewel he'd risked his life to get.
When the ball was at its height
On that still and tropic night,
She thought of him and hastened to his room.
As she crossed the square
She could hear the air
Of a waltz tune softly stealing through the gloom.
His door was open wide, with silver moonlight shining through;
The place was wet and slippery where she trod;
A knife lay buried in the heart of "Mad" Carew—
Twas the vengeance of the little yellow god.

There's a one-eyed yellow idol to the north of Kathmandu;
There's a little marble cross below the town;
And a brokenhearted woman tends the grave of "Mad" Carew,
While the yellow god forever gazes down.

Sounds just like a cowboy.

113

CHAPTER FIVE

About Love

LOVE IS ONE OF THE WESTERN recitations' greatest and most frequently employed themes. Performances describe love throughout life: hoping for love, unrequited love, first love, young love, love after fifty years of marriage, and love after death.

66   *A Young Girl's Prayer*

LaVelle Whiting DeSpain: I was asked to give a talk or a reading to a group of young girls, and I couldn't find what I wanted, and my daughter was about seventeen at the time, and I just thought of her and wrote this. I send them out when a young girl is graduating from high school, and we had a store at the time, an interior decorating store, and people liked them. They said, "Why don't you sell them?" So we started printing them, and they sold a lot. So they were used quite a lot for young girls' graduations.

Oh, Lord, I ask Thy blessings
On this time I am a teen.
Help me, Lord, to do Thy will
And to keep my body clean.

Bless me each new day to seek Ye,
When I would awake,
To do the right and not the wrong
When a decision I would make.

And may each day be challenged
To live a better life
And not become discouraged
With worldly care and strife.

May You always find me willing
To work in that gospel plan,
To take each job I'm asked to do
And do the best I can.

And help me, Lord, to be loyal
To friends who are so dear,
To always tell the good about them
And not the bad I hear.

And though the time seems distant,
I know it's very near
When I'll choose life's partner,
Someone to me so dear.

So this partner I would want
The very best there be
To share the joys of this life
And of eternity.

Help me, Lord, to keep
My body clean and undefiled
For the man that I would marry
For him would have a child.

Give me courage to stand by my ideals,
The finer things, I pray.
Give me knowledge and understanding
To brighten up life's way.

All of these I ask of You
For alone I can't temptation fight,
But with Your help I can make life worthwhile,
With You my guiding light.

67   *Not the Old Maid's Prayer*

**Grant E. Brown: Some of these young maidens get kind of a kick out of the
"Old Maid's Prayer." No, let's see, that's not the name of it, I don't think.
That's something else. Anyway, she says:**

Oh, unknown man, whose rib I am,
Why don't you come for me?
A lonely, homesick rib, I am,
That would with others be.

I want to wed. Now, there, 'tis said.
I don't deny it and fib.
I want my man to come at once
And claim his rib.

Oh, don't you sometimes feel
A lack, a new rib needed there?
'Tis I; do come and get me real soon
Before I have gray hair.

Come get me, my dear, I'm homesick here.
I want, and I won't fib,
I want my man to come at once
And claim his rib.

68   *My Life's History*

Van N. Holyoak: I learned this one from old Don Jackson over here.

I was borned way up in the mountains
Beneath the lonesome pine
Where the quaking aspen grows thick as hell
And so does that old grape vine,

I've hunted saddle horses
Through the valley, hill, and dale,
Till I wore out my eyes hunting tracks
And my ears listening for bells.

Now, cowboying used to be a pleasure
When there was a lot of real good hands
And a lot of real good horses
That seemed to know their brands.

We rode them bucking ponies,
Talked about Billy the Kid,
We popped them maidens' coattails
After the sun was hid.

When the roundup was over,
It was into town we'd go,
We'd take a drink of whiskey,
Maybe a dozen or so.

Them bartenders, they all knew us,
And the girls would ask us in.
What we once called a pleasure,
They now call a sin.

But my old life's seen many changes
Since I'm come upon the soil.
There ain't nothing left but heartache.
I'm lonesome. Life's a toil.

I'm all by my lonesome.
Live up here in a tent.
Another year's come and gone
That seems poorly spent.

I roll out my old bedroll.
It's neither soft nor warm.
It's never felt the presence
Of a woman's lovely form.

But then I guess the cards will change,
Or at least that's what I think,
And I'll have a pretty woman
And lots of booze to drink.

Or else I'll go into Old Mexico
And there I'll buy some mescal
And either join the Mormons
Or marry a Mexican gal.

But it's farewell to old Hell's Canyon
And its god-forsaken life,
Where I live up here in the mountains
With a pack mule for a wife.

69   *A Shack in the Mountains*

Don Jackson: There was only one person I remember who seemed to enjoy my singing, and that was Joe Holyoak, Van Holyoak's dad. I used to go down there and chat with him, and we shared songs and stories, and I'm pretty sure that this is one recitation Van got from me. It's just a kind of a story to make somebody laugh.

I'm snug in a shack in the mountains
Where winds and wild wolves love to howl.
My feet know the swales and the far winding trails
That the cougars and the wolverines prowl.

My mind is never burdened with worries.
I'm happy and footloose and free,
And this blissful state I wish to relate
Is a gift from my buddy to me.

My buddy and I rode together
When only the stars knew our quest.
We shared in the fun when the law of the gun
Was helping to tame the wild West.

We weathered a hundred hot battles,
And I know I once saved his life,
A staggering debt, but he paid it, you bet,
He saved me from taking a wife.

One day when we rode into Rio,
We met a fair miss from the East
With soft golden hair and a big baby stare,
Her beauty was fairly a feast.

My freedom of life was forgotten,
Forgotten the blue of the skies.
My heart, if you please, I tossed to the breeze
For one long look from her eyes.

She had me roped, hogtied, and branded.
Right soon would wedding bells chime.
I was surely blind to my fate most unkind.
I parted from her hand just in time.

I might have been stuck in some city,
Cooped up in a two-by-four flat,
With sickly steamed heat and canned goods to eat;
My buddy, he saved me from that.

I'm snug in a shack in the mountains.
I'm happy and footloose and free,
This heaven complete I wish to repeat
Is a gift from my buddy to me.

By saving me from my folly,
Reserving my throne at the cost of his own,
My buddy, he married the gal.

70   *The Face on the Barroom Floor*

Grant E. Brown: Some of the readings or poems that I say I learned when I was in high school. And my mother was always called upon and was good at giving these kind of things. I thought I had to. I learned "The Shooting of Dan McGrew," "'Osler Joe," and "The Face on the Barroom Floor." Those three I learned in high school, and I supplemented those with other poems from Robert Service and Edgar Guest, and some I've used their poems but don't

even know who wrote them. (I haven't given them any credit at all.) And some of them I'm sure if the authors heard me give them, they'd wonder if it was theirs anyway because I've dealt kind of free and put what I thought they ought to have said in there.

Would you like to hear "The Face on the Barroom Floor"?

'Twas a balmy summer evening, and a goodly crowd was there,
Which well-nigh filled Joe's barroom on the corner of the square;
Songs and witty stories come through the open door,
A vagabond crept slowly in and plopped on the floor.

"Where did it come from?" someone said. "The wind has blown it
    in."
"What does it want?" another cried. "Some whiskey, rum or gin?"
"Here, Toby, sic 'em, if your stomach's equal to the work.
I wouldn't touch him with a fork, he's filthy as a Turk."

This badinage the poor wretch took with socially good grace;
In fact, he smiled as though he thought he'd struck the proper place.
"Come, boys, I know there's kindly hearts among so good a crowd.
To be in such good company would make a deacon proud.

"Give me a drink—that's what I want—I'm out of funds, you know,
When I had the cash to treat the gang, this hand was never slow.
What? You laugh as though this pocket never held a sou;
Why, I once was fixed as well, my boys, as any one of you.

"There, thanks, that's braced me pretty nicely; God bless you one
    and all;
Next time I pass this good saloon, I'll make another call.
Give you a song? No, I can't; my singing days are past;
My voice is cracked, my throat's worn out, and my lungs are going
    fast.

"I'll tell you a funny story; in fact, I promise to.
Say! Give me another whiskey, and I'll tell you what I'll do—
That ever I was a decent man not one of you would think;
But I was, four or five year back. Say, give me another drink.

"Fill her up, Joe, I want to put some life into this frame—
Such little drinks to a bum like me are miserably tame;
Five fingers—there, that's the scheme—corking whiskey, too.
Well, here's luck, boys, landlord, and my best regards to you.

"As I told you, once I was a man, with muscle, frame and health,
For a blunder ought to have made considerable wealth.

"I was a painter—not one that daubs on bricks and wood,
But an artist, and for my age, was rated pretty good.
I worked hard at my canvas and was bidding fair to rise,
For gradually I saw the star of fame before my eyes.

"I painted a picture perhaps you've seen; 'tis called the 'Chase of
  Fame.'
It brought me fifteen hundred pounds and added to my name.
And then I met a woman—now comes the funny part—
Her eyes have petrified my brain and sunk into my heart.

"Boys, did you ever see a girl for whom your soul you'd give,
With eyes like the Milo Venus, too beautiful to live;
With a form that would beat the Koh-i-noor, and a wealth of chestnut
  hair?
If so, 'twas she, for there never was another one half so fair.

"I was working on a portrait, one afternoon in May,
Of a fair-haired boy, a friend of mine, who lived across the way;
And Madeline admired it, and, much to my surprise,
She said she'd like to know the man that had such dreamy eyes.

"It didn't take long to know her, and before the month had flown
My friend had stole my darling, and I was left alone;
And ere a year of misery had passed above my head,
The jewel I had long treasured was tarnished and was dead.

"That's why I took to drink, boys. Why, I never saw you smile,
I thought you'd be amused and laughing all the while.
Why, what's the matter with you? There's a tear drop in your eye,
Come, laugh like me; 'tis only babes and women that should cry.

"Say, boys, if you give me just another drink, I'll be glad,
And I'll draw right here a picture of the face that drove me mad.
Pass the piece of chalk with which you mark the baseball score.
You shall see the lovely Madeline upon the barroom floor."

So with another drink and with chalk in hand the vagabond began
To sketch a face that might well buy the soul of any man.
As he placed another lock upon the shapely head,
With a fearful shriek, he leaped and fell across the picture—dead.

71 *Socrates Snooks*

Don Jackson: This is a kind of a comical recitation. It's just something I read somewhere once.

Mr. Socrates Snooks,
The lord of creation,
The second time
Entered the marriage relation.

Antippe Cahlorie
Accepted his hand,
And for a time he felt himself
The happiest man in the land.

Scarce had the honeymoon
Passed over his head,
One morning to Antippe
Mr. Socrates said,

"I think for a man
In my standing in life
This house is too small
As I now have a wife,

"So as early as possible
Carpenter Parry
Shall be sent for to widen
My house, and my dairy."

"Now, dearest,"
The lovely Antippe replied,
"I hate to hear
Everything vulgarly 'myed.'

"In speaking of our chattel hereafter
Say, 'our pigpen, our farmhouse.' "

"By your leave, Mrs. Snooks,
I'll say what I please—
My house, my orchard,
My land, and my trees."

"Say 'ours,' "
The lovely Antippe replied.
"I won't, Mrs. Snooks,
Though you ask for an age.

"Oh, my woman is only
A part of man's rib,
If the story in Genesis
Don't tell a fib.

"Should your male companion
Quarrel with you,
You're certain to prove
The best man of the two."

In the following story
This was certainly true,
For the lovely Antippe
Just pulled off her shoe

And laying about her
On all sides at random
The scene was verified
In near desperatum.

Mr. Socrates Snooks,
After trying in vain
To ward off the blows
That descended like rain,

Crept under the bed
Like a terrified Hessian.

But the dauntless Antippe
Not one whit afraid
Simply turned the siege
Into a blockade.

At last after reasoning
The thing in his pate,
He decided it was useless
To strive against fate.

Protruding his head
Like a tortoise, he said,
"My dear, may we
Come out from under our bed?"

"Ha! Ha!" cried Antippe,
"You came to my terms.
I can tell by your looks.

"Now, Socrates, hear me,
After this happy hour
If you'll always obey me,
I will never look sour."

'Tis said the next Sabbath
They were going to church.
He chanced for a new pair
Of trousers to search.

Having found them
He asked with a few nervous twitches,
"My dear, may we put on
Our new Sunday britches?"

72   *Brought Back*

Don Jackson: My mother had a book of recitations, and I learned from it, but it's lost. The old poems had more meaning, and I learned a few. (I learned mostly cowboy songs, and I sing them all to the same tune, you might say.) And I used to recite to myself or to the coyotes, or to whoever would listen:

She wandered alone at midnight
Through alley and coiling street,
Through the heart of a wealthy city,
Yet she starved for food to eat.

Still on though her feet were weary,
And the winter wind blew keen.
Her heart was nearly breaking
At the thought of what might have been.

Through her mind old scenes are passing
So vivid and quick and clear.
She can see the stile where Harold
First met her and called her dear

In the old sweet country village
Where she lived in days long gone,
Where not a pang of sorrow
Ever caused her a tear or sigh.

And then there's a fancy painting,
A picture of that day's scene
When wedding bells rang sweetly,
And she was a sailor's queen.

The vision melts and quickly
There flits through her haunted mind
The sight of her love departed
Leaving her, sad, behind.

He'd gone for his duty bravely
Away over the salting sea.
"Oh, God," she prayed when he left her,
"Bring Harold again to me."

Months went by, and he came not,
And now two years had fled.
She had given up all hope,
For, Lord, he was surely dead.

She had wed against parents' wishes.
They had renounced her long ago.
A poverty strong had forced her
To take to the needle and sew.

As she who had lived in the country
And thrived in its pure air
Soon pined in the crowded city
When left in a workroom there.

Still on did she wander slowly
Till weary and well-nigh spent
To one of the broad recesses
On London Bridge she went.

And peering just over its coping,
She strained her eyes to scan
The place beneath where swiftly
The cold black river ran.

What horrible thoughts were passing
Held her a-leaping there.
Leave her own life's burdens,
Pain and wandering and care.

"Only one leap," she murmured,
"No more to be starved, oppressed,
And maybe I'll meet my Harold,
In the far off land of rest."

She sprang on the ridge as cold as she could be
Just to glance around.
No one in sight.
'Twas then her sharp ear caught a sound.

It was a footstep coming quickly.
Should she wait till it passed her by?
"No!" she replied that instant.
What mattered who saw her die,

But a voice cried, "Hold, for God's sake!"
She starts and falls off the ridge.
Not into the rushing water
But onto the hard stone bridge.

A man's strong arms had caught her
As she gently raised to her feet.
She turned and they both were startled
As soon as their glances meet.

"Harold!" "My Bess, my darling!"
A husband and wife are met.
What pen can describe the gladness
Such feelings as these beget?

Bess could hardly believe her senses.
She felt so serene and blessed,
As her weary head lay pillowed
On her sailor husband's breast.

He told how the ship foundered,
And how he managed to reach the shore
Where he eked out an existence
For eighteen months or more.

When rescued he came to England
To search for his poor, young wife,
And now at last he'd found her
And brought her back to life.

73   *A Chinese Poem*

Grant E. Brown: This is "A Chinese Poem." I always wrote it and do it so it was in a long column like the Chinese write instead of across, and the way it goes is:

Nice
Night
In
June;
Star
Shine,
Big
Moon;
In
Park
On
Bench
With
Girl
In
Clinch.
Me
Say
Me
Love.
She
Coo
Like
Dove.
Me
Smart,
Me
Fast.
Never
Let
Chance
Pass.
Get
Hitched.
Me
Say
Everything
Okay.
Wedding
Bells
Ring
Ring
Honeymoon
Everything.

Settle
Down.
Happy
Man.

74 *Once Upon a Time*

LaVelle Whiting DeSpain: This is a little poem I found today, and I had forgotten it. I had written it for my daughter Claudia to give at her friend's reception. Her friend's name was Gordon Wheat, and I'll tell you he worked for Sears, so you'll understand it.

Once upon a time
Not too long ago
There was a girl named Polly
Who was looking for a beau.

Now I knew that Polly was a prize
And planned that she would be
Among the topmost branches
On our illustrious family tree.

Claudia had introduced Polly to all her fine relatives, but it didn't work.

So I tried to lure her
With my cousins by the score,
But alas, she'd already placed her order
At Sears and Roebuck store.

I told her the order could be canceled,
And she could send him back,
But I found sweet Polly has a temper,
For she fairly blew her stack.

But still I couldn't relinquish
The claim we had on her
And tried to point out some of the finer features
Of our Whiting's grocery store.

I pled with her, "Polly, you can get your groceries wholesale
With nothing down to pay."
"But Gordon's all I ever wanted,"
Was all that she would say.

When Polly showed me her order,
I knew that all was lost.
She had ordered Gordon Wheat
No matter what the cost.

The order was marked urgent
And read something like this,
"No substitute will be accepted;
Just send the top man on your list."

Catalog number? Number one, of course.
The one that is tall and neat.
In case there is a question,
The name is Gordon Wheat.

Quantity? This matters little to me.
It's quality I'm after,
As you can plainly see.

Size? When it comes to width, he may be lacking,
But he makes it up in height,
So just send him six foot two.
I'm sure he'll be just right.

Color? Tall, dark, and handsome.
Liz couldn't ask for more.
And just to think I found him
At a Sears and Roebuck store.

And the lifetime guarantee
Means very much to me
Because, you see, I want this fellow
For all time and eternity.

Please mark "fragile"
And handle him with care.
He is now mine forever
And the answer to my prayer.

Now since Polly placed that order
At Sears and Roebuck store,
It not only gave her Gordon Wheat
But many, many more.

There's little Shredded Wheat,
The oldest of the clan,
Not to forget German Wheat,
A manly little man.

Then the little Wheathearts,
The twins they all adore,
Are the last of this year's wheat crop
And even up the score.

I almost forgot little German Wheat,
The delinquent little Wheat,
And though he's always in trouble,
He still is very sweet.

One day in desperation
Gene and Corrine took him to the track.
He slipped away and placed his bet,
And to their horror, he won the stack.

Besides being a father
And having many cares,
Gordon quit his job with Sears and Roebuck
And is helping Gene with mares.

The years have come; the years have gone,
And life has changed, I'm sure,
But they will both be truly grateful
To Sears and Roebuck store.

The order brought happiness
They never thought could be
Not only in this life
But in eternity.

There's a moral to this story, girls.
When all else does seem to fail,
Just pick up a Sears and Roebuck catalog
And order your own male.

75 *My Mother-in-Law*

**Horace Crandell: Just a few years ago I heard somebody do this. I was
delighted because it's kind of an extension of ''Young Jacob Strauss.'' It's in a
German dialect, and I just kind of make it up, I guess.**

There's strange tings done in dis land a da free,
I jus' can't quite understand.
Da peoples all seem so different ta me,
Then they does in mine own fadder land.

They gets plenty troubles and into mishaps
Without the least bit of a cause,
And would you believe it, them mean Yankee chaps
They fight mid their mudder-in-laws.

Can you tink of a white men so vicked as dat?
Why not gib the old lady a show?
Who vas it got up ven de night was so hot
With my baby? I'd like to know.

Den in de winter when Katrine was sick,
When de mornin' was snowy and raw.
Who made right away that big fire up so quick?
Huh! That was mine mudder-in-law.

I vas one of dem wimen rights fellas. I was.
Dey wadn't anyting mean about me,
But ven dat old lady vants to run dat machine,
Vell, I just let her run it, you see.

And when dat young Jacob was cutting some tricks
A block off de ole chip he vas. Ya!
But when she took to him mit some thousand bricks.
Vell, dat's all right, too. She's mine mudder-in-law.

Veek in and veek out, everyting was da same.
Dat women vas boss of da house,
But never mind dat, I vas glad dat she came.
She vas kind to mine young Jacob Strauss,

And ven der vas vater to bring from da spring
And firewood to split up and saw,
She vas velcomed to do it. There's not anyting
Dat's too good for mine mudder-in-law.

76   *Betty and the Bear*

Joseph C. Bolander: Now, this is one I think as near as I know is the first one I ever memorized (I might have memorized "The Night Before Christmas" before this one), and I've forgotten part of it. It is entitled "Betty and the Bear."

Into the pioneer cabin out West, so they say,
A great big black grizzly trotted one day.
He seated himself on the hearth and began to lap up the contents
Of a two-gallon pan of milk and potatoes, an excellent meal,
And then look about to see what he could steal.

**Now, this is the part I've forgotten in it, and you'll just have to use your
imagination, but eventually the lord and lady of the house returned home
only to find their little cabin occupied by this great big grizzly bear, and of
course there was some discussion as to what to do about the situation, and
somebody suggested that somebody might go in and chase the grizzly out, to
which somebody replied:**

"Yes, Betty, I will if you'll first venture in."
So Betty leaped up and the poker she seized,
And the man shut the door and against it he squeezed.
Betty then laid on the bruin her blows
Now on his forehead, now on his nose,
And her man through the keyhole kept shouting within,
"Well done, my brave Betty, now hit him again."

With rapping and poking, brave Betty alone
At last laid old bruin dead as a stone,
And when the man saw the bear was no more,
He ventured to poke his nose out of the door,
And there was the bruin stretched out on the floor.

And off to the neighbors he hastened to tell
Of the wondrous things which that morning befell,
"Oh yes, come and see it. All the neighbors have seen it.
Come and see what we did, me and Betty, we did it."

77 *William and Mary*

**Ada Holyoak Fowler: This was written around Christmas time for a little
man and his wife. This woman had had about seven strokes, and her husband
had been hurt real seriously on a fire engine (he used to be a fireman), and
everything, but it's just like, I don't care where you see them, it's, "Hi!"
She's always cheerful. I just kinda wrote it for them as a Christmas present,
I guess. It says:**

There are times in a person's life.
Some things go wrong, some right.
Then you meet that special person
Who gives your life a special light.

There are all kinds of people in love around.
We all see and feel things differently,
And then you meet a special person.
Their "howdy" and their sound are all so heavenly.

They never change from day to day.
No matter where you meet them, they're always the same.
They always keep their bright happy smiles
And always remember and speak your name.

I've had the pleasure of such a friend,
And I thank you for your strength and your will.
You are a very special loving couple,
And I thank you, my friends, William and Mary Campbell.

I met them at the clinic where I work.

78 *Lady, Queen of My Heart*

**LaVelle Whiting DeSpain: I'll read you one I had written the words to and
someone else set to music. The first part my brother read; the other part was
a duet.**

Lady, queen of my heart,
You were my lady
Right from the start.

You were my everything,
A lady so fine.
I thank the dear Lord
That He made you mine.

Mother of my children,
Fifty years my wife,
You'll still be my lady
In that other life.

Then they sang this part.

Yes, you were my lady,
And I was your beau.
You knew it the first night,
Thought I didn't know.

You knew it the first night
You sat by my side
That someday I'd ask you,
And you'd be my bride.

We made a vow together
That evening in June.
Mother Nature smiled down
And gave us the moon.

Yes, you were my lady,
And I was your beau,
And you were so coy,
Thought I didn't know.

Fifty years, my lady,
And also my bride,
We've traveled down life's highway
Side by side.

The vows we made together
That evening in June
Are as lasting and binding
As the stars and the moon.

Love songs have been written
Since first time began
'Bout love for his lady
And hers for her man.

But none can compare
With my love for you.
It's been tested and tried,
And still it is true.

And though we're growing older,
It's still nice to know
That you are my lady
And I'm still your beau.

Mother gave lots of readings when she was a girl, and she wrote some beautiful speeches to give.

79 *Hands*

LaVelle Whiting DeSpain: I'll read you my "Hands" which I wrote for my parents' fiftieth wedding anniversary.

Your hands, they tell the story
Of fifty years of love and strife.
They tell of sorrow borne and victories won
Together in your life.

Fifty years ago
When you clasped your hands in love,
God smiled on both of you
His approval from above.

So He sent you precious spirits
Because He alone did know
The love, the care, the attention
Your precious hands would show.

These hands have served your God
And fellow man as well.
The lines, the wrinkles, and the roughness
Alone the story tell.

Your hands will go on serving
Till in death they are folded there.
"Well done, thou good and faithful servant,
Be free from earthly care.

"For in My celestial kingdom
Your hands have work to do,
As you travel heaven's highway
Hand in hand, the two of you."

80 *Anona's Golden Wedding Day*

Alida Connolly: This is "Anona's Golden Wedding Day." It tells all her life history.

Byron's and Anona's golden wedding day
Has rolled around.
Looks like a more popular couple
Couldn't be found.

You folks either like them,
Or you're just hungry for meat.
With prices so high,
It's a very rare treat.

Of course, the jolly Barbecue Sam,
Bill, Larry, and Dapper Dan,
They'll draw a crowd
If anyone can.

With LaRue, Maxine,
Olivia, Marilee, Zora, and the rest,
That dinner tonight
Was really the best.

Fifty years ago
When these two were young,
The wide world unexplored,
Their love song unsung.

Just look at their pictures.
Time has not yet left its traces.
With eyes full of dreams,
No lines on their faces.

Their future so rosy
Just coming in view.
Of course, Byron's vision
Included a cow or two.

Byron's sophistication consisted of
A few puffs behind the barn of various things,
Dating some girl in the old Model T,
And at dances having some flings.

And 'Nona had worked in a cafe
And gone to several schools,
And at flirting and dancing
Broke a few rules.

The first time Byron saw her,
She was working at the cafe.
He explained, "Who's that pretty, plump girl?
How can I meet her? What shall I say?

"I've never liked skinny girls.
Nothing to hold on to when you dance.
Boy! I'd like to date her
If I had a chance."

But he was dating another girl,
And Anona had one or two,
So just a friendly relationship
Was the best that he could do.

In fact, when the crowd went camping,
They were with different people,
But they kept feeling
This compelling force.

And so when their dates both left town,
They felt elated, it's true.
They started sympathizing with each other,
And you can see what sympathy can do.

Their gang used to meet at our house
To party and dance.
Our parlor was known to each flapper and sheik.
Us kids would sneak down in our nighties to listen and peek.

"Beautiful Ohio," "Peg o' My Heart," "Oh, My Dardanella,"
"Oh, Johnny, Oh, Johnny, Oh, Johnny, Oh," "Sheik of Araby,"
All the songs which were played, waltzed, fox-trotted, and
     one-stepped to
Still mean so much to me.

Byron was our favorite suitor.
He brought us candy when he came to call,
And he talked to us like we were somebody,
Not just brat kids, at all.

When I had pneumonia,
I'd only take the medicine from him, and oh, my,
When I burped it all over his partying suit,
I wished that I could die.

But in spite of bratty kids
And things that happened, he took a chance
And popped the question—
Hence this fifty year romance.

Oh, they've had their ups and downs
And plenty of heartaches along the way,
But they faced them bravely and well,
Or they just couldn't smile here today.

They were married at Fern Johnson's house,
Four of them together.
Anona wore a blue serge dress.
It was very cold weather.

They'd asked Levi Udall to officiate,
But he was held up in Concho, and it got very late,
So they sent for E. I. Whiting
Whose task that day was to irrigate.

They wouldn't let him change his clothes,
So they were married to their delight.
They wanted to surprise
The crowd at dinner that night.

Byron had dated Fern some,
So George Waite wrote the license that way.
They had to change the names,
Or Byron and Fern would have been wedded today.

Next day all the four decided to make it for eternity at the Salt Lake
       temple,
Each traveling in their own Model T,
They had their own camp outfit
And were as independent as they could be.

They spent one whole day stuck in the mud in Zuni.
The Indians just passed them by,
Wouldn't loan them a horse or anything,
Wouldn't even try.

When they got to Salt Lake,
It all seemed so big, so bright, so rushed, it was a shock.
These country kids said,
"This is just too hectic. Let's park the cars and walk."

They visited relatives
On all sides while there.
They had their great sport
Floating in the salt water at Salt Air.

When they returned, they lived at the meadows,
And life was hard.
They had their first boy, a girl named Alma,
And Byron had his reward.

She loved farming, the outdoors.
He forgot he cried 'cause she wasn't a boy.
He said she was the best boy he had
And such a joy.

'Nona used to put Alma in ruffles, and she'd come down out of a tree with her ruffles all torn, and here was Wallace sitting in the house reading a book.

They lived at L. R. Gibbons' farm
In a little red house under the hill.
They had Wallace, Dan, Billy, and Dennis,
And of boys Byron finally had his fill.

'Nona made butter, sold it for thirty cents a pound,
Yellow, fresh, sweet, good as gold.
She'd put it in the well
Each time before it was sold.

Sold milk for ten cents a quart
Delivered to the door.
She canned, gardened, raised calves and lambs,
Cooked for hired men galore.

She never got bored,
Or for idleness felt any guilt.
For she was always sewing
Or making a quilt.

Byron worked on the highway
For many long years.
Our kids always watched for Uncle Byron's grader
And gave him big cheers.

There is a big tree on the Show Low road
Where he ate his lunch.
We always called it Uncle Byron's tree.
You can't fool our bunch.

Well, if this sounds like an obit,
Just look around.
A more active couple
Just can't be found.

Byron raises lambs, cows,
And his own, what's more,
He worked on his mountain cabin, built a fence,
And laid some floor.

Anona has hobbies that
Would keep ten women going.
If she isn't planning a trip, decorating something,
She's cooking or sewing.

Of course, they both have a leg
That gives them a twinge or a slip.
I suppose that's from waltzing, square dancing,
And doing the dip.

So on this golden wedding day
Before it's o'er,
Golly, we all wish you great happiness and joy,
And may you have many, many more.

And here's the pictures that will prove it. This is their wedding, and this is their golden anniversary.

81 *Let the Damn Grass Grow*

Joseph C. Bolander: This was written by Owen Sanders down at Hurricane. He's a pretty good amateur poet. Anyway, it's entitled "Let the Damn Grass Grow."

He, enthusiastically, "Come on, my dear,
Let's take a trip so we can be together.
We'll leave our many friends in town
To talk about the weather."

She, reluctantly, "I have so many
Household chores, it's hard for me to go.
Plants to water, pets to feed,
Weeds to chop, and lawns to mow.

"Besides, my dear, the girls would meet,
And I'd miss my club.
I'd miss my hair appointment,
Massage, and facial rub.

"Let's wait a little longer
Till social duties alter.
We've been so very busy since
We journeyed to the altar."

A little later he, hopefully, "Come on, my dear,
Let's take a stroll and hobble around the block,
And while we are strolling,
We'll have a good long talk."

She, dejectedly, "I've got a hitch in my get-along
My corns and bunions throb.
Arthritis is so painful
I almost can't but sob.

"Let's wait a while. I'll take a pill.
Tomorrow we may go.
Then maybe we can stroll a block
If we take it very slow."

Tomorrow he, dejectedly, "Farewell, my dear,
Please wait for me. I'll find you some bright day,
Then we can stroll together
Down some grand celestial way.

"If you would return to be with me,
I want the world to know,
We'd take a thousand little trips,
And let the damn grass grow."

Isn't that the way?

82 *Lorenzo Brown's Poem*

**Anona Heap: I wrote a drama on the life of Lorenzo Brown, compiled from
the direct words of his journals. I merely made up the scenery, and I'm his
great, great granddaughter, and it ends with a poem he wrote.**

Farewell, my partner, my life, my love,
When death is done;
When death's dark stream I ferry o'er,
And that time surely will come, I know.
In heaven above I'll ask no more
Than just an eager welcome.

He lived in Eagar, Arizona, you know.

83 *Building for Life Eternal*

**Alida Connolly: The husband of a friend of mine died, and she was quite
devastated. I just wrote this to comfort her. It fit her husband 'cause he was
always carpentering.**

141

Daddy's not gone,
He's just away.
Building a home
For a future day.

He took his carpentry apron
From a cloud there in the sky,
And he's gone ahead into heaven
Where you'll be by and by.

I seem to hear him whisper,
"Now, Mama, please don't fret.
It'll take a while to finish,
But I'll come and get you yet.

"I'll have to put some windows in
And lay a little floor,
And make a pretty pathway,
For some roses round the door.

"I have finished the foundation
Strengthened by love throughout the years.
The walls are cemented with laughter,
Moistened by happy tears.

"The roof stands open to the heavens
So Father's angels may wave good night.
There's space enough for all our dear ones,
So, Mama, keep them in your sight.

"Now, Honey, when I get it finished
And all your earthly tasks are through,
I'll need you to hang the curtains
And arrange the furniture, too.

"For it never could be heaven
Without you, Mama, you know,
So look after all the children
Till your time comes to go.

"Now, Mama, please don't worry.
Sweetheart, don't you fret.
I'm building for life eternal,
And I'll come and get you yet."

CHAPTER SIX

About Children

AFTER THE MYSTERY OF love between men and women comes the mystery of children: the mystery of life beginning anew and "the kid part" in the adult. There are as many recitations about children as there are recitations for children.

84 *A Grandson's Love*

Delbert D. Lambson: Being a grandpa and having a lot of grandkids, you kinda live for them. The kids are all gone, and you've got that behind you. I live next door to my little old grandkids, and I wrote a few poems about them, to them, for them, and mainly for myself. And this is just a small one I wrote about my grandson. It's "A Grandson's Love."

When my little grandson greets me
With the early morning rising,
The big wide smile upon his face
Is always surprising.

He comes to me with arms outstretched.
I return his salutation
With a smile, a kiss, and a little squeeze
That meets his expectation.

He looks right past my old slouch hat
And my clothes with smell abiding.
He only knows there's a real big hug
And a knee that's good for riding.

My day is better, my day is blessed,
And my burden now is lighter.
Someone loves me, and I know who.
It's my grandson, and my life is brighter.

85 *The Ocean Voyage*

Margaret Witt: My mother had a recitation book, and I learned a lot from it, but it got destroyed, and I don't think anyone else has them. I'll give the "The Ocean Voyage."

Two little children grown tired of play
Roamed to the sea one summer day.
Watching great waves come and go
Prattling as children will, you know,
Of dolls and marbles, kites and strings,
Sometimes even graver things.

Alas, they spied within their reach
An old boat cast upon the beach.
Helter-skelter with merry din
Over its sides they clambered in,
Ben with his tangled dark brown hair,
Bess with her sweet face flushed and fair.

Rolling in from the briny deep
Nearer and nearer the great waves creep.
Higher, higher upon the sands
Reaching out with their giant hands
Grasping the boat with boisterous glee
Tossing it up and out to sea.

The sun went down mid clouds of gold.
Night came with footsteps damp and cold.
Now across the starry sky
A black cloud stretches far away
And shuts the golden gates of day.

A storm comes on with flash and roar,
While all the sky is shrouded o'er.
Still floats the boat through driving storm
Protected by God's powerful arms.

A home-bound vessel lies
In ready trim 'twixt sea and skies.
Her captain paces restless now
A troubled look upon his brow.
While all his nerves with terror thrill
The shadow of some coming ill.

A mate comes up to where he stands
And grabs his arm with eager hands.
"A boat has just swept past us," says he,
"Bearing two children out to sea.
'Tis dangerous now to put about,
Yet they cannot be saved without."

"Naught but their safety will suffice.
They must be saved," the captain cries.
"By every hope that's just and right,
By lips I hope to kiss tonight.
I'll peril vessel, life, and men,
And God will not forsake me then."

With anxious faces one and all
Each one responded to the call.
And when at last through driving storm
They lifted up each little form,
The captain started with a groan,
"My God!" he cried, "They are my own."

86   *Quick As a Telephone*

**Margaret Witt: I just recited anytime anybody asked me. Most now they ask
people to sing or something else. They don't ask people to recite or anything
like that anymore. The last time I recited was to a party up here, and there
weren't very many there, and some of them, too, had parts but didn't turn
up, so then another lady and I just took turns reciting. Somebody said there
that I should have had them recorded.**

One night a well-known merchant of a town in the West who had
been traveling for some time a downward path came out of his house,
for tonight a crowd of some old companions he'd promised to meet.
His young wife had resolved him with imploring eyes to spend the
evening with her and had reminded him of a time when an evening
passed in her presence were all too short. Little daughter'd hung
about his knees and coaxed in her pretty, willful way for Papa to tell
her some bedtime stories, but habit was stronger than love for wife or
child, and he eluded their tender questionings with deceits and
excuses which are the intemperate ravage for the intemperate and so
went on his way.

When he was some distance from the house, he found that in
changing his clothes he had forgotten his purse, and he could not go
on a drinking bout without any money, so he hurried back and crept
past the window of his own home in order that he might sail in and

obtain it without running the gauntlet of other questioning caresses. As he looked in at the open window, something stayed his feet, for there was fire in the grate within (the night was chill), and it lit up the pretty little parlor and brought out the pictures in startling effect; but these were nothing to pictures on the hearth where knelt his little daughter at mother's knee small head bowed, small hands clasped: "Now I lay me down to sleep."

His thoughts ran back to boyhood hours, and as he compressed his bearded lips, he could see in memory the face of that mother long ago gone to her rest who taught his own infant lips prayers he had long forgotten to utter.

The child went on, completed her little verse, and then continued, "God bless Papa, Mama, and my own self." Then there was a pause, and she lifted her troubled blue eyes to her mother's face.

"God bless Papa," prompted mother softly, "and please send him home sober." He did not hear the mother as she said this, but the child followed in a clear, inspired song.

Mother and child both sprang to their feet in alarm when the door opened so suddenly, but they were not afraid when they saw who it was returned so soon. That night when little Mary was being tucked into bed after a romp with Papa, she said in the sleepiest and most contented of voices, "Mama, God answers almost as quick as the telephone, doesn't he?"

87 *A Child's Prayer*

Margaret Witt: The poems you get nowadays, they don't have any sense to me, no meaning. It's just like a lot of the songs today don't have a lot of meaning like the old ones. Now, I'll tell you "A Child's Prayer." It's got meaning.

On the pleasant sunshine
Of a bright October day
Rollicking, frolicking, through the woods
Scaring the birds away,

A group of laughing girls and boys
To play till the sun was set,
Martha, and Tony, and Bob, and Will,
And Dolly, the household pet.

They played tag and follow-the-leader
And scampered up and down
When at last they settled down

To talk and rest
And plan some pleasure new
While Martha unpacked the goodies
For the hungry, bright-faced crew.

"I'm too little to work," said Dolly,
Tossing her curls away.
"You make the dinner, Mattie dear,
And I'll be papa and pray.

"I know just how he does it
'Cause I looked through my fingers so,
And God will hear me better outside
Than He would in the house, I know."

Then clasping her baby's fingers
And bowing her little brown head,
After the children's father
Folded this childish prayer.
"We thank thee, God, way up in the skies
For these nice things to eat,

"For fathers and mothers to love us,
Only Bobby, his mother's dead.
But I guess you know all about that, God;
You took her away, they said.

"If you please, don't let my mother die,
For I shouldn't know what to do.
I'm afraid you'd have
To get me, too.

"Make all our days just as good as this,
And don't let Bobby cry.
That's all little Dolly knows to pray,
So our Heavenly Father, goodbye."

88 *My Young Jacob Strauss*

**Horace Crandell: I got this out of that red history book. I just kind of liked it,
so I learned it. I did it for years.**

I have vun funny little boy
That comes just to my knee.
Da cutes' chap, the greatest rogue
As ever you did see.

He runs and yumps and smashes things,
In all parts of da house.
But what of dat, he was mine son,
Mine little Jacob Strauss.

He catch de measles and da mumps
And everything dat's out.
He spills mine glass of lager beer,
Throws snuff into mine kraut.

He stuffs mine pipe mid Limburg cheese,
He was the greatest taus.
I'd take dat from no other boy
But little Jacob Strauss.

He takes mine milk pan for a drum
And cuts mine cane in two
To make the sticks to beat it mit.
I'll tell you dat was true.

He asked me questions such as dese,
What make mine nose so red?
Who vas it dat cut dat sleek place out
From the hair on top o' mine head?

And vhere de blaze goes from de lamp
Venever de gleam I douse?
How can I such things explain
To dat little Jacob Strauss?

Sometimes I tink I shall go vild
With such a naughty boy.
I vish again I might have rest
And quiet times enjoy,

But ven he vas asleep in bed
As quiet as a mouse,
I pray de Lord, "Take anytings,
But leave dat Jacob Strauss."

89 *Freckles*

Ralph Rogers: I sure was lucky; I spent twenty-six years rodeoing before I got hurt bad enough I had to quit. I still like to ride broncos, though.

This is one of my favorite recitations or songs. I did it on that record as a song, but I'll recite it for you.

He was just a kid,
A little pug-nosed, redhead kid.
Though he was his mother's pride and joy,
He was worse than Peck's Bad Boy.

Freckles was his name.
Young Freckles always got the blame
For every broken window pane.
Oh, how they'd fan him and tan him.
How he'd tease the girls
When at school he'd pull their curls.

His marks were lower
Than kids much slower,
But he was a whiz
With the old bean blower.

People used to coax
Young Freckles not to play jokes.
Oh, how he'd fool the village folks.
It was a shame.

And when the teacher found a tack in her chair,
Though a hundred scholars were there,
She said, ''Freckles!''
'Cause he always got the blame.

In a marble game
He'd shoot and never miss his aim.
At spinning tops he was sure to win
Because his top had the longest spin.

And at the old swimming place
You could always see his smiling face,
And at the old church picnic
He'd win every race.

Freckles was his name.
Young Freckles always got the blame
For every broken window pane.
Oh, how they'd fan him and tan him.
How he'd tease the girls
When at school he'd pull their curls.

His face was ruddy,
But not from study,
And the other kid's nose
Was always bloody.

People used to coax
Young Freckles not to play jokes.
Oh, how he'd fool the village folks.
It was a shame.

And when the old cat had kittens in the hay,
One was black and seven were gray.
Everybody said, "Freckles!"
'Cause he always got the blame.

90   *Dad Book, Number One*

Joe S. Holyoak: I wrote this one when Vandee was a baby; it goes on:

I talked to my father,
Listened to all that he had
On being a good father
And a successful dad.

I read all that is written
Heard all that was said,
And kept all the secrets
In an old canvas bag.

My defense was patience,
And the offense I had
Was, "Charge at full steam.
You're the world's best dad."

The first month of action
I was doing all right,
A few bumps and scrapes
And a fall late at night.

She was sound in bed
And sleeping tight.
The second month
I was doing all right.

Tore up the hall
And a telephone line
Over a cough and a whinny,
And dad's little girl was just fine.

The third month I was getting in shape.
The hives were all gone,
And the ulcer didn't ache.
Along came four.

She fell out of bed.
I hauled and screamed
And pulled the hair
Out of my head.

Then at five
Was a sleepless night
When the doctor said,
"Your baby's all right.

"We'll keep her here
For a little while.
You get some rest."
And I left with a smile.

I should of rebelled
And been a bum.
This playing daddy
Isn't fun.

I wrote that the night Vandee spent the night in the hospital.

91   *The Moon Shines Brighter*

Joe S. Holyoak: One Sunday night I came home and the moon was shining on my pickup as I did my chores, and I sat out there and thought of this poem.

The moon shines brighter on a Sunday night
As it dances across the city's light.
The cares of tomorrow seem far away;
I thank my God for the Sabbath day.

Things seem clearer in the dimmer light.
The soul can ponder on the things that are right.
The moon shows the outline of our Father's hand
And covers the blemishes here of man.

Am I teaching my children there's a better way?
Do they understand Resurrection Day?
Will they see the beauty of God's great plan?
Can they live the mission here of man?

God bless the children;
They'll do what's right.
God bless the beauty
Of a moonlight night.

92   *The Auction*

**Margaret Witt: I'll give "The Auction." I get a little mixed up in it sometimes
and have to start over. When you get eighty-two—when you get twenty-eight
years old—you sometimes forget.** *(Laughs.)*

The auctioneer lifted down a chair.
Bold and loud and clear
He poured his cataract of words
Just like an auctioneer.

An auction sale of furniture
Where some hard mortgagee
Was bound to get his money back
And pay his lawyer's fee.

He knocked down bureaus, beds, and chairs,
And clocks, and chandeliers,
And a grand piano which he swore
Would last a thousand years.

He rattled out the crockery
And sold the silverware.
At last they passed him up
A little baby's chair.

"How much? How much? Come make a bid.
Is all your money spent?"
Just then some fast city swag
Came up and bid one cent.

Just then the sad-faced woman
Who had stood in silence there
Broke down and cried,
"My baby's chair! My poor dead baby's chair!"

"Here, Madam, take your baby's chair,"
Said the softened auctioneer,
"I know its value all too well.
My baby died last year.

"And if our friend,
The mortgagee,
Objects to these proceedings,
Let him send the bill to me."

Gone was the tone of raillery.
The softened auctioneer turned
Shamefaced from his audience
To wipe aside a tear.

The laughing crowd was awed and still.
Not a tearless eye was there
When the weeping woman reached
And took her little baby's chair.

93   *To Ramah and My Father*

Anona Heap: I took a creative writing class a few years ago through the local junior college, and this is a story I wrote for that class. I wrote a longer, fuller version just for the family, and this shorter one to read to people.

I have often wondered why Father decided to leave Eagar, the place of his childhood and young manhood, to go out to a place as uninviting and as unpromising as Ramah. Was it the pioneering urge to build up a new country? Was his pride hurt? I remember he ran for office and was defeated. Or just what was the reason he left in the cold month of February in 1915 with my mother expecting within a month, myself nine, my brother Lorenzo five, Geneva four, Alida two, with extra horses, a cow and a cat and a dog. And the dog's name was Dash.

I remember looking back over the valley of Eagar just as we went around the hill east of town, the hill where the Round Valley Rodeo Ground now stands. I don't know how far we traveled. I was only nine. I don't remember where we first camped, but I do remember the afternoon we arrived at Atarque Flat. Oh, it was cold! There was so much snow, great drifts everywhere. I don't know how Father found the road. Once when we were going around the point of a hill, the horses that were tied on the side of the wagon missed the road and fell into the great big wash that was nearly filled with snow. That's how near the wagon was to going off.

There were a few Mexicans living in Atarque Flat, and we camped in a house that night. It hadn't been used for a long time, but we were so tired of camping out that we were very grateful for this chance. I guess the reason I remember that night so well is for two things. One, they had a tall scaffold for hanging up the slaughtered beef, I guess, but in my childish mind I knew it was a scaffold for hanging people, and I scarcely slept that night I was so frightened. And then our cat! I guess there hadn't been a cat there for a long time because there was so many mice. The next morning our cat had caught so many she made neat piles of them in each corner of the room.

Then we went across the Flat the next day. The sticky clay would ball up on the wagon wheels until Dad would have to stop and dig it off every little while.

We arrived at Ramah after ten days of traveling. Sometimes I would like to go back over that road again and see if things are there as I remember it, but I never have. We moved into a little tumbled down shack, the only empty house in town, on a hill. Here one cold blustery night Johnny was born on March the twentieth, 1915, my first introduction to the facts of life. Dad went after the midwife and left Mother with a labor lady. Things began to get rushing, so she called me, a girl of nine. I was kept very busy building fires, trying to keep the snow from blowing in on Mother through the quilt that served as a door, and holding Mother's hand. I remember the lady said something about me being there when I was so young, and Mother said, "Well, I don't care. Maybe she'll have sense enough not to get married."

Well, Johnny was born before Dad and the midwife got back. Poor kid! That was a terrible night to be brought into this world.

We lived in this little shack for awhile, and Dad helped farm in what they called the Upper Valley. That was a beautiful place, a valley surrounded on three sides with hills of pines and facing the reservoir. To reach it, you had to go around a big high cliff the base of which rested in the water. They had built up a road of rocks around this point, and when the water was high, we really went into the water about four feet deep, but it was always clear, and you could see where the roadbed ended under the water.

Later we moved to town across from the schoolhouse. I remember one day at school, I looked up and there was Ren who was four years younger than me toddling across the square, dirty face and all. I jumped up and took him home and then had to stay in at recess once or twice for not asking the teacher's permission to leave.

The next day we moved out and homesteaded three hundred twenty acres. This was ten miles southeast of Ramah. At first Dad built a house near the northeast corner of the section and quite near to Fred Lewis's house, but after digging a well down forty feet and finding no water, he moved the house nearer to a place where he found water about a fourth of a mile away. Our house was just one thickness of lumber left with the studding inside to be lined later, but it never got done. There was only one room and a porch. There were four of us. Part of the porch was boarded up and used later as a bedroom. There must have been a bed of rattlesnakes near that first house. We killed thirty or forty. I remember watching one charm a bird one day.

Dad built a small dam near the house, and we watered some garden and potato patches from it. The rest was dry farm. I would judge about forty acres were under cultivation. The first year we raised quite a few spuds and had some to sell, but how we worked—plowing, harrowing, planting, and poisoning the prairie dogs—there were millions of them. Many a night I've cried myself to sleep with a leg ache.

Then Dad would freight in between times so we could have something to eat and wear. I went with him to Gallup once or twice. Once I drove a four-horse outfit alone; of course, he was just ahead. My, Gallup looked like a big place to me!

One fall there were so many pine nuts that Mother and we kids gathered enough to buy all of our winter's flour. We used to turn our pigs out and herd them as we picked nuts. These they fattened on, but the fat was never hard; it was just like oil.

In the winter we moved into town for school. Frank, my younger brother, was born October 3, 1917. They must have had plenty of help this time because they didn't even ask me. Before Mother was out of bed, I came down with typhoid fever. There had been an epidemic there a few years before, and no one would come near to help us, so she had to get up and take care of me. While I was sick, the Lewises needed their house that we were living in, and so we had to move. They moved me on a cot all covered up. Of course, I peeked out a little. I guess I was sick a long time. All my hair came out, and I had to learn to walk again. Remember, there was no doctor.

We moved back to the homestead in the spring and filed on three hundred twenty additional acres, six hundred and forty acres in all. We put in crops again, and things looked a little brighter. Then the World War I broke out. Four of Mother's brothers joined. Grandfather and Grandmother LeSueur and Harvey came to see us. They lived in Mesa. I remember how they used to send us corn flour, rye flour, potato flour, and milo flour all from Mesa. I remember the milo flour was very dark, and the corn flour tasted real good. It was just like corn meal only ground really fine. Because of the war, we weren't allowed to use wheat flour and very little sugar. Dear Grandma's packages were the highlights of our existence. The gum, the candy, the clothes she used to send us there three or four times a year—it was just like Christmas.

My dad was very fond of candy and always managed to bring us some when he came from Gallup. He didn't smoke, or drink tea or coffee, but he did love his candy. We always had family prayers in the morning, blessed the food, and said our prayers at bedtime. Although we didn't get in to Sunday school every Sunday, we always had Sunday school at our house.

For a wedding present Grandpa LeSueur had given Mother a piano which was always in our house. Imagine a piano in a one-room house! But I guess most of the time Mother was too tired to play. We were taught the ways we should be taught. I don't remember my dad ever working on Sunday. If we were traveling and Sunday came, he rested and had services. Dad was very strict, and none of us disobeyed him the second time or ever talked back, yet he never spanked us. He loved horses; of course, he needed many to farm and freight with, but I expect it took more to feed them than it did his whole family. The Indians would often drive them off, and Dad would always hunt for them for days, and then after he offered a reward of a dollar, the Indians would bring them back in. We were living among the Indians—Navajos on all sides of us. They'd run their sheep on our crops when Dad was gone freighting. They'd graze off the grass in the pasture and deal us misery in general.

The Fourth of July, a real celebration, what fun! We were going to Ramah to stay all night. About noon on July the third, Dad said it looked like it had rained up at the draw several miles above us, so he had better go and see if his ditches were all right because we needed the water so bad in the lake. He told me that if he didn't get back by three o'clock, to get the horses, and we would go to town as soon as he returned. I remember going after the horses. It was across a big old muddy flat and about a mile and a half.

There was some lightning and light showers about one o'clock, but it was nothing very serious. When it was time to go for the horses, Dad hadn't returned, so Mother told Ren he'd better go see what was the matter while I went after the horses.

About a mile from the house I could hear Ren screaming and calling and waving to me. I went toward him, but there was a big flood of water between us, so I couldn't hear what he was saying until I waded through the water. It was about three-quarters of a mile wide. When I finally got across, I could hear Ren crying, "Papa's dead! Papa's dead!" Ren was always such a big pest and always trying to scare somebody, and he made me real mad. I thought, "I'll spank him when I get there. He shouldn't fool about things like that." As I got closer, however, I could see that he wasn't fooling, and something was very wrong. When I got real close, I could see that Dad's head was above the water. Nothing else was showing. His head had hit on a grass bump and was out of the water. The water wasn't very deep there but was rising all the time. Dad was a large man, so we two small kids couldn't move him, so I sent Ren to the house for help three-fourths of a mile away, while I held Dad's head as high as I could to keep it out of the water. Oh, how my arms ached before Ren got back. Dad groaned every minute, and he couldn't understand me. After what seemed like hours, Mother came, and we dragged Dad a little higher up on higher ground. Ren had gone on to Lewis's for help. As they soon arrived, they began working with Dad thinking he had drowned but soon found marks on his body showing that he had been struck by lightning, they figured, around one o'clock, and it was nearly six o'clock. One thumb, the left, was torn nearly off, and a dark streak went up his arm, across his body, missed his heart, and went out of the heel of his right foot. The back of his head was crushed. While they were working with him, I caught a horse and went to get Frank and Frances Lewis. They lived three miles away. This was all the neighbors we had. Then I got the team ready, so we could take him to town.

It was dark before we got away, dark and rainy. Fred Lewis went with us. They made a bed in the covered wagon and laid Dad on it. How different from the trip we had planned! I never remember seeing such a dark night. We had a lantern and had to trust to it and the horses to find the road. Ten miles of the longest road I have ever traveled. Dad moaned and groaned with every breath. The mud balled up on the wheels, and the rain poured down. I don't know what time we reached town—it seemed years—but it was still dark.

We went to Fred Lewis's home. Everyone came, but no one could help. The nearest doctor was at Zuni, twenty-five miles away. He came—he was a Negro—he came but he could do nothing. All the while Dad lay and groaned, never regaining consciousness.

At ten o'clock on the night of the Fourth, the moans stopped and Dad was dead, leaving Mother thirty-six years old with six small children, no welfare, no social security, and six hundred and forty acres of nearly worthless land and no home. Dad was laid to rest at

Ramah bringing to close a little better than three years of life in the area.

My granddaughter teaches the primary class, and they try to have lessons about history every so often. She asked me to do one, so I rewrote this story, made it shorter, and gave it as a sort of moving diorama. I had everyone in the family and all my friends collecting all the little figures they could find, and I made covered wagons out of matchboxes. I even had a tiny copper lantern to hang in the back of the covered wagon. I had little sheep, a cat, and dog, cows, everything. I moved them along as I told the story to illustrate it. You know how hard it is to keep four- and five-year-old boys interested; well, this worked so well, I've been asked to give it several more times.

94   *Busy Little Mother*

Alida Connolly: This is advice from a grandmother to a young mother.

Busy little mother
Rising at the break of day,
Fix the breakfast, dress the babies,
Get them out to play.

Curl sister's hair, fix the lunches,
No time to yawn,
No time to smile or joke
Till the last chick is gone.

Busy little mother
Can't see her favorite roses bloom,
Make the beds, sweep the floor,
Pick up the boys' room.

Set the bread, mend a while,
Wash a batch of clothes,
Oh-oh, baby's running away again,
Down the street he goes.

Busy little mother,
Children all home at the close of day,
Cherish well this moment.
Too soon it will fly away.

Stop and listen to their little tales,
Sympathize and smile,
And laugh a laugh and sing a song,
And dance a little while.

Then put your arms around them
As you kneel to pray
And thank Him for each other
And for a fresh new day.

Busy little mother,
Live and love while yet you can,
For sonny's legs are elastic
And soon he'll stretch into a man.

And sister won't need you around
As you'll soon know.
For mothers are old-fashioned
And not as interesting as a brand-new beau.

Then the rugs stay put, the clothes hung up
For like mothers, they're outgrown.
Then mother has time to sit among the shining order
With a heart that's turned to stone.

Busy little mother,
It's hard to adjust to growing old and slow.
That cake that used to disappear,
Why, you couldn't even keep the dough,

Now grows moldy,
And that pie so fluffy and light
Remains uncut, and the cookie jar lid
Fits down so terribly tight.

The meals pass by in boring silence
With never a childish tale
To brighten grown-up conversation
Businesslike and stale.

Busy little mother,
All your fledglings flown,
So many hours in every day,
Too many to live alone.

The clock runs slower than it did
When there was much to do.
The house breathes quietly at night,
And it's much bigger, too.

Busy little mother, love them, kiss them, hold them close,
With all their adorable ways,
For their fat little legs will carry them away,
And they'll all be gone tomorrow, next week, or just one of these
    days.

95 *Memories of Vernon*

Alida Connolly: We were raised at Vernon when our stepdad took us up there.

Oh, little town of Vernon
Surrounded by cedar and fragrant pine,
However long I live or wherever I go,
Part of my heart is thine.

For though I have seen fair cities
As through this wide world I roam,
Their bright lights could never equal
The warm welcoming lights of home.

Yes, dear little mountain valley,
So close to my homing heart.
When I think of the good people we knew so well,
It makes the teardrops start.

So, let's have a party like we used to,
Inviting everyone in town,
Or build a big bonfire on Serviceberry,
Roast corn and chicken crisp and brown.

Let's ride horses in the moonlight
To Bannon, Piñon, or Floy.
We'll talk and sing as we ride along
Filled with youthful vigor and joy.

Let's play fox-and-geese in the snow,
Have a snowball fight before the school bell rings
And dance at recess with just anyone at all
Just for the pleasure it brings.

Let's have a ciphering match
With the other little schools.
Maybe even study a bit
To prove that the Vernon kids are nobody's fools.

Let's walk to school while the snowflakes
Fall slightly, softly, and white.
No matter if we're half frozen,
The pot-bellied stove will thaw us out all right.

Let's take a drink from the same dipper
From the bucket someone brought in from the well,
Pouring back what we can't drink,
For water is scarce in Vernon as any good Vernonite can tell.

Let's take valentines to everyone's door
Even though we live miles apart.
The wallpaper ones, the catalog ones, the boughten ones,
And the jerk one, the red heart.

Let's dress up now in scary clothes
For now it's Halloween.
Such upset johns, overturned gates,
The town has never seen.

Let's rob rats' nests, eat piñons
While the snow piles up deep and white.
There's only three or four kerosene lamps
Blazing in the winter night.

We ate what we raised
And we raised corn, squash, beans, and a little meat.
With honey and molasses, wild grape and algerita jelly,
And homemade candy for sweet.

We ate squash pie, squash butter,
Squash boiled, baked, sizzled, and fried.
I used to stick out my tongue
To see if I wasn't turning orange inside.

They say Cinderella's coach was made from a pumpkin,
And that's a fairy tale, but gosh!
There's been many a cinderella at the Vernon balls
Created from nothing but squash.

Come on, let's have a dance.
Crawl in the old schoolhouse window and ring the bell.
Throw cornmeal over the knotholes in the uneven floor.
Let the fiddlers weave a spell.

Oh, those good old days in Vernon!
Why couldn't they always last?
And as I start to reminiscin',
I feel like a woman with a past.

For though there's been some changes in the Vernon kids
Like graying hair, false teeth, and falling chests,
By golly, the kids who were raised on beans, and corn, and squash
Are the ones who have held up best.

And you know the ghosts of those Vernon kids
Still haunt those beloved hills,
And you can see their shadows and hear their laughter
When all is quiet and still.

For once you've been a kid in Vernon
And then you go away,
It's only the grown-up part that leaves;
The kid part will always stay.

So now my tale is ended, my glasses are fogged,
I'm feeling sentimental. That's very true,
And I'll say goodbye to the good old days in Vernon
And the friends so tried and true.

CHAPTER SEVEN

About Home and Place

WESTERN RECITATIONS AGREE with the idea that it is a heap of living and dying which makes a house a home and affirm also that it is a heap of living and dying, laughter and tears, which make a town, a state, a nation *my* town, *my* state, *my* country, and they describe the process and the resulting emotions.

96   *Home*

Anona Heap: Well, I'll start. I'll give the title and by whom. This is "Home," by Edgar A. Guest.

It takes a heap o' livin' in a house t' make it home,
A heap o' sun an' shadder, an' ye sometimes have t' roam
Afore ye really 'preciate the things ye lef' behind,
An' hunger fer 'em somehow, with 'em allus on yer mind.
It don't make any difference how rich ye get t' be,
How much yer chairs an' table cost, how great yer luxury;
It ain't home t' ye, though it be the palace for a king,
Until somehow yer soul is sort o' wrapped round everything.

Home ain't a place that gold can buy or get up in a minute;
Afore it's home there's got t' be a heap o' livin' in it;
Within these walls there's got t' be some babies born, and then
Right there ye've got t' bring 'em up t' women good, an' men;
And gradjerly, as time goes on, ye find ye wouldn't part
With anything they ever used—they've grown into yer heart:
The old high chair, the playthings, too, the little shoes they wore
Ye hoard; an' if ye could ye'd keep those thumb-marks on the door.

Ye've got t' weep t' make it home, ye've got t' sit an' sigh
An' watch beside a loved one's bed, an' know that Death is nigh;
An' in the stillness o' the night t' see Death's angel come,
An' close the eyes o' her that smiled, an' leave her sweet voice dumb.
These are scenes that grip the heart, an' when yer tears are dried,
Ye find the home is dearer than it was, an' sanctified;
An' tuggin' at ye always are the pleasant memories
O' her that was an' is no more—oh, you can't escape from these.

Ye've got to sing an' dance fer years, ye've got t' romp an' play,
An' learn t' love the things ye have by usin' 'em each day;
Even the roses around the porch must blossom year by year
Afore they 'come a part o' ye, suggestin' someone dear
Who used t' love 'em long ago, and trained 'em just t' run
The way they do, so's they would get the early morning sun;
Ye've got to love each brick an' stone from cellar up t' dome:
It takes a heap o' livin' in a house t' make it home.

97 *At Grandma's House*

LaVelle Whiting DeSpain: We always went to our Grandma Whiting's on Christmas Eve and to my parents', and I wrote this for one of my children to give, and it's just quite descriptive of what we always enjoyed at Grandma's house.

There's a feeling of Christmas
Strong in the air.
It's a feeling of friendship
And love that we share.

There's a feeling that comes to me
Year after year
When I open Grandma's door
And see you all here.

There's an aroma of cinnamon spice
In the air.
If you look in the kitchen,
You'll find Grandma there.

She's been there each Christmas
That I can recall
Serving doughnuts and milk
To the old and the small.

Even though I am getting older,
It wouldn't seem right
If I didn't take my turn
On Grandpa's knee Christmas Night.

The grandchildren gather round him
In hopes he will tell
"Big Klaus and Little Klaus."
He tells them so well.

And now to the living room
For a program of fun.
Here's a program of talent
That includes everyone.

First on the program
A skit from the Grants
Starring Ronny, the villain.
How he raves and he rants!

With Merwin, Howard, and Rita,
His supporting cast,
This skit takes top billing.
It's really a blast.

Aunt Mable couldn't decide
Just what they should do,
So she decided on four numbers
Instead of just two.

There's so much talent in my family
It's hard to decide,
So we had numbers from all
Including Rex and his bride.

I've heard Uncle Sherwood
Prepared a song for each year,
But Aunt Melba always says,
"Maybe next year, my dear."

So Kathy and Linda will dance.
From the boys a song we'll hear,
And we're hoping, Uncle Sherwood,
Next year is the year.

This number from Uncle Forrest's family
Included grandkids and all.
The music they make
Sounds like Carnegie Hall.

Lane and David will fiddle
While Penny and Webb sing.
With Karen and her kids,
They make the air ring.

My family want to do something different
Or we felt that we should.
No matter what we thought of,
Pam always said a dramatic reading would be good.

But I have some talent.
I'm sure you'll agree.
Why, Pam probably got her talent
From little old me.

Well, I've had my turn.
I've enjoyed the spotlight.
Merry Christmas to all
And to all a good night.

This is just typical of things that go on at our Christmas Eve program at our grandpa and grandma's house.

98   *The House by the Side of the Road*

Delbert D. Lambson: My brother Marion lived on a ranch just out north of El Morro right in the Zuni Mountains just below the Notches, and everybody that came through knew where there was a meal, a night of entertainment, and a good time, and they stopped at my brother's place, and Lucille, my sister-in-law, would stop what she was doing and prepare a meal for who-ever came, and they would come in the middle of the night. Time and time again I was there asleep, and here they would come, and I could hear them in the kitchen and Lucille preparing food. And then they would get the old fiddle out, and they'd start, and they'd dance till morning.

My brother Almie had a stroke about a year before he died, and we went to Ramah on a Fathers' Day outing, and this was two weeks before my brother died, and he had lost his ability to really express himself, and that was really sad because there was not a more dynamic speaker than my brother. Now, after he had the stroke, he could speak perfect Navajo still, but he couldn't speak English very well at all. He was very hard to communi-cate with. That day he got up and gave this poem absolutely perfect and with expression, and those were the only words I heard him say without slurring real bad. It was "The House by the Side of the Road."

166

There are hermit souls that live withdrawn
In the place of their self-content;
There are souls like stars, that dwell apart,
In a fellowless firmament;

There are pioneer souls that blaze their paths
Where highways never ran—
But let me live by the side of the road
And be a friend to man.

Let me live in a house by the side of the road,
Where the race of men go by—
The men who are good and the men who are bad,
As good and as bad as I.

I would not sit in the scorner's seat,
Or hurl the cynic's ban—
Let me live in a house by the side of the road
And be a friend to man.

I see from my house by the side of the road,
By the side of the highway of life,
The men who press with the ardor of hope,
The men who are faint with the strife.

But I turn not away from their smiles nor their tears,
Both parts of an infinite plan—
Let me live in a house by the side of the road
And be a friend to man.

Let me live in my house by the side of the road,
It's here the race of men go by—
They are good, they are bad, they are weak, they are strong,
Wise, foolish—so am I;

Then why should I sit in the scorner's seat,
Or hurl the cynic's ban?
Let me live in my house by the side of the road
And be a friend to man.

99   *Are the Hills Still Green?*

Horace Crandell: Just a few years ago I was teaching Sunday school, and this just impressed me, so I learned it to tell my Sunday school class. Not too long ago Christine Perkins, a lady in Clay Springs, she was a school teacher, and

she made it as a pianologue, and she wanted me to learn it and say it to her class, and that's what I did.

Are the hills still green?
Do the cows still graze?
Do the children still laugh?
Are there peaceful days?

Is the air still pure and sweet?
Is there solitude and quiet?
Is clean rain still the source
Of Mother Nature's diet?

Do the squirrels still chitter-chatter
As they hide away their nuts?
Is the harvest moon still silver?
And the dirt road still full of ruts?

Do the snowflakes still make white castles
When drifted by the wind?
Does the ice still form as smoothly
On the pond around the bend?

Does spring still come in slowly
With a hope for little things?
Do the young birds still work bravely
To try their new-found wings?

Are the hills still green?
Do the cows still graze?
Do the children still laugh?
Are there peaceful days?

These days I recite most often in people's homes. We have what you call "home teaching." The last two years that's all I've done in these visits is recite or play the fiddle, and they get a big kick out of it. I have a companion go with me, and he gives the spiritual thought and like that, and they holler at me to give a reading or play the fiddle or something. That's where I do most of it nowadays.

100 *Putting a Town on the Map*

Margaret Witt: I was born in Taylor and lived on the ranch till I was five, and I've been here in Clay Springs for seventy-seven years. There's nobody else left in Clay Springs as far as I know that recites. My brother Don Jackson does a little, and of course, Van Holyoak did and he sang, too, but I don't know anyone else.

Two fool jackasses
Said, "Get this, dope,
We're tied together
With a piece of rope."

Says one to the other,
"You come my way,
And we both eat hay."

"I won't," said the other.
"You come my way,
For I, too, have
Some hay, you see."

So they got nowhere
Just pawed the dirt,
And, oh by golly,
That rope did hurt.

Then they turned about
These stubborn mules,
And said, "We're acting
Like two human fools.

"Let's pull together.
You come my way,
Then I'll go your way,
And we both eat hay."

So they ate their hay
And liked it, too,
And just at the close of day,
They were heard to bray:

"Now this is the end of a perfect day."
Now get this lesson; don't let it pass.
Learn from a poor jackass
That you must pull together.

'Tis the only way
To put your town on the map
And put it to stay.

101 *Jerome*

Alida Connolly: This is one I wrote about Jerome when we used to live in Cottonwood.

Perched high on the mountaintop
Not far from my home,
Lies a ghost of a city
Called Jerome.

At night from the valley
Its lights twinkle away
Bidding its ghostly inhabitants
To come out and play.

And as I sit here dreaming,
The buildings come to life as they used to be,
And as I peer through the dust and the cobwebs,
Many strange sights I'm permitted to see.

I can hear ghostly fingers playing ragtime
In the old Kentucky Bar across the way
And smell the beefsteaks a-fryin'
In the Copper Star Cafe.

I can hear the wagons creaking
As they come in from gulch and hill,
Hear the shouts of ghostly laughter
From throats I thought were dead and still.

I watch their fancy dancing,
Those lively ghouls of long ago,
The Vesuvian, the schottische, my-little-gal,
With a bow and a do-si-do.

They all wolf, sit on the curb,
And spit tobacco juice and stare
At the ladies' curves, and bony ankles,
Their thin and wispy hair.

But suddenly a piercing shriek
Breaks the stillness of the night.
Be danged, if it ain't two ghostly miners
Having themselves a fight.

As they punch and poke
And roll on the ground,
There should be blood shed,
But none can be found.

The women shriek and holler
And gesture and wave,
Making the most of each moment
Before they return to the grave.

Then there's the ghosts of the pious ones
Who remain dressed in the shroud.
Their fleshless faces are solemn.
Their bony heads are bowed.

On wraith-like feet
They enter their churches one by one
To pray for their lusty brethren
Who they are afraid are having too much fun.

And, brother, their prayers are needed,
For in the middle of the fight,
They tied a rope around a gambler's neck
And pulled it up very tight.

And as over old Mingus
Comes the first streaks of dawn,
I rub my eyes and gaze around.
All the ghostly figures have gone.

The wagons, the horses, the laughter and light
Have vanished away, and sad is my plight,
And I'm left to worry and ponder and fret.
Did I really see all this, or was it something I et?

But there's one thing for certain,
If ever at night I'm tempted to roam,
It won't be through those ghost-ridden,
Curving old pathways of old Jerome.

102 *Our Fair Nutrioso*

**Alida Connolly: This is one I wrote for Nutrioso. I've written one for almost
every place we've lived, and I've lived all over.**

171

Oh fair Nutrioso, land of our beginnings,
Our heritage, our youth,
So many stories and histories,
So many people of valor, courage, and truth,

Stories of father, mother, grandparents,
Kindred, acquaintances, and friends,
Our gratitude is endless as our roots
Which grew in this soil and never ends.

Oh, lovely mountain meadows where we picnic
Relaxing from the city's strain and stress.
Oh, pine scented hills and mountains
Where we roam with freedom and happiness,

Surely there must be other places where the snow falls softly
And home is cozy as fires are lit
And one can toast their shins,
Or read, or sew, or watch the flames and dream and knit.

Surely there must be other places where the birds
Are nesting and singing in the tall pine trees,
And wild flowers bloom on hills and in valleys,
For memories are made of these.

There must be other places where the sound of silence
Makes one reminisce and really think
And other places where the water from the well
Is so cold it's ever so slow to drink.

Yes, there must be other places as beautiful,
But right now I can't think where or why,
Unless it's that lovely land called heaven
Just beyond the mountain sunset in the Nutrioso sky.

103 *St. Johns*

Alida Connolly: Well, I don't know which one to do now. Oh, I've got one about St. Johns.

Sometimes when the world seems against me
And my new friends let me down,
I have the strangest longing
For a little friendly town.

For the old friends that I've cherished
As I've moved from place to place
Seems like every time I get discouraged,
I see every friendly face.

Oh, it isn't much to boast of,
Just a quiet little town
Where everyone knows about you,
Why you smile and why you frown.

It's just a place where you know your neighbor
As a friend across the way,
And you run over in your apron
To pass the time of day.

Sure, you know most all the gossip that goes on,
And all the while
You have a little heartache
For the tears behind the smile.

And when sickness hovers over you
And you're feeling pretty blue,
Your friends come in and take your hand
And suddenly the sun shines through.

You have a little house
Nothing grand, just small and neat,
A stranger would hardly glance at it
As he passes on the street.

He doesn't know the wealth of living
That goes on from day to day,
The tender family gatherings,
And your friends and things they say.

He doesn't know the children that it shelters
Or the happiness that's there
From the finger-printed woodwork
To the footprints on the chair.

And sometimes I think that heaven
Must be like a little town
With shady old trees
And flowers and sunshine all around.

Children playing peacefully,
Grownups smiling sweet
At them and at each other
Whenever they chance to meet.

So is it any wonder
Sometimes I feel a little sad
When I think about the old days
And the joys that I've had?

And I get the strangest longing, tugging, tugging in my heart,
For that little town on a quiet street
Where family and friends
Would make my life complete.

104 *St. Johns' Pioneers*

**Wilford J. Shumway: I had heard something like this poem, and I just
changed it to fit this area. I recite it, but I didn't write it.**

In the 1880s the Mormons came
To settle the valleys and wilderness tame;
They charted a course for you and me
And left their mark on history.

Names of those hardy pioneers
Have multiplied throughout the years;
Names which you all will surely know,
Your neighbors' names, not long ago.

Sherwood, Slade, Hunt and Cherry,
Ramsey, Rencher, Rogers, Berry,
Bushman, Brimhall, Brewer and Becker,
Babbitt, Ballard, Neal and Decker.

Freeman, Owens, Haws and Hall,
Maxwell, Tanner, Bigelow, Udall,
Westover, Hansen, Turley and Flake,
And many others, for goodness sake!

Schuster, Shumway, Gibbons and Hatch,
Stratton, Wakefield, Smith and Patch,
Rhoton, Reidhead, Willis and Greer,
Raban and Richards, Plumb and LeSueur.

Penrod and Pierce, Zulick and Zeek,
And Bazan, the bishop of Silver Creek.
Perkins, Wilbur, Palmer and Bates,
Gardner and Hancock, and their mates.

Solomon, Burk, Kemp and Kay,
Broadbent and Merrill, Knight and Day,
Gillespie, Noble, Nielsen and Pond,
Gibson and Colter, Lambson and Bond.

Coleman, Cowley, Cooley, Crandall,
Jennings, Jones, Thurber, Randall,
Hale, Heward, Slaughter and Biggs,
Crosby, Duke, Stradling and Driggs.

Tenney, Eagar, then Porter's name,
Kartchner and Youngblood of music fame.
Hulsey, Richey, Larson and Farr,
Blazzard, Blevins and Pulsipher.

Mineer and Laney, Webb and Waite,
High tribute to them all this date.
Overson, Ollerton, DeSpain and Brown.
These names from every little town.

Peterson, Patterson, Platt and Fish;
Recall them all—my fondest wish!
Wiltbank and Whipple—no rhyme to fit—
Whiting, Wilhelm, Allen, DeWitt.

Spurlock, Butler, Baldwin and Pace;
Lopez and Baca of Spanish race.
Hamblin, Standifird and Isaacson,
Wilkins, Waters and Anderson.

Hubbell and Heap, and others? Yes!
There's Ellsworth, Woods and Divelbess.
Prentice, Ashcroft, Lee and Scott,
Adam and Eve, and "Pinch me not."

Howela Polacca, the Navajo;
Cochise, Billigodi, Geronimo.
Remember their cousins of long ago?
Shadrach, Meshach and Abednego.

Jarvis, Barth, Shreeve, McLaws,
Naegle, Collier—and Santa Claus.
Davis, Heywood, Lund and Frost,
And several others I must have lost.

Pena, Montoya, Chavez, Madrid,
Garcia, Gutierrez and Billy the Kid.
There's Woodruff, Taylor and Brigham Young,
And other heroes still unsung.

Forgive omission if there be
No mention of your family tree.
My memory dulls in passing time!
But some names simply will not rhyme.

I hope my list has brought to you
A pleasant thought, or maybe two!
Or loosed a latent memory dear
Of cherished friends of yesteryear!

105 *This Was a Harsh and Barren Land*

Delbert D. Lambson: We had a Pioneer Day, twenty-fourth of July; I don't know if you're familiar with that or not. And they had me take some slides of the old town and show them, but what I did was write this poem about the St. Johns' pioneers.

This was a harsh and barren land
Graced hard by sun and wind and sand,
Uncoveted, unkempt, unyielding strand,
But lightly touched by God's own hand.

The call was made to a chosen few,
Faithful souls who were tried and true,
"Go till the land and see it through
And do what God wants you to do."

With a vision of hope and a steady hand,
They turned their face to this fruitless land.
Though foulers came, they took their stand
And put their trust in His guiding hand.

With a firm resolve to stand the test
To build a refuge of peace and rest
For the families with which they would be blessed,
This was their call, their sacred quest.

Tried and true they faithful stood.
They filled their mission the best they could.
They honored the Prophet, he knew they would,
And built a lovely neighborhood.

So God bless you, St. Johns' pioneers,
For the faithful service you render here.
Our eyes are filled with joyful tears.
We thank you, blessed pioneers.

Utah's Dixie (106-107)   **Joseph C. Bolander: Now this is a couple I picked up when I was working out at Pipe Springs, and they went with the folklore of Utah's Dixie. They give a picture of the country and the experiences of the people: the sacrifices, the impossible country, the primitive roads if they could be called such; and it expresses the way the people felt about their call to Cotton Mission. They were the ones on the firing line. One of these was Charles L. Walker. He was generally accorded the honor of being the poet laureate of Dixie, and this is his description of St. George evidently in the 1860s. He called it "Dixie."**

106   *Dixie*

Oh, what a desert place was this
When first the Mormons found it;
They said no white man here could live.
Indians prowled around it.

They said the land, it was no good,
And the water was no gooder,
And the bare idea of living here
Was enough to make men shudder.

Mesquite, soap root,
Prickly pears and briars,
Ere long St. George will be
A town everyone admires.

Now green lucerne in verdant spots
Protects our thriving city,
And vines and fruit trees grace our lots
With flowers sweet and pretty.

Where once the grass in single blades
Grew a mile apart in distance,
And it kept the crickets on the jump
To pick up their subsistence.

The sun it is so very hot
It makes the water siz, sir,
And the reason it is so hot
Is just because it is, sir.

The wind like fury here does blow,
And when we planted her so, sir,
We place one foot upon the seed
And hold it till it does grow, sir.

And this other one is by George Hicks. He and his wife Betsy got a call to go to the Cotton Mission, and this is the story of his experiences on the journey and while they was there. It has various titles: "Once I Lived in Cottonwood," "The Red Hills of November," and "I Was Called to Dixie," the one I'm going to use:

107 *I Was Called to Dixie*

Once I lived in Cottonwood
And owned a little farm,
And I was called to Dixie
Which caused me much alarm;

To raise the cane and cotton,
I right away must go;
But the reason why they called on me,
I'm sure I do not know.

I yoked old Jim and Bolly up
All for to make a start,
To leave my home and garden,
It almost broke my heart.

We rolled along quite slowly,
And we often looked behind,
For the sand and rocks of Dixie
Kept running through my mind.

At length we reached the Black Ridge
Where I broke my wagon down,
We didn't find a carpenter
So far from any town,

So with a clumsy cedar pole
I fixed an awkward slide;
And the wagon pulled so heavy then
That Betsy couldn't ride.

Now she was a-walking,
I told her to take care,
When all upon a sudden
She struck a prickly pear.

She began to blubber out
As loud as she could bawl,
"If I was back in Cottonwood,
I wouldn't come at all!"

Then we reached the Sandy,
Where we could not move at all,
And poor old Jim and Bolly
Began to puff and bawl.

I whipped and swore a little,
But I couldn't make them rout,
For myself, the team, and Betsy
Were all of us give out.

But we finally got to Washington
Where we stayed a little while
To see if April showers
Would make the country smile.

But, oh, I was mistaken,
And so I went away,
For the red hills of November
Looked just the same in May.

It's oh so sad and lonely here;
There isn't much to cheer
Except prophetic sermons
Which we very often hear.

They'll hand them out by dozens
And prove them by the book,
But I'd rather have some roasting ears
To stay at home and cook.

Now, George Hicks got in Dutch with the church leaders over that verse. Those sermons didn't make up for an empty stomach.

I feel so weak and hungry now,
I think I'm nearly dead.
It's seven weeks next Sunday
Since I have tasted bread.

Of carrot tops and lucerne greens
I have enough to eat,
But I'd like to trade that diet off
For buckwheat cakes and meat.

I brought this old coat with me
About four years ago,
And when I'll get another one,
I'm sure I do not know.

May providence protect me
Against the cold and wet;
I'm sure myself and Betsy
These times will ne'er forget.

My shirt is dyed with wild dock root,
With greasewood for a set.
I fear the colors all will fade
If it ever does get wet.

They said we could raise
Madder and indigo so blue,
But that turned out a humbug;
The story wasn't true.

The hot winds whirl around me,
And they take away my breath;
I've had the chills and fever
Till I'm nearly shook to death.

But "all earthly tribulations
Are but a moment here;
And if I can prove faithful,
A righteous crown I'll wear."

My wagon's sold for sorghum seed
To buy a little bread,
And poor old Jim and Bolly
Long ago are dead.

There's only me and Betsy left
To hoe the cotton tree.
May heaven help the Dixie-ite
Wherever he may be!

Now that caught on with the common people over there, and they set it to music and danced to it, and the leaders got kinda worried, afraid it might harm their faith, but I don't guess it did.

108   *Arizona*

Kristi Hodge: This one was written as a school project. They wanted us to write an essay about Arizona, and I wanted to do something a little different, so I wrote a poem about it.

Arizona began its state history in 1912.
I have heard many stories, but I wasn't there myself.

And then it grew so very fast
That there's much to remember of Arizona's past.

Now in the next twenty-five years
People will overcome most of their fears.

I am afraid the drug problem will increase,
And high school dropouts will not cease.

The number of homeless will increase greatly
Because fancy houses are being built lately.

The population will almost double,
Then job opportunities could be in trouble.

The major disease will be the A.I.D.S. virus
If we never stop the dissemination by us.

Soon the schools will go all year,
And then you will have even more peers.

The jobs will all be computerized,
Saving us from having to memorize.

I hope Arizona will get a pro team.
It would help build our state esteem.

I wish the future would bring great cheers,
So no one of us would have to shed any tears.

109 *Fair California*

Madeline Collins: Reminiscing again, I came up with this poem about California which I learned fifty-two years ago. I was lonely at the time; my sister who had been very close to me had married and left home. This was a framed poem which an older brother had, and that day I learned it all, complete with author's name. This is "Fair California" by Marie K. Stokes.

California, land of beauty,
Lovely valleys, scented rain,
How I love your rock-bound sea coast,
Wooded hillsides, fertile plains.

Thou hast all the wondrous riches,
Fair Golconda of the West,
And thy children ever call thee
Fairest land so dear and blessed.

Where the gold sun is sinking
In a flood of shining light,
And fair Tamalpais shadowed
In rare tints of rose and white

Fades from view and softly lumbers
In her bed of clouds and dew
Lulled to sleep by soothing sea songs
Floating over waves of blue.

There I long to be forever
Gazing on thy beauties rare,
Listening to the happy wavelets
Easing sorrow, soothing care,

Gaily culling golden poppies,
Straying on thy windswept strand,
Resting blessed, safe, contented
In my fair, dear western land.

110 *When the Frost Is on the Pumpkin*

Horace Crandell: I used to sing this in glee club. I kind of like the words to it, so I learned it. That was all. That's when I was going to high school. It was about 1915.

When the frost is on the pumpkin and the fodder's in the shock,
And hear the cluck and gobble of the struttin' turkey-cock,
And the clackin' of the guineas and the cluckin' of the hens,
And the rooster's hallelujah as he tiptoes on the fence;
It's then the time a feller is a-feelin' at his best,
With the risin' sun to greet him from a night of peaceful rest,
As he leaves the house, bareheaded, and goes out to feed the stock,
When the frost is on the pumpkin and the fodder's in the shock.

There's somethin' kind o' hearty-like about the atmosphere
When the summer heat is over and the autumn chill is here—
Of course we miss the flowers, and the blossoms on the trees,
And the hummin' of the hummin'birds and the buzzin' of the bees,
But the air's so appetizin', and the landscape's in a haze
Of a crisp and sunny mornin' of the early autumn days.
It's a picture no painter livin' has got the colorin' to mock,
When the frost is on the pumpkin and the fodder's in the shock.

The husky, rusty rustle of the tassels of the corn,
And the raspin' of the tangled leaves, as golden as the morn,
The stubble in the furrows, sort o' lonesome-like, but still
A-preachin' sermons about the barns they growed to fill;
The straw-stack in medder, and the reaper in the shed,
The horses in their stalls below, the clover overhead,
Sets my heart a-clickin' like the tickin' of a clock,
When the frost is on the pumpkin and the fodder's in the shock!

When the apples all is gathered, and the ones a feller keeps
Is poured around the cellar floor in red and yaller heaps;
And your cider-makin's over, and the wimmen folks is through
With their mince and apple butter, and their sauce and sausage, too!
I don't know how to tell it—but if such a thing could be
As the angels wantin' boardin', and they'd call around on me—
I'd want to 'commodate 'em all—the whole-endurin' lot—
When the frost is on the pumpkin and the fodder's in the shock!

111 *Bacon*

**Joseph C. Bolander: I've got one entitled "Bacon." This was written by
Badger Clark. He's quite a well-known poet.**

You're salty and greasy and smoky as sin,
But of all the grub, we love you the best.
You stuck to us closer than nighest kin
And helped win out in the West.

183

You froze with us up on the Laramie Plains,
And you sweat with us down in Tucson.
When the Indians was painted and the white man was pale,
You nerved us to grip our last chance by the tail
And load up our colts and hang on.

You sizzled on mountains and mesas and plains
Over campfires of sagebrush and oak.
The breezes that blow from the Platte to the Maine
Have carried your savory smoke.

You're friendly to miners and punchers and priests
You're as good in December as May.
You always came in when the first meat had ceased,
And the rough road of empire westward was greased
By the bacon we fried on the way.

Here's to you, old bacon,
Fat, lean, streak, and rin',
All Westerners join in the toast
From mesquite and yucca to sagebrush and pine,
From Canada down to the Mexican line,
From Omaha out to the coast.

112 *Winds!*

Anona C. Heap: Milo Wiltbank was my cousin, and I've got four of his books, and there's one in there that was really good about the winds. Well, it's just like we have. This is called "Winds" by Milo Wiltbank.

Winds! Playful summer winds,
Playing tag with the clouds,
Playing leapfrog in the treetops,
Pushing the thunderheads,
Pleasant, joyful winds.

Winds! Harvesting autumn winds,
Shake the laden branches,
Scurrying around the leaves,
Hurrying over the land,
Prying, greeting, grasping winds.

Winds! Snow-loaded winter winds,
Nipping ears and fingers,
Riding the mountains on icy steeds,
Driving the storm clouds,
Chilly, frost-bearing winds.

Winds! Destructive spring winds,
Harassing the earth,
Building dust clouds,
Scurrying through the barren branches.

Winds! Soft gentle East winds,
Sunny, thirsty South winds,
Hot, dust-laden West winds,
Cold and hungry North winds.
Winds! Winds! Winds!
Nothing but winds!

How many springs have you felt that?

113   *Jeff Hart*

Joseph C. Bolander: Now, if you like drama (I'm not very good at drama—I should just stick to comedy), this is a different type I picked up by Badger Clark. It's entitled "Jeff Hart," and it's the story of the first World War and how it affected a little Arizona mining town that went simply by the name of the Gulch.

Jeff Hart rode out of the Gulch to war
When the low sun yellowed the pines.
He waved to his folks in the cabin door,
And he yelled to the men in the mines.

The Gulch kept watch till he dropped from sight,
Neighbors, and girl, and kin.
Jeff Hart rode out of the Gulch one night.
Next morning the world came in.

His dad went back to the clink and drills,
And his mother cooked for the men,
And the pines branched black on the eastern hills,
And black to the west again.

But never again by dawn or dusk
Was life in the Gulch the same,
For back up the trail Jeff Hart had rode,
The trample of millions came.

185

Then never a clatter of dynamite
But echoed the guns of the Aisne,
And the coyote howls in the hills at night
Were bitter with Belgium's pain.

We heard the snarl of a savage sea
And wind in the pines as the wind swept through,
And the strangers Jeff Hart fought to free
Grew folks to the folks he knew.

Jeff Hart has drifted for good and all,
And the ghostly bugles blown
In the far French valley that saw him fall
Blood kin to the Gulch has grown.

These foreign folks are ours by right,
The friends that he died to win.
Jeff Hart rode out of the Gulch one night.
Next morning the world came in.

114   *His Guiding Hand*

Delbert D. Lambson: My mother recited "Bingen on the Rhine" and "The Hell-bound Train." Remember that one? She was a natural-born actress. She'da been right along Bette Davis if she'd had the chance. In fact, she reminded me of Bette Davis. She raised a family of twelve children, though, and she didn't have much time to really develop her talents, but if she had been in the right place at the right time... She was a ham.

She was a Five Star Mother. Mom never had worked away from home. She still had three children, but during the war when her sons were over there, she went to work at Williams Field and went to washing down airplanes, washing the grease and gasoline and stuff off the airplanes to help her boys come home. She didn't set down and cry, no sir, but at night she'd get down on her knees, and it was that faith, that strength that sustained us and brought her boys home, all five of them. There was three of us wounded. I was wounded the most severely, but there was never any doubt in my mind that I would come home, there never was, because that was the faith my mother and family gave me.

I was shot down over Germany in a B17 and was hospitalized in France and came very close to losing my life. Hey, there were times I could have literally laid down by the side of the road and died. We left prison camp the sixth day of February, five thousand men strong. We marched for three months in the dead of winter sleeping in the fields. We left five thousand strong. We crossed the Elbe River with two thousand men. I could have just as easily been one of those three out of five that didn't make it. The only thing that kept me going was the love, strength, and prayers of those at home. That's what made the big difference in me coming home.

This is one I wrote. It's entitled "His Guiding Hand," and it says something.

America, the beautiful,
Choice and promised land,
Protected by the will of God
And caressed by His guiding hand.

We gave our sacred promise,
We pledge our heart and hand
To keep our country strong and free.
We pray for His guiding hand.

We owe our precious freedom
To those who made their stand
Who conquered the evil tyrant
With the help of His guiding hand.

In battle our choicest young men fell.
They died in a foreign land.
May they know peace at last
And rest in His guiding hand.

May those who mourn their precious sons
Called home to that golden strand
Find sweet consolation and strength
In His guiding hand.

To keep the freedom they have won
Now side by side we stand
And continue the fight for liberty
With the help of His guiding hand.

We know that freedom's not free.
God help us to understand
That a constant vigil's required
Plus the help of His guiding hand.

As wise men of the past have said,
"Carry a big stick in your hand
And speak with quiet, convincing voice
And lean on His guiding hand."

Lord, help us fulfill our destiny
As a bastion of freedom stand.
To those who yearn for liberty
Stretch forth Thy guiding hand.

As a nation may we trust in Thee
And may we understand
That all good gifts come from Thy love
Borne by Thy guiding hand.

May peace be published in the earth
May war by all be banned,
This is our humble prayer to Thee,
"Thanks, God, for Thy guiding hand."

**That's just my own personal feeling about my country, my flag, and our
relationship to God as a nation.**

115 *The Stars and Stripes*

**Delbert D. Lambson: I consider myself a patriot. I have written a book about
my war experiences, and I hope one of these days to have the finances to
publish it. I do love my country, this great United States of America, I love it,
and every time the old flag goes by, my heart skips a beat. It is an emblem of
freedom to me, an emblem of right and justice in the world, and so I love the
flag.**

**This is my special poem. I just wish I had written it, but it's anonymous.
It's about the flag, and it's entitled "The Stars and Stripes."**

I rode into an old
Cow town courthouse square,
And I saw an old cowboy
Sitting on a bench over there.

So I rode up, and I said,
"You know, your old courthouse is awful run-down."
He just smiled and said,
"Son, it'll do for our little town."

So I said, "But your flagpole
Is leaning quite a bit,
And that's a ragged old flag
You've got a-hangin' on it."

He said, "Son, climb down off your horse
And take a seat." And so I did, and I sat down,
And he said, "Son, is this the first time
You've been to our little town?"

"Well," I said, "Yes, sir, it is."
"Well," he said, "Son, we don't like to brag,
But we're kinda proud
Of that ragged old flag.

"You see, that flag
Got a hole right there
When Washington carried it
Across the Delaware.

"Got powder burns
When Francis Scott Key
Sat a-watchin' it
And writing, 'Oh, say, can you see?'

"And that tear right there,
That's from the Battle of New Orleans
With Packingham and Jackson
A-tuggin' at her seams.

"She nearly fell
At the Alamo,
But she kept
Right on a-wavin', you know.

"She got cut with a sword
At Chancellorsville,
And she got cut again
At Shiloh's Hill.

"And there was Robert E. Lee
And Beauregard and Bragg.
The south wind blew hard
On that ragged old flag.

"In Flanders' Field
In World War One,
She got a big hole
From a Bertha gun.

"Turned blood red
In World War Two
And hung limp and low
A time or two.

"She's been to Korea
And Vietnam.
She goes where she's sent
By her Uncle Sam.

"She waves over our ships
On the briny foam,
But they've kind of stopped
Waving her here at home.

"Here in our
Own good land
She's been burned and abused,
Criticized and refused,

"And the government
For which she stands
Has been scandalized
All across the land.

"Ah, she's threadbare
And a-wearin' thin,
But she's in good shape
For the shape she's in.

"So we bring her up every morning,
And we bring her down every night.
And we never let her touch the ground,
And we fold her up just right.

"Well, I guess on second thought
I do like to brag
'Cause I'm mighty proud
Of that ragged old flag."

Thank you for listening to me.

Down at Mesa, outside of Mesa, they have an old-time, I don't know what to call it. They have a barbecue and a show, and they have just a kind of a setting of the Old West. I was out there one night, and some old cowboy said this, and I said, "I've got to have a copy of that," and so I persisted till he gave me one.

CHAPTER EIGHT

About Mothers, Fathers, Sons, and Daughters

MOTHERS AND FATHERS, sons and daughters, brothers and sisters share a special love in the West's view of itself. In the reality of the West, and world, sons and daughters lose mothers and fathers to death when they are young and when they are old, mothers and fathers lose children to death as babies and adults, sisters and brothers are separated by death and despair, and loss cries out through and for poetry and story. Story and poetry, performed orally or based on oral performance, is the language by which the unspoken and the almost unspeakable find their voices.

116 *Recompense*

Stanley Shumway: Many of my poems have significance in the family. Here's one called "Recompense." I'll read it and then maybe make a comment about it.

Springtime, sunshine,
Happiness everywhere
With lovely flowers'
Fragrance on the air.
But of a sudden
Winter's icy blast,
Lovely flowers die
In a dreary world's clasp.

Soul's content,
Hope from above,
Radiant expectation,
Motherhood inspiring love.
But of a sudden
The clutch of death,
Despair replacing hope,
Grief at halted breath.

So with all God's nature,
With flowers or humanity,
Shadow after sunshine,
Sadness after glee.
But we must learn to bide the shadows,
The sadness and the grief,
For surely as springtime follows winter,
God will send relief.

My wife's sister had just lost her first baby in childbirth, and so I wrote that poem.

117 *A Prayer for a Cowboy*

Van N. Holyoak: I wrote this for my dad's funeral.

My dear brethren and sisters,
We've gathered here today,
To try and give our last respects
To a friend who passed away.

Now we all know he had some faults
To make a preacher frown,
But you must remember he's a cowboy,
And I'm not here to tear him down.

He spent his life out in the hills.
He felt that God was there.
It didn't matter how hard the task.
He always did his share.

He never harmed a neighbor
Nor cheated on a friend.
If a man would help himself,
He stayed with him to the end.

He never misused horses.
He had no greed or hate.
If he rode through your pasture,
He would always close the gate.

But now he's gone to meet his Maker
In the land up in the sky,
Where I hope he has good horses,
And springs are never dry.

I hope he has a bedroll
Where he'll be warm at night.
He'll need that same old happy heart
And that same old smile so bright.

I don't think he cares to play a harp
Up in the heavenly choir.
Just let him have some old cow hide
To while away the hour.

But let him have some cattle
With calves to rope and brand.
I know if you do this, dear Lord,
He'll try to make a hand.

He wouldn't ask this much for himself,
But he is our "dear Friend."
Just treat him like he treated us;
That's all we ask—Amen.

118   *The Telephone Conversation*

Joe S. Holyoak: Dad called me up the morning he was killed and said he had to wire up a big three-phase motor, so we talked about it for a little bit. So when they called me up and said, "You dad's been in an accident on the highway and you better get home," I couldn't figure it out 'cause I knew he'd been planning on playing electrician.

But the whole deal of it was this guy had a dentist appointment and then one with a chiropractor, and he wanted the morning off. "Well," they said, "if you can find somebody to run that sweeper for you," they said, "you can."

And Dad says, "Well, I can do my job in the afternoon." He says, "I can do that job for you." And that's how come he was riding the sweeper when the bus hit it.

Nobody told me, just that there was an accident. So I borrowed a pickup at work and went home. Somehow I figured I had time to clean up (I'd been working with a coal crusher, and I mean I was black.) So I walked through the shower, got dressed, and started out of town. The first person I passed was Paul, no, I guess it was Barbara and Dan, and I waved, and both of them just looked at me. Then I went on up the hill, and I ran into somebody else I knew in their Suburban, and I waved, and they just slowed down and watched me go by, and I thought, "There's something worse here than I had any idea." Just before I got to the bus wreck, I saw the smoke coming off of the bus, and I heard a highway employee had been killed, and I pulled up there, and the cop said, "You just stop here. Don't go on down." And I saw Pete, and I just said, "Did my dad get killed?" And old Pete just broke down and put his arms around me, and I guess that's as close as I came to getting told.

He'd called me up that morning, and afterwards I thought about it and tried to write it down.

Van N. Holyoak: Hello, son. Did I wake ya?

Joe S. Holyoak: Uh huh.

Van: Did they work the packin' out of you last night?

Joe: They tried, but you know how that is.

Van: What did they have you do?

Joe: Boy! I worked on a chlorine heater. That crap will kill you. It's weird stuff.

Van: Be careful.

Joe: I will.

Van: Can you finish planting the wheat tonight?

Joe: Yeah, I'll get it.

Van: We need to get it in before it rains.

Joe: We will.

Van: How's Debbie?

Joe: Okay.

Van: Still pregnant?

Joe: Ha! Yes, I guess, or just getting fat.

Van: You be good to her.

Joe: All right! Did you do last night?

Van: Shod one and trimmed one. I was give out. These ten-hour days are going to kill me.

Joe: Man, I wish we worked those hours. A three-day weekend would be hard to take. Yeah.

Van: But I'm not as young as I used to be.

Joe: I'd like to try it for awhile.

Van: Today I'm going to wire a three-phase three hundred horsepower motor with dual controls.

Joe: Can you do it?

Van: With a little help from Quakenbush, I can; he loaned me some books last night.

Joe: Any cow buyers yet?

Van: Supposed to be one here Thursday, but it don't look good.

Joe: I never seen it like this before.

Van: It's different. Hey, son, it's time to go back to the salt mine.
Joe: Okay, we'll see you.
Van: Plant that wheat.
Joe: We'll get it.
Van: Go make a hand.
Joe: Okay. Bye, Dad.
Van: See ya, son. Bye.

I tried real hard to remember it and write it down just the way it was.

119   *A Shadow*

Joe S. Holyoak: This one is spooky; this one even scares me.

Sometimes late in the evening
A shadow comes riding off from the hill.
He checks on the cows and the pasture,
Makes sure everything has had their fill.

He sees if the family has what they need,
And he watches my children grow.
I think they're a harvest from his seed,
But then I really don't know.

It's no thief out there in the shadow.
It's no monster or anything bad.
He's just checking on his children.
That shadow out there is my dad.

Whichever direction you're riding,
May the wind always be at your back.
May the trails be soft and sandy,
So maybe I can cut your track.

Or, whatever your lot will be,
I hope they treat you
Just as good as
You've treated me.

There are different times I miss Dad, you know, out riding horses or cutting firewood, things that were close to you. I don't dig a posthole or saddle up a young colt without thinking of him because those were the things we did together, and I believe it makes the loneliness easier to deal with to write it down.

120 *Hello, Mr. Tombstone*

Joe S. Holyoak: Well, I look at people that's got kids that's got granddads, and I remember my granddad and the closeness I had with him and my dad, and I feel my kids kinda got short-changed here. He left more than most people do for a kid to remember, but they still won't know him and what he meant to me, and sometimes I just get lonely and write it down.

Hello, Mr. Tombstone,
How are you today?
Me? I'm feeling lonely
On this stormy sort of day.

You know, you're just a marker
Of a friend that passed away.
At least you're here to listen
To the things I want to say.

You'll never answer any questions
Or soothe my fears away.
My kids can't call you grandpa
Or follow you around someday.

To them you're just a big old rock
That sticks out of the ground,
A place were Daddy comes and talks;
He cries and stomps around.

I know that they don't understand
The hollow in my heart,
But then they'll never know the man
Except for the record part.

So, Mr. Tombstone, it's up to you.
I hope you do your part,
For buried here with this man
Is all the goodness of my heart.

I just write poems to read to my kids or my wife, and I read them to my mom every once in a while.

121 *Farewell to Daddy*

Ada Holyoak Fowler: Losing Daddy was one of the hardest things I ever lived through. We did everything together. We were talking before he ever died. He kept telling me he was going to die. It was really awesome. He just kept

telling me he was going to die. One day I got really mad at him, you know. He just kept telling me he was going to die, and I looked at him, and I said, "Daddy, why do you keep saying that? I'm sick and tired of hearing that. If you're so sure, give me a time."

And he goes, "Within a year. I won't make another year," and this was only about two months before he got killed.

And I said, "That really bothers me, but if I got a year, I can handle it."

He says, "Yeah."

We were out riding one day, and he said something—I don't even remember what he said—but he said something about his dad, and you could just hear the longing in his voice. Granddad had been dead almost eleven years, and I said, "Man, you still miss him, don't you?"

And he goes, "Oh, Ada, more than you'll ever know."

And I said, "Well, Daddy, if anything ever happens to you, I'll be the same way."

And he says, "No, you won't."

And I said, "Why?"

And he said, "'Cause I loved my dad." That was just like him. He cared, and he made it clear without ever saying it. In fact, he said insulting things to show that he loved you.

Well, Daddy, it has been a long time
Since I laid you to rest.
You and I both know that
I haven't given life my best.

I feel so lost and scared
Since you left me alone,
And I often wonder if I'll always hurt
Clean to the bone.

I can't keep my life functioning
Since you went away
In your fiery death on that
Early morn's day.

The memories I have are good,
But, Daddy, some are sad.
With this life you have given me,
I have done some things bad.

Without you to lean on
And to hold me tight,
I can't seem to keep from
Thinking at night.

I am so thankful for
The privilege of your love.
I know God sent you to me
From way up above.

I have so much of that love
In my heart.
I can't seem to give love
Now that we are apart.

Oh Daddy, I am so afraid of
That awful hurt
That I felt while watching them
Cover you with dirt.

How can I let you
Lay down to rest
When my memories of you
Are my best?

Daddy, I know I need
To let you die,
But my heart can never
Say good-bye.

Oh Daddy, I am so sorry
For letting you down.
When I get to Heaven,
Don't greet me with a frown.

You were always there to help me
With my children to raise,
And Daddy, they have nothing of you
But good memories and praise.

You were always there
When my life got rough.
You always said wisdom
Would make me tough.

Don't worry, Daddy,
Your wisdom has never let me down.
It was my doing, not yours,
That let me hit ground.

Daddy, I promise you on this
Near anniversary day
That I will gather my strength
And make my own way.

With the good memories of you
Held tight in my heart,
I will take my life and make
A brand new start.

The things that I have done
To make us both sad
Will be things of the past.
Now, aren't you glad?

Oh Daddy, I have always loved you.
You were the best.
How great I must be to have
To face this great test.

Thank you, Daddy, for all
The good times we shared.
For as long as I can remember,
I will always know you cared.

Now with life
I must continue to grow,
And I thank you. Daddy,
I still love you so.

122   *My Hill*

**Ada Holyoak Fowler: I don't know. I just started after Daddy died really.
Just things were bothering me, and he was a poet, and you know we had just
been around it all our lives, and it just seemed the right thing to do.** *(Laughs.)*
**How else, you know, could I leave anything to him without saying or doing it
in poetry? The first one I wrote was right after he died. I couldn't sleep at
night, you know. I was just having a hard time, and I just got up, and I just
wrote it, and it just came. Course, it wasn't that good!** *(Laughs.)* **I start with
pencil and paper. Daddy always would have it go through his head for a week
or so and then go write it. Yeah, I've tried doing it the other way, and I can't
remember what I thought of the first time. I use mostly four lines and
sometimes two. One of these times, maybe I can get six. I don't know.**
(Laughs.) **I rhyme the last words. Yeah, I can always do that.** *(Laughs.)* **Not
really.**

   **What do you want me to do? Some of these are bad. The one about my
hill, I'll do that.**

How do I tell you
How I feel?
How can I explain
My love is so real?

Everyone says my love
For you is wrong!
How can that be
When my feelings are so strong?

Everyone else at one time
Has let me down.
But not you,
You were my glowing crown.

For you, and only you,
Did I dare to cry.
I would come to you
When I wanted to die.

You would comfort me
In times of need.
You would open my eyes
And make me see.

Without you what chance
Would life have had?
For your love and mine
I will always be glad.

As a child growing up,
You held my hand.
You offered solid ground
For me to stand.

Now the time has come
I must say good-bye.
My heart is broken,
And my eyes, they cry.

When you are gone,
I will no longer be.
It hurts me so,
But I can't let them see.

For as long as I live
And still have a will,
In my heart you will always
Still be my hill.

**That was written because Mom was selling the ranch and the hill was going.
When I was growing up, I always helped Daddy do chores. There was this hill
out behind our house, and I loved it, the way the trees were set, and every-**

thing. I had a living room, my kitchen, my bedroom without really doing anything except laying a couple of logs down. I could sit up on that hill, and I could see for miles, and I could hear people even in town talking. And anytime anything ever happened to me or I was upset (as a child I was really melodramatic), I would run away to my hill, and I always could just go up there and feel the serenity, and I always told Daddy that I was going to live up on that hill, and every night when I saw him doing chores, I would run down and help, so Daddy gave me that hill. I would say my poetry is a way of dealing with emotions, with life, but generally it has to do with some sort of ah-h-h-h. *(Laughs.)* I don't know the word for it. You know, it's just when you kind of feel... I'm not the kind of person who can walk up to somebody and say, "I really love you," or "I really care about you," but I can write you a poem.

123 *Granddad*

Kristi Hodge: I always get my poetry after I go to bed. Then things just come to me, and I have to get up in the middle of the night and write them down. Writing poetry just helps me get my feelings out.

Although I know
He's up in heaven,
I wish he could have waited
Till I was twenty-seven.

The memories of him
Will be the best
Because they are better
Than the rest.

You could always tell
That he cared;
He was never selfish;
He always shared.

There's never a day
That goes by
That I don't think of him
And want to cry.

I know I shouldn't
Feel so sad
Because he's with God
And very glad.

I know he's up there
Doing what's right,
But I still can't help
From crying at night.

I want to do
The best I can,
So when I die
I can see him again.

124   *My Granddad*

**Kristi Hodge: All of the poems that I have written except for the one about
Arizona that I did for school are about my granddad, but I don't like this one
because when I wrote it, I didn't really feel it. I just wanted to write about
Granddad, so it wasn't something I was really feeling.**

Van Holyoak was my granddad.
He never did anything really bad.
Sure he had a few faults.
He's only human not a vault.

He had the best advice around
That wouldn't tear anyone down.
I've never met anyone who didn't like him,
But I accidentally laughed when he was hit with a limb.

He had a memory that wouldn't quit.
He could recite poems for people until they split.
Now, I'm not good at writing poems,
But I know what I feel when it comes.

Now my granddad is dead and gone,
But his spirit lingers on.
Now, I will tell you this.
He is someone you don't want to miss.

He is so special in my heart.
I want to tell you, but I don't know where to start.
Now that he's gone, our family is lost.
They fight and argue about who is boss.

I miss and love him so much
Because he is my very special Granddad.

125 *A Little Parable for Mothers*

Anona C. Heap: This is a thing I've always loved. It's just so much like my mother that I have always cherished it.

A young mother set her foot on the path of life. "Is the way long?" she asked.

And the guide answered, "Yes, and the way is hard, and you'll be old before you reach the end of it, but the end will be better than the beginning."

Oh, but the young mother was happy, and she would not believe that anything could be better than these years, so she played with her children and gathered flowers for them along the way and bathed them in the clear streams, and the sun shone down on them, and life was good, and the young mother cried,"Nothing will ever be lovelier than this."

Then the night came and the storm, and the path was dark, and the children shook with fear and cold, and the mother drew them close and covered them with her mantle, and the children said, "Oh, Mother, we are not afraid, for when you are there, no harm can come."

And the mother said, "This is better than the brightness of the day for I have taught my children courage."

And the morning came, and there was a hill ahead, and the children climbed, and they grew weary, and the mother grew weary, but at all times she said to the children, "A little patience and we are there."

So the children climbed, and when they reached the top, they said, "We could not have done it without you, Mother."

And the mother when she laid down that night looked up at the stars and said, "This is a better day than the last, for my children have learned fortitude in the face of hardship. Yesterday I gave them courage. Today I gave them strength."

And the next day came a strange cloud which darkened the earth—clouds of war and hate and evil. And the children groped and stumbled, and the mother said, "Look up! Lift your eyes to the light."

And the children looked and saw above the clouds and the darkness and saw the Everlasting Glory, and it guided them and brought them beyond the darkness.

And that night the mother said, "This is the best day of all, for I have shown my children God."

And the days went on and the weeks and the months and the years, and the mother grew old, and she was little and bent, but her children were tall and strong and walked with courage, and when the way was hard, they helped their mother, and when rough they lifted her. At last they came to a hill, and beyond the hill they could see a shining road and golden gates swung wide. Their mother said, "I have reached the end of my journey, and now I know that the end is better than the beginning for my children can walk alone and their children after them."

And the children said, "Oh, you will always be with us, Mother, even when you have gone through those gates." And they stood and watched her as she went on alone and the gates closed after her, and they said, "We cannot see her, but she is with us still. A mother like ours is more than a memory. She is a living presence."

And that's just like my mother's life.

126 *The End of a Perfect Day*

Anona Heap: I have one that's very sentimental to me. When that song "The End of a Perfect Day" first came out, you know, that was when my father was killed, and the first time I ever heard that was at his funeral when I was eleven. Then it's gone down, and we had it sung at Mother's, and then my oldest daughter was killed, and we sang it at hers, and I love that as a reading.

When you come to the end of a perfect day,
And you sit all alone with your thoughts,
While the chimes ring out with a carol gay,
For the joy that the day has brought,
Do you think what the end of a perfect day
Can mean to a tired heart,
When the sun goes down with a flaming ray
And dear friends have to part?

Well, this is the end of a perfect day,
Near the end of a journey, too,
But it leaves a thought that's big and strong,
With a wish that is kind and true,
For memory has painted this perfect day
With colors that never fade,
And we find at the end of a perfect day,
The soul of a friend we've made.

127 *You Ask Me Am I Sad*

Alida Connolly: Since my sister Anona told you about our dad dying, I'll start out with one I wrote about my mom when she died.

You ask me am I sad
Now my mother's gone
Up beyond the sunset
With her husband John?

Up beyond the mountains,
Way up past the sky,
Where she'll know only laughter
And never have to cry.

Where young John is waiting
Filled with a young man's pride
For Alice in her white wedding gown
Once more to be his bride.

There never more to sorrow,
Bear trouble or suffer pain,
But dwell in peace forever
With her loved ones again.

You ask me do I want her back again?
No, not I,
Though I'll miss my little mother
Until the day I die.

But those tiny hands that nurtured me
And calmed my troubled brow
Are needed elsewhere,
And those tiny feet are treading holier places now.

Dear Mother, it is over,
All the agony and pain,
And I look forward to the time
I'll be with you and Dad again.

See you two reunited
As you were meant to be
With glory upon glory added
Throughout all eternity.

128 *Happy Birthday, Billy*

Alida Connolly: I've got that one from Bill's book. This is the last one I'll do. This is for Anona's boy Billy that we all loved so well. He was six foot four, big grin from ear to ear, always dressed Western with boots. The last time I saw him we had a family reunion in Mesa, and he danced me all over the place, and we laughed so hard we could hardly dance. We all loved Billy.

Happy Birthday, Billy,
I would like to say today.
You lived among us nearly twenty years
Before you went away.

I'm so very glad I knew you,
Though it was just a little while.
It would have been a sad old world, Billy,
Without your great big smile.

Though you left your tall brown boots
And your new straw hat,
The coiled up rope and your saddle
Worn hollow where once you sat.

Your horse looks over the barbed wire fence
And neighs for you at the gate.
The cows all wonder,
"Where is Billy and why is he so late?"

The spurs you carried in the back of the car
You won't be needing now.
Someone else will ride herd for you
And see about that cow.

The brand you chose as your very own,
The Quarter Circle Dart,
Is a brand your parents carry
Burned on their aching heart.

But, Billy, we who know you
Know you would never shirk,
And you'll soon be doing
Your Heavenly Father's work.

You'll be rounding up and sorting out
The valiant ones from that heavenly herd
And burning a brand everlasting
Of that great and glorious word.

You'll have loved ones there a-plenty,
And I guess they needed you
With your winning ways and clean young life
For the work they have to do.

So, Bill, we'll take care of your saddle
And all of the things you left
And treasure them because they were yours,
And though we feel bereft,

Just wait for us by that open gate
And when it's opened wide,
Why, there will be all of us critters reunited,
Herded together and branded a family
To graze in God's peaceful pasture together forever side by side.

There's his picture and there's a picture of his horse. Maybe I should have brought some more to read. I have a trunk full.

129 *I Like to Think in That Far Land*

LaVelle Whiting DeSpain: This is to my mother.

I like to think in that far land
Before I came to earth
That I a choice did make
To whom would give me birth.

There had to be a waiting list
Of spirits by the score
Hoping to be chosen soon
As Gibbons number four.

But somehow, heaven only knows,
I was the lucky one.
Was it chance or fate
Or my reward for something I had done?

I'm sure I knew her very well,
My mother who would be
My mother in this earth life
And through eternity.

I think we had a lot in common
That endeared her from the start.
Her gentle ways, her kindness, too,
Found a place within my heart.

God gave her many virtues
And talents by the score,
But when He gave her motherhood,
She never needed more.

She did magnify her calling
By bringing to the fold
Eight of His spirit children,
Each life to gently mold.

And this has been my blessing
To travel by her side
Down earth's well-worn highway
With Mother as my guide.

But now I travel onward
Without hesitancy or fear
Though she is not beside me,
Her presence still is near.

Yes, she has gone ahead of me
As she has done before
To set her house in order
And wait there at her door.

And one day when life is over,
This message I hope to send,
"Mother, I am coming
For I have endured to the end."

130   *To My Dad*

LaVelle Whiting DeSpain: My dad had a real sense of humor, and he loved to
dress up. He'd call home, and he would say, "If you girls will press my suit,
there's a quarter or fifty cents waiting for you." All you had to do was just
take it out of the closet, just dust it off a little bit, and it just pressed perfect
because he pressed his pants every morning. That's how he wore them out.
The creases on the seams would just finally fall apart. He just took pride in
the way he looked. And this is how I thought of him.

These are the things
I like best about my dad,
His happy smile, his gay hello,
And seldom was he sad.

I first remember him
As principal of the school
Slipping me a candy bar
Which was against the rule.

When I asked him for a nickel
Which I knew he couldn't afford,
He never did refuse me,
For his pockets couldn't hoard.

These are the things
I like best about our dad,
His hacking cough, his polished shoes,
And never being mad.

I often think of him.
When Norm and I did fight,
We'd pinch and kick, and sure enough,
On would go the light.

Never did he spank us.
I wish he would, by heck,
'Cause he always pulled
The shortest hair growing on the neck.

I think that was from his school teaching days.

These are the things
I like best about our dad,
His funny jokes, his gift to thrill
Since he was a little lad.

And I remember how
When courting I did go,
If I wasn't home by twelve o'clock,
I was sure to lose my beau.

'Cause when he came to hunt me,
I really didn't care.
But it was a romance killer
When he came in underwear.

He never bothered to put on his shirt after midnight.

These are the things
I like best about our dad,
His sense of humor, his love for us,
For these things I am glad.

And I remember him
As always in a hurry.
I won't forget the night we wed,
He had me in a flurry.

It was a lovely wedding.
The rush I didn't mind,
But when the ceremony started,
Our dad we could not find.

Hunted all over the temple for him.

These are the things
I like best about our dad,
His gay, bright ties, his love for sports,
The cross word he seldom had.

And now his grandchildren know him
As a grandfather who will never grow old,
For his sunny smile, his loving ways,
And for his heart of gold.

Happy Father's Day. We love you.
Our love you've always had,
And now you know a few things
We like best about our dad.

**I gave it to him on Father's Day. I probably wrote it out and handed it to him
because I would have cried if I had read it to him.**

131   *To Helen*

**LaVelle Whiting DeSpain: This is one I wrote to my sister to thank her for
being such a help when I was so discouraged.**

She's had her share
Of trials and strife
While walking down
This road called life.

And yet to see her
You'd never know
She had a care.
It doesn't show.

Oh, her hair is gray.
It's nearly white.
Each gray hair added
In the life we fight.

No, she's not old.
She's still a queen
And has the sparkle
Of sweet sixteen.

To know her,
You'd feel her world is right.
To meet her each day
Makes your day seem more bright.

Her shoulders aren't broad.
She's very small,
Yet she carries a burden
Of all that call.

When there's sickness or trouble,
You'll find her there
Lending a hand,
Doing her share.

How do I know this?
I've had my grief,
And she was there
To give relief.

Relief and comfort
Were hers to share.
When I wanted to die,
She made me care.

The road is hard
And black as night.
She opened the door
To let in the light.

A tiny light
That seemed to say,
"Life will be brighter
Than it is today.

"Life will have meaning
And purpose, I'm sure,
If you'll but let it.
Open the door.

"The door you've shut
On all that care,
Your family and friends
Who want to help and to share."

In my stupidity
She made me see
They did all they could;
Now it was up to me.

And I know someone
Who's thanking her, too,
For doing the things
He couldn't do.

I'll help you, Blessing,
And do all I can
If you'll help me
In the world of man.

Some call her Blessing,
To others she's a queen,
To me she's a sister
On whom I can lean.

Thanks, dear sister,
You were so right.
Where there was darkness,
Now there is light.

Mother always called my sister Blessing, and some of the high school kids heard, and they started calling her Blessing, and then she was queen for a couple of years at Flagstaff where she went to college, and so some called her Queen.

132 *That Silver Haired Daddy of Mine*

Reinhold "Tex" Bonnet: Okay, now I'll do "Silver Haired Daddy." It always makes me think of my dad. I left home young to cowboy.

In a vine covered shack in the mountains
Bravely fighting the battle of time
Lies the dear one whose weather lines battle.
It's that silver haired daddy of mine.

Ah, now I broke up. I'm sorry. I just can't do that without crying.

CHAPTER NINE

About All of That

FROM CHILDHOOD AND CHILDREN, from love and adventure, from life and death arise the ultimate questions concerning this world and beyond: sin and redemption, creeds and codes, the now and the forever. Western recitations deal with these questions, too.

133   The Old Plantation Mule

Margaret Witt: Let's see. I'll do "The Old Plantation Mule." It starts out funny and then changes to a serious ending.

A very funny fella
Is the old plantation mule,
And nobody'll play with him
Unless he is a fool.

The best a'thing to do
When you meditate about him
Is kinda sorta calculate
You can get along without him.

When you try to 'proach that mule
From the front end wise,
He look as meek as Moses,
But the look is full of lies.

He doesn't move a muscle.
He doesn't even wink,
And you think his disposition's
Better than people think.

Then you cosset him a little,
And you rub and pat his other end,
And you has a revelation
That he ain't so much your friend.

You have made a great mistake,
But before the heart repents
You is hitched very sudden
To the other side of the fence.

Now you feel like you been standin'
On the locomotive track
And the engine come and hit ya
In the middle of the back.

Now, sin in the soul
Is precisely like the mule,
And nobody will play with it
Unless he is a fool.

134 *Life*

Stanley Shumway: Our church encourages us to write our life's story, and I love to write. It's a joy for me, not a burden. For my life's story, I didn't follow the usual trend. It isn't chronological. I organized the chapters around various phases of my life—how I've earned my living and various other facets—and I included some poems in one chapter, and this is one of them.

What is life?
The poet answers, "Life is love;
Life is romance and all that's beautiful."

The philosopher speaks, "Life is friendship;
Life is devotion to duty and to self."

And still I hear the peasant in some war-torn
Country cry, and the prisoner in his cell,
"Life is bitterness; life is misery;
Life is hell."

What is life?
Ah, I know the answer,
For oft it has been told to me
As I have sat beside the dying embers of a lonely campfire
On some far-off mountain side,
Or been borne into my soul on the strains of
Some sweet melody,
Or looking into the blackness of my
Lonely chamber at midnight? Yes, oft
Has it been told to me
As I have seen my soul
A speck, floating on the wings of Eternity.

135   *Storm Tossed*

**Stanley Shumway: This one would be kind of meaningless without explana-
tion. We lived in a house that was sort of creaky, and there was a storm, and
it inspired this poem.**

Last night I awoke from slumber deep
To a howling and raging storm,
And the chill of the wind through my soul did creep,
Though my cover was amply warm.

As I lay there, I heard on the voice of the gale
Tales of the ages, of wisdom and woe,
And I said to the gale, "Go on with your tale.

"There are mysteries that I would know,
Of life and death, of the spirit and soul,
Of heavens and the earth below."

But with one final shriek the storm was done,
And the elements silent became,
Though the strife continued within my soul
For my questions unanswered remain.

**My wife slept through the storm. Well, maybe not, but anyway she didn't
think of it as a subject fit for poetry.**

136   *My Symphony*

Stanley Shumway: I'll do one more. It's called "My Symphony."

On fleeting occasion when I have known small pain
Or some small sadness hath on my spirit lain,
I have but to listen to a far-off echo,
And to my waiting ear is borne
The soft, sweet melody of my symphony.

A symphony of life, of love, of beauty—
Of beauty and love and life.
And I am carried aloft on wings of music rare.
Oh, that my symphony I could share.

The Overture is Beauty.
Dear land of home,
The land in which I walk is to my eye
A marvel of beauty
Of sky and mountain and starlight and moonlight,
Of vistas unsurpassed by anything my vision can conjure.
As day by day and night by night I view
The panorama of its mighty majesty;
As I listen, the overture fades, and the theme begins.

The Theme is Love.
I love music and I love beauty,
But love is more than beauty seen and music heard.
My symphony is a symphony of love;
The love of kindred, sweet wife and daughters fair,
Son and sons-in-law of stature with me a name to share,
And of new small spirits sent
That the enduring theme of love in my life may not be spent.
Until with one great blend and burst of tone
Beauty and love, overture and theme,
Mingle their voices in one great symphony of life.
Life in which the sum of love and beauty blend
Played by a thousand instruments,
And a hundred strains transport the cares and sorrows,
Small sadness and small pain.
With arms upraised and eye on far-off horizon,
I stand and hear again the echo of my symphony.

I wrote that in Reserve, New Mexico, during the May of 1960.
     **You know I went to college at Northern Arizona; it was Arizona State
Teachers College then. There was a lady English teacher who taught my
class. She had what we called bobbed hair; it was quite unusual in those
days. And she would make us recite. There was one little girl in the class—
sort of consumptive-looking, hollow chest—and every day the teacher would
make this little girl say this line. (Isn't it amazing! I can't remember the girl's
name or the teacher's name, but I remember the line.)**

"Roll on, thou deep and dark blue ocean, roll!"

"No!" she'd yell, "Louder! Louder! 'Roll on, thou deep and dark blue ocean, ROLL!' "

Before the quarter ended, that little girl could shake the walls, so I learned about reciting in college, and I wouldn't consider myself a performer because I don't shake the walls.

137   *The Snow*

Joe S. Holyoak: I started poetry when I was a little kid in school. Basically, writing poems was the only thing that got me through English. Dad wrote a lot and that influenced me. It just kinda comes to you once in a while, and you sit down and write it, or you forget it, but I may have it in my mind for a month or so before I put it down. Basically, I get an idea of what I want to write about, and then as I start thinking about it, either it becomes a little western or a little religious or something. You know, it's like a trip. You want to know where you're going to, and then you figure out the route you're going to take to get there.

It's five o'clock in the morning.
The snow's still filtering down.
It's the first that fell this winter
Like a satin blanket on the ground.
The whole world in its virtue,
Not a blemish to be found,
A ghostly white world to look to,
No breeze or earthly sound.
There's no footsteps here to follow,
Nor are there any roads here to be found.
You can start out here a beginner
And turn your world around.
So pray unto your Maker.
Repent of what you do.
The tracks you make this morning,
Each and every one, are up to you!

All your cowboys had a lot of religious philosophy. I've never sat down and tried to write a poem with philosophies, theology, or anything like that in there, but like I said, that's in the root of most people, so I end up getting that way.

138   *Silver Jack*

Van N. Holyoak: This is about cowboy religion.

I was on a drive in eighty
Working under Silver Jack
Who's now in jail in Jackson
And ain't soon expected back.

Now there was a man among us
By the name of Robert White.
He was smart and cute and tonguey.
I guess he was a graduate.

He could talk on any subject
From the Bible down to Hoyle.
His words flowed out as slick and smooth
As if they's made of oil.

One day when we was camped out
In that Godforsaken land
Smokin' Nigger-head tobacco
And hearing Bob expand.

Hell, he said it was a humbug,
And he made it plain as day
That the Bible, it was a fable,
And we vowed it all looked that way.

Miracles and suchlike was
Too rank for him to stand,
And as for Him they called the Savior,
Hell, He's just a common man.

"You're a liar!" someone shouted,
"And you've got to take it back."
I turned my head all startled.
'Twas the words of Silver Jack.

He'd cracked his fists together,
And he stacked his duds and cried,
"It was in that same religion
That my mother lived and died.

"Though I haven't always
Used the Lord exactly right,
Yet when I hear things about Him,
A man's got to eat his words or fight."

Now old Bob, he wasn't cowardly,
And he answered bold and free,
"Stake your duds and cut your capers;
There ain't no flies on me."

Now they fought for forty minutes,
And the crowd would whoop and cheer
When Jack spit up a tooth or two
And Bobby lost an ear.

At last Jack got him under,
And he hit him once or twice.
Right soon Bob started to admittin'
The divinity of Christ.

But Jack kept reassuring him,
Till he made that poor cuss yell,
And he vowed he'd been mistaken
On his views concerning hell.

When the fierce encounter ended,
And they raised up from the ground,
Someone brought a bottle out
And kindly passed it round.

We drank to Bob's religion
In a friendly sort of way,
And the cry of infidelity
Was checked in camp that day.

139   *The Cowboy's Prayer*

**Joseph C. Bolander: Did you ever hear "The Cowboy's Prayer"? "The Cow-
boy's Prayer" is one that's always been quite popular around here. Let me
try it.**

Oh Lord, I never lived where churches grow.
I love creation better as it stood
The day You finished it so long ago,
And looked upon Your work and called it good.

I know that others find You in the light
That's filtered down through tinted window panes,
And yet I seem to feel You close tonight
In this dim, quiet starlight on the plains.

I thank You, Lord, that I am placed so well,
That You have made my freedom so complete;
That I'm no slave of whistle, clock or bell,
Nor weak-eyed prisoner of wall and street.

Just let me live my life as I've begun,
And give me work that's open to the sky;
Make me a pardner of the wind and sun,
And I'll not ask a life that's soft or high.

Let me be easy on the man that's down;
Let me be kind and generous with all.
I'm careless sometimes, Lord, when I'm in town,
But never let 'em say I'm mean or small!

Make me as big and open as the plains,
As honest as the hoss between my knees,
Clean as the wind that blows behind the rains,
And free as the hawk that circles down the breeze!

Forgive me, Lord, if sometimes I forget.
You know about the reasons that are hid.
You know about the things that gall and fret;
You know me better than my mother did.

Just keep an eye on all that's done and said,
And right me when I sometimes turn aside,
And guide me on the long, dim trail ahead
That stretches upwards toward the Great Divide.

Bud Ogle's Recitations (140-141)

Billy Simon: There were a lot of cow camps where we used to pass the guitar around, and some of the boys could sing a little and knew some old cowboy songs. One time we were down camped in the bottom of Buckskin Canyon. It's below Walnut Grove between there and Castle Hot Springs. And there's quite a bunch of cowboys there, and we didn't have any guitar in that camp, and we came round singing these songs, and it came to ol' Bud Ogle's turn. He's the man who owned the J Bar outfit down on Castle Creek. Bud said he couldn't sing, but he knew how to recite a couple of things or two. I didn't think much of it at the time till after it was all over, and I think that maybe you'll agree with me that it was sort of an unusual recitation for an old flea-bitten cowboy to say. But here's the way it went:

140   *She Was a Woman Long and Thin*

She was a woman long and thin
Whom the world condemned for a single sin.
They cast her out on the King's Highway,
And they passed her by as they went to pray.

He was a man, more to blame,
But the world spared him one breath of shame.
Under his feet he saw her lie,
But he raised his head, and he passed her by.

Now these were the people who went to pray
In the temple of God on His holy day.
They condemned the woman, forgave the man.
It was ever thus since the world began.

Now time went on, and the woman died.
On the cross of shame she was crucified.
The man died, too, but they buried him
In a casket of cloth with a silver rim.

And they said as they turned from the grave away,
"We have buried an honest man today."
Two mortals knocking at heaven's gate
Stood face to face to inquire their fate.

The man had a passport of earthly sign,
But the woman a pardon from the Lord Divine.
"Oh, ye who judge 'twixt virtue and vice,
Which think ye entered paradise?"

So the song business went on, and when it came Bud Ogle's next turnaround, why, he came up with this:

141   *Blue Eyes, Brown Eyes*

Blue eyes, brown eyes, green and gold eyes,
Eyes that falter, doubt, deny,
Sudden flashing, sweet young bold eyes.
Here's your answer. I am I.

Not for you and not for any
Came I into this man's town.
Barkeep, here's my golden penny,
Come who will and drink her down.

Now, I'm not one to lend or borrow.
I'm not one to overstay.
I shall go alone tomorrow
Whistling as I came today.

142   *The Touch of the Master's Hand*

Leon Lambson: I don't have a good recall at all. I don't have a photographic memory, but I can learn things, and I'll use them, and then I'll pick up something for another occasion, and I'll use it, and then I put this one out of my mind. If the occasion comes, I have to redo it—you know, relearn it.

Now, this is a tape of me reciting with my band. Give me one of your empty cassettes, and I'll make you a copy with my fast copy machine while we talk.

(The band plays "Sweet Hour of Prayer" on piano and guitar throughout the recitation.)

I live in the little town of Ramah
Out in New Mexico.
I've been up the river and over the ridge,
And I want to tell you about some old fiddlers that I used to know.

First I want to tell you a beautiful story
I heard about an old violin
(It was carried to the auction all covered with dust),
And how it came to life again.

I'll do it to the tune of "Sweet Hour of Prayer,"
The most beautiful song in our land.
Let's see now; it goes something like this,
And it's called "The Touch of the Master's Hand."

'Twas battered and scarred and the auctioneer
Thought it hardly worth his while
To spend much time on the old violin,
But he held it up with a smile.

"What am I offered, good folks," he cried,
Who'll start the bidding for me?
A dollar, one dollar, two?
Two dollars, and who'll make it three?

"Three dollars once, three dollars twice,
Going for three?" But no!
From the back of the room a gray-haired man
Came forward and picked up the bow.

Then wiping the dust from the old violin
And tightening up the loose strings,
He played the melody as pure and as sweet
As the caroling angel sings.

*(Leon plays "Sweet Hour of Prayer" on fiddle accompanied by his
    band.)*

The music stopped and the auctioneer
In a voice that was quiet and low,
Said, "Now, what am I offered for this old violin?"
And he held it up with a bow.

"A thousand dollars, and who'll make it two,
Two thousand, and who'll make it three?
Three thousand once, three thousand twice;
Going and gone," said he.

The people cheered, but some of them cried
They didn't understand
What changed its worth.
Then someone replied, "It was the touch of the master's hand."

So it is that many a man with life out of tune,
All battered and scarred with sin,
Is auctioned cheap to a thoughtless crowd
Much like the old violin.

A mess of pottage, a glass of wine,
A game, and then he travels on.
He is going once, he's going twice,
He's going and he's almost gone;

But the Master comes, and the foolish crowd
Still don't understand
The worth of a soul and the change that's wrought
By the touch of the Master's hand.

(Plays "Sweet Hour of Prayer.")

143   *The Volunteer Organist*

Horace Crandell: I got this out of that same red book. I never heard anyone say it. I just go over these things in my mind until I have them about as good as I can.

There was an old fellow who lived in Pinedale when I was a kid by the name of Solomon Robinson. He was a widower with three or four girls, and I heard him recite a lot, but I didn't get any of his pieces, only just partial. He impressed me a lot because he was a kind of a loner and nobody paid attention to him, but he could really recite. He gave me the impression that I was right there with him saying it, you know, and that's what I liked mostly. He had a lot of influence on me.

The great big church was crowded full
Of broadcloth and of silk,
And satin rich as cream that grows
On our old brindle's milk,

Shined boots, biled shirts, stiff dickeys,
And stovepipe hats were there,
And dudes with their trousers loomed so tight
They couldn't kneel down in prayer.

The elder in his pulpit high
Said as he slowly riz,
"Our organist's kept home today,
Laid up with rheumatiz.

"And since we have no substitute
And Brother Moore ain't here,
Will someone in the congregation
Be so kind as to volunteer?"

And then a red-nosed, drunken tramp
Of slow and lowly style
Gave an introductory hiccup
And staggered up the aisle,

And on that holy atmosphere
There appeared a sense of sin,
And on the air of sanctity,
The odor of old gin.

Then Deacon Purlington, he yelled,
His teeth all set on edge,
"That man profanes the house of God.
Why, this is sacrilege!"

But the tramp didn't hear a word he said
But slouched with stumbling feet.
He reeled and staggered up the aisle
And reached the organ seat.

He then went sprawling on the keys
And soon there rose a strain
That seemed to just bulge out the heart
And electrify the brain.

Then he come down on the thing
With hands and head and knees.
He slambashed his whole body down,
Kaflump, upon the keys.

The organ roared, the music flood
Went soaring high and dry.
It swelled up to the rafters
And bulged out into the sky.

The old church shook and trembled
And seemed to reel and sway.
The elders shouted, ''Glory!''
And I yelled out, ''Hooray!''

And then he touched a tender strain
That melted in our ears.
It brought up blessed memories
And drenched them down with tears.

We thought of the old-time kitchen
And Patty on the mat,
Of love, and home, and baby days,
And Mother, and all of that.

And then he touched a streak of hope,
A song of souls forgiven,
That barred the prison doors of sin
And stormed the gates of heaven.

The stars of morning sang together,
No soul was left alone.
It seemed the universe was safe,
And God sat on His throne.

And then a song of deep despair
And darkness come again.
A long black crepe hung on the
Doors of all of the homes of men.

No love, no peace, no joy, no hope,
No songs of pure delight.
Then the tramp he staggered down
And reeled into the night,

But he knew he'd told his story
Though he never spoke a word,
And 'twas the saddest story
Our ears had ever heard.

He had told his own life's history.
No eye was dry that day.
When the elder rose, he simply said,
"Brethren, let us pray."

144   *Where Is My Wandering Boy Tonight?*

Horace Crandell: I don't have any recitations to speak of that are specifically about my religion except for some hymns, but this comes close.

Where is my wandering boy tonight?
The boy of my tend'rest care,
The boy that was once my joy and light,
The child of my love and prayer,

Oh, where is my boy tonight?
Where is my boy tonight?
My heart o'erflows, for I love him he knows.
Oh, where is my boy tonight?

Once he was pure as the morning dew
As he knelt at his mother's knee.
No face was so bright nor heart more true,
And none was as sweet as he.

Oh, could I but see him now,
My boy, as fair as in olden time
When prattle and smile made home a joy,
And life was a merry chime.

And go for my wandering boy tonight,
Go search for him where you will,
But bring him to me with all his blight,
And tell him I love him still.

Oh, where is my boy tonight?
Where is my boy tonight?
My heart o'erflows, for I love him he knows.
Oh, where is my boy tonight?

145   *'Twas a Few Weeks Before Christmas*

LaVelle Whiting DeSpain: When I was Relief Society President, I wrote this and gave one to all the ward relief society presidents.

'Twas a few weeks before Christmas
And in Sister Relief Society's house
Everyone was busy
Including her spouse.

She had shopped and she had baked
For days now it seems
Trying to please all
With their rare Christmas dreams.

The last present she had wrapped
And sent her last card.
My, Christmas is fun,
But it's also been hard.

The stockings yet to hang
And decorate the tree,
She should be pleased
As pleased as could be.

But hark!
The feelings just aren't right.
Had she failed in her shopping
Each one to delight?

She went over in her mind
Her long Christmas list,
But not one of her loved ones
She'd found she'd missed.

Then why couldn't she thrill
And have satisfaction, too,
With Christmas so near
And her work almost through?

With all of her shopping,
Cooking and baking,
It had been such fun,
But a great undertaking.

Then, "Ba! Humbug!" she heard,
"You're a selfish one, too.
You thought only of your loved ones
And the things you should do."

"Oh, go away, Scrooge,
You're ruining my fun
In trying to undo
All the good things I have done."

"'Twas told me one Christmas
By a wise Christmas elf
That we should love our neighbor
As much as our self."

Then what to her
Wondering mind should appear
But the names of her neglected neighbors.
How her heart raced with fear!

She knew he was right,
As right as could be.
Her Christmas plans included
Only her precious family.

Then the words of the Christ Child,
Oh, why didn't she see!
"When you've done it unto the least of these,
You've done it unto me."

So she went right to work,
A much happier self
Thanks to old Scrooge
And a wise Christmas elf.

They'd helped to make her
A strong believer
That Christmas is for both
The giver and receiver.

146 *Lady Yardley's Guest*

Madeline Collins: This is a poem about the early days of our country when people from England came here in 1620. They built rude cabins in the deep forest, very much like our own Coconino forest. One cabin, a little larger, set in a clearing, housed Lady Yardley and her children; her husband Sir George had returned to England many months before to bring back much needed supplies to the colonists. Besides the bitter cold, the settlers had to contend with the threat of hostile Indians.

And so we come to Christmas Eve, about the year 1622, and the story:

'Twas a Saturday night, midwinter,
And the snow with its sheeted pall
Had covered the stubbled clearing
Which girdled the rude built hall.

High in the deep-mouthed chimney
'Mid laughter and shout and din,
The children were piling Yule logs
To welcome the Christmas in.

"Ah, so, we'll be glad tomorrow,"
The mother half musing said,
As she looked at the eager workers
And laid on a sunny head

A touch, as of benediction.
"For Heaven is just as near
To Father at far Patuxent
As if he were with us here.

"So choose ye the pine and the holly
And shake from their boughs the snow.
We'll garland the rough-hewn rafters
As they garlanded long ago,

"'Fore ever Sir George went sailing
Away o'er the wild sea foam
To my beautiful English Sussex
The happy old walls at home."

She sighed as she paused. A whisper
Set quickly all eyes a-strain.
"See! See!" and the boy's hand pointed.
"There's a face at the window pane."

One instant a ghastly terror
Shot sudden her features o'er.
The next and she rose unblanching
And opened the fast-barred door.

"Who be ye that seek admission?
Who cometh for food and rest?
This night is a night above others
To shelter a straying quest."

Deep out of the snowy silence
A guttural answer broke,
"I come from the Three Great Rivers.
I am Chief of the Roanoke."

Straight in through the frightened children
Unshrinking, the red man strode
And loosed on the blazing hearthstone
From his shoulder a light-borne load.

Then out of the pile of deerskin
With look as serene and mild
As if it had been his cradle
Stepped softly a little child.

As he chafed at the fire his fingers
Close-pressed by the brawny knee
The gaze that the silent savage
Bent on him was strange to see.

And then with a voice whose yearning
The father could scarcely stem
He said, to the children pointing,
"I want him to be like them.

"They weep for the boy in the wigwam.
I bring him a moon of days
To learn of the speaking paper
To hear of the wiser ways,

"Of the people beyond the waters,
To break with the plow the sod,
To be kind to papoose and women,
To pray to the white man's God."

"I give thee my hand,"
And the lady pressed forward with sudden cheer,
"Thou shalt eat of my English pudding
And drink of my Christmas beer.

"My sweethearts, this night remember
All strangers are kith and kin,
The night when the dear Lord's mother
Could find no room in the inn."

Next morn from the colony belfry
Pealed gaily the Sunday chime,
And merrily forth the people flocked
Keeping the Christmas time.

And the lady with bright-eyed children
Behind her, their lips a smile,
And the Chief in his skins and wampum
Came walking the narrow aisle.

Forthwith from the congregation
Broke fiercely a sudden cry,
"Out! Out with the crafty redskin.
Have at him! A spy! A spy!"

And quickly from belts leaped daggers
And swords from their sheaths flashed bare,
And men from their seats defiant, sprang
Ready to slay him there.

But facing the crowd with courage,
As calm as a knight of yore,
Stepped bravely this fair-browed woman,
The thrust of the steel before.

And spake with a queenly gesture
Her hand on the Chief's brown breast,
"How dare ye impeach my honor?
How dare ye insult my guest?"

They dropped at her words their weapons
Half shamed as the lady smiled
And told them the red man's story
And showed them the red man's child.

Then pledged her their broad plantations
That never would such betray
The trust that a Christian woman
Had shown on a Christmas Day.

147   *Abou Ben Adhem*

Ralph Rogers: This is the second recitation I remember learning. I got this in the district school when I was going to the sixth grade. I liked it then, so I learned it, and I still like it.

Abou Ben Adhem (may his tribe increase!)
Awoke one night from a sweet dream of peace
And saw within the moonlight in the room
An angel writing in a book of gold.
Exceeding peace had made Ben Adhem bold,
And to the presence in the room he said,
"What writest thou?" The angel raised his head and said,
"The love of God for Everyman."
"I pray thee then," said Abou,
"Write me as one who loves his fellow men."
The angel wrote and vanished,
But the next night he came again,
And with a smile of love he said,
As he opened the book, and lo,
Ben Adhem's name led all the rest.

148   *Not Enough*

Stanley Shumway: I traveled extensively on business because we were in the sawmill business, and if you go anywhere in Arizona or New Mexico, it's a long ways. I would often have to go to Albuquerque or El Paso, two hundred or three hundred miles, leaving early in the morning and getting back after midnight, and sometimes I would in my mind concoct some little poem or something.

'Tis not enough to walk life's road
Disgruntled by your heavy load;
To only think of self, no more,
And count life's task a dreary chore.
No, not enough through life to go
With eye cast down and head bent low.
Sweetest joy will not be known
If you aim to live by bread alone.
A happier life will be for you
If you'll a nobler goal pursue.

Then greet each day with faith serene,
Let virtue guide, keep body clean,
Know happiness as you go along,
Fill the empty hour with song,
Think lofty thoughts, do worthy deed,
Give heart and hand to those in need,
And let this be your motto and your creed,
            "To Give Enough."

The Master said the life worthwhile
Is builded on the second mile.
When duty calls, be quick to hear,
Serve state and church with equal cheer.
Then walk life's road with eager tread,
Lift up the eye, unbow the head,
And let it in truth of you be said,
            "He gave enough."

I wrote that about ten years ago.

149   *Homecoming*

**Alida Connolly: I don't know which one to do. I've got a hundred here, but I
think I'll get serious now. This is going to be read at my funeral if I ever turn
up my heels and die. I know this one real well. I'll get up from my coffin and
read it myself.**

When my time has come to shuffle off,
Please don't anybody cry.
It's been a lot of fun, this life,
But I'm not afraid to die.

And if I'm still hovering around
Between you and the atmosphere,
I'd like to see fond, loving smiles,
So don't let me see a single tear.

I'd like you to sing some lovely songs
And tell of fond, funny things I've done.
It will make me happy as I linger there
Before my journey has begun.

For what is death but a short, sad parting,
The opening of a half-closed door
To find old friends and loved ones waiting
To guide you across that misty shore.

To me it will be
The most glorious experience this girl ever had
The day I step through that half-opened doorway
Into the arms of my dear old dad.

I never had a chance to know him
For he was called when I was young.
Oh, it will be the most glorious meeting!
How glad the day! How bright the sun!

And there will be another Father,
Oh, lucky me having two.
I hope He'll take my hand and say,
"Come in, my child, there's much that you can do."

So just wish me joy as you gather round,
Rejoice and happy be,
And hurry and finish your small tasks,
And come on over and visit me.

150 *This is My Creed*

Alida Connolly:

A little work,
A little fun,
A little laughter
When day is done,

A little home
With an open gate,
With friends coming in
Early and late,

A little family
Of girls and boys,
For this is one
Of the greatest joys,

A touch of sadness
With joy to blend,
The better to know
The comfort of a friend,

A loving heart,
A desire to reach
All those in need,
Inspire and teach.

Give me a spirit
Meek and mild,
Let me help and inspire
A suffering child,

So I may say
With the setting sun,
"A life well lived,
A race well done."

151 *The Harvest of Leaves*

Alida Connolly: This is one I wrote for the family reunion.

I'm just a leaf
On the family tree,
But my days are numbered
In eternity,

And deep go my roots
Vital and strong,
Oh, proud grows the tree
To which I belong,

And though among millions
I am just one,
Like all of the others,
I have my day in the sun

To sparkle and glisten
In the bright summer day
Till the cold autumn winds
Carry me away

And change my green dress
To scarlet and gold
As the chill winds whisper,
"Growing old! Growing old!"

And as if in a dream I drift
Silently from the tree,
Hark! My falling was noted
In eternity.

Not a second do I wait
In the chill, icy breeze,
But gloriously I arise
In the harvest of leaves.

152   *Don't Fence Me In*

Reinhold "Tex" Bonnet: This is the way I feel.

Oh, when I die,
You just bury me
Way out West
Where the winds blow free.
Let cattle romp
My tombstone down,
Let coyotes mourn their kin,
Let horses come
And paw the mound,
But, please, don't fence me in.

CHAPTER TEN

And I'll Tell You Another

THE FIRST CHAPTER OBSERVED that this book is a mystery asking who done it, what they did, and why they did it. The clues have presented themselves, and it is time to deduce answers to the questions.

There were twenty-eight reciters who created and controlled stages and spoke their speeches. The reciters ranged from 3 to 92 years of age at the times they were recorded, but they fit into three age groups. Van, Deedra, Sara, and Vandee Holyoak and Kristi Hodge were all between 3 and 13 years old when they were recorded. Van N. Holyoak, Joe S. Holyoak, Ada Holyoak Fowler and Alice Tripp were all 30 to 50 years old when they were recorded. The remaining nineteen performers were all over 60 years of age at the times of their lives represented in the book. There were fifteen male and thirteen female reciters.

Twelve of the performers lived in or around Clay Springs, Arizona. Ten came from the St. Johns, Arizona, area. Billy Simon lived just outside the Prescott, Arizona, city limits. Austin, Texas, is Alice Tripp's home. Joe Bolander lives in Orderville, Utah. Winnemucca, Nevada, is Tex Bonnet's home. Leon Lambson resides in the little town of Ramah out in New Mexico. Madeline Collins retired to Flagstaff, Arizona.

Twenty-four of the twenty-eight performers are members of the Mormon Church and live in Clay Springs, Arizona; St. Johns, Arizona; Orderville, Utah; or Ramah, New Mexico, which are all Mormon communities in terms of history and settlement. Madeline Collins is an active member of a Flagstaff, Arizona, Catholic Church. Tex Bonnet and Alice Tripp live in predominately non-Mormon communities, and so did Billy Simon.

For many of the performers, recitation scripts and the tradition of recitation were gifts of inestimable value sanctified by the fact that they were presented through example by beloved parents or grandparents from childhood on. Margaret Witt, Don Jackson, Leon and Delbert Lambson, Anona Heap and Alida Connolly, and Ralph Rogers fondly remember that their mothers were reciters. Elda Brown, Madeline Collins, Joe S. Holyoak, and Ada Holyoak Fowler all explained that their fathers were major influences and examples who led them to recite. Other performers stressed that recitations were a vital, natural, and widespread phenomena of their childhoods.

Joe Bolander and Anona Heap learned and performed recitations within the context of their high school educations. Joe Holyoak wrote poems as a part of his high school education. Kristi Hodge wrote a poem and entered it in a junior high school English contest. Stanley Shumway remembers recitations and recitation being taught in his college English courses.

Joe Bolander and E. Z. Nielsen learned recitations from phonograph records. Margaret Witt, Don Jackson, Horace Crandell, Anona Heap, and many more performers learned recitations from books. Billy Simon and Ralph Rogers learned recitations from the performances of others. Delbert Lambson and Kristi Hodge learned recitations from handwritten or photocopied texts furnished to them by performers whose performances they admired.

There are eight communities and five states presented as examples of homes of the recitation in the American West. Recitation as traditional performance is today both more widespread and more vigorous in Mormon communities than in other Western communities. The fact that Madeline Collins, Billy Simon, Tex Bonnet, and Alice Tripp are not Mormon, however, demonstrates that the recitation tradition is not exclusively Mormon. The fact that Alice Tripp learned her recitations from her Southern grandmother in the South demonstrates that the recitation tradition is not exclusively Western. Reciting is a traditional talent learned within tradition by the traditional method of seeing and hearing family members or others recite. Popular and folk, official and unofficial culture are united in presenting and preserving recitation as a performance option for the performers.

There are similarities and differences in what the reciters recite. The most obvious distinction is that 134 of the 153 texts are poetry and only 19 are prose. Of the 19 prose recitations, 15 were learned by their performers from recordings, books, pamphlets, or other sources. Only LaVelle Whiting DeSpain's "Good Morning, Dr. Martin," Anona Heap's "To Ramah and My Father," and Joe Holyoak's unusual reporting of a dialogue in "The Telephone Conversation" are prose recitations written by their performers. These are also the only prose recitations except for "A Little Parable for Mothers," performed by Anona Heap but not written by her, that are serious in tone.

Frank Desprez's "Lasca," for a long period of time the most popular recitation in the American West; "Green Eye of the Little Yellow God," the most popular British recitation from its composition to the present; and Thayer's "Casey at the Bat," quite possibly the best known poem in America today, are all examples of the 58 percent of the recitations in verse in the book that entered tradition from popular poetry. Poetry written by the people who perform it or by other folk poets makes up an equally impressive 42 percent of the total verse recitations. Many of the poems, "Sheridan, Twenty Miles Away," for example, are dramatic and serious in tone; others like "My Last Request" are predominately humorous, and a small number, "Putting a Town on the Map" or "Memories of Vernon" for instance, blend humor and seriousness.

Recitations include examples of many forms of traditional literature. Van Holyoak, Ralph Rogers, and Tex Bonnet, among others, all recited items that they quite correctly reported were more often performed as songs. They also sometimes sang these items. Joe Bolander does not sing, but he recites a number of songs. The performers distinguished between songs and recitations based on how the items were performed.

Elda Brown's "Willy and The Giants" and LaVelle Whiting DeSpain's "Big Klaus and Little Klaus," which traces to the same source, are classic European folk tales recited in Arizona. Alice Tripp's "The Tree Deedle" is a Texas transplant of the same literary form.

Joe Bolander's "Let Us Spray" is a joke based on word play and has minimal narrative content or introduction. He recited it and employed it as a transition between longer items as a part of the recitation "set" or program he regularly performs.

E.Z. Nielsen's "Uncle Josh Gets a Letter from Home" and his "Coonskin Huntin' Down in Moonshine Holler," both learned from early 78-rpm recordings, are popular culture comic monologues. Joe Bolander learned his popular culture comic monologue "The Revival Meeting at Pumpkin Center" from an even earlier Edison cylinder record.

Anona Heap wrote three versions of "To Ramah and My Father" for three different audiences. She wrote them, she recites them, and they are autobiography or family history.

Most of the poems adopted by reciters from popular poetry are narratives and tell stories. Many of the poems written by their performers are lyric and concentrate upon expressing emotions rather than upon telling stories.

What all the one hundred fifty-three recitations have in common is performance. Elements of performance run through all of them. Most of them are actually performed before an audience. Those that are not performed before an audience adhere to performance characteristics and could be. The size of the audiences for the performances ranges from a few family members to fairly large groups that are a part of family or community gatherings, but they share a basic familiarity with the conventions of recitation performance. Performance is introduced, indicated, and communicated in various subtle and not so subtle ways. The performers and their performances are formally introduced by others or they introduce themselves. They stand while their audience remains seated. By their performance, they create and command an invisible stage so that their audiences recognize recitation in progress, enter the performance, play their role. A theatrical or subtle gesture, a twinkle in the eye, words that tumble over each other, a shout, a whisper, the rising and the falling of pitch, silence—all call into being a world of the imagination wherein the audiences feel the hot breath of cattle gaining and share with the performers joy and sorrow, laughter and tears. Recitation is performance. Recitation is drama.

All one hundred fifty-three recitations are scripted, fixed form, non-extemporaneous performance. Sometimes the performers have memorized their recitations. Sometimes the performers read their recitations. In either case, both the reciters and their audiences have a clear concept of a script, a correct form of that which is being performed. Scripts often include introductions, conclusions, and "asides" that may appear spontaneous but are also fixed form. Joe Bolander's "Blue Hen Chicken," Grant Brown's "Setting a Hen," Horace Crandell's "Lasca," and Van Holyoak's version of the same poem indicate that each performer develops his own script, and that the term "fixed form" must not be understood too rigidly; but recitation is scripted performance. Performers correct themselves when they have made even minor departures from their written or internal texts. Wilford Shumway's audience each time anticipates the points during his performance of "Casey at the Bat" when he will spit water in imitation of Casey's spitting tobacco juice by getting out of the line of fire (or water).

Dramatic oral performance of scripted poems and stories from a variety of sources has been a British and Anglo-American popular culture and folk art form from at least the mid-seventeenth century on. Many early phonograph records, both cylinder and 78-rpm disks, produced and distributed across America in the first quarter century of the history of the media were recorded recitation performances. Professional popular entertainers from Cal Stewart to Johnny Cash wrote, performed, and recorded recitations, and many reciters learned items from popular records.

Recitations are still a part of popular culture and popular entertainment in the British Isles and the United States. Programs as varied as the Celi held at Bunratty Folk Park in Shannon, Ireland, and the Old West Show held in Mesa, Arizona, continue to feature recitations as a part of their performances. The recitation is not as common in popular entertainment in either the British Isles or America in the 1980s as it was in the 1880s, and recitation performances are not as common in the folk cultures of the two areas as they once were. Wherever there are opportunities for reciters to perform, and their performances are valued by their audiences, however, recitation continues.

Recitations use language in special ways. Many comic prose monologues employ pseudo-dialects as a major source of their humor. Others use departures from standard English in the same way for the same purpose. "He asked me he didn't care," serves as a chorus for "Coonskin Huntin' Down in Moonshine Holler." "Quick as a Telephone" uses Victorian English. "A Little Parable for Mothers" draws upon the language of the King James version of the Bible. Poems written by their performers often utilize a poetic diction with archaic words and inverted sentence structures and special pronunciations.

There has long been an offical Anglo-American art poetic based upon the normal, accepted pronunciations of individual words and their syntactical relationships. *Pronunciation,* for instance, is usually pronounced as a five-syllable word with stresses on the second and fourth syllables. Conjunctions and articles are rarely accented in this poetic, which considers and counts both accented and unaccented syllables.

Alongside the official Anglo-American art poetic, Anglo-American folk culture has preserved another poetic based upon recurring patterns of stresses. This poetic, like the art poetic, is based upon normal pronunciations of words and their syntax, but it is much less restrictive. The stresses may fall upon a syllable which would normally be accented or upon one which would normally be unaccented or upon an article or conjunction. The major difference between the Anglo-American folk poetic and the Anglo-American art poetic is that the folk poetic, like many others of the world, does not consider or count unaccented syllables, which may occur in any number and relationship to the accented syllables.

You've seen how they "DA da DA da DA da DA-A." This basic Anglo-American oral formula is often written by folk and popular poets as a long line with seven stresses and with the last words of each line rhyming. For example:

DA   da   DA da   DA   da DA-A
She's grunting and groaning, and her eyes are glazed.

DA da   DA da   DA da DA-A
Her color's not good, and her hair has raised.

Performed—no matter how it is written—as a four-line unit with the first and third lines having four stresses and the second and fourth having three stresses and end rhyme, this basic oral formula is indicated in writing by punctuation reflecting speech patterns and serving as a guide to oral performance. The first and the third lines of this poetic pattern each have four major stresses. The second and the fourth lines each have three major stresses. The last word in the second line rhymes with the last word in the last line. The basic oral pattern includes four units. For example, LaVelle performs her "The Day Mother Saved Our Bacon" as follows:

DA   da   DA da
She's grunting and groaning, (pause)

           DA   da DA-A
And her eyes are glazed. (longer pause)

DA da   DA da
Her color's not good, (pause)

           DA da DA-A
And her hair has raised. (major pause)

Recited poems which have been adapted by their performers from popular culture sometimes were written following the conventions of the Anglo-American art poetic. Stanley Shumway, Milo Whitbank, and Delbert Lambson also sometimes created within the conventions of the Anglo-American art poetic.

Many of the poems created by their performers and many of those adopted and adapted by them from popular poetry, however, march to the beat of the Anglo-American folk poetic. To some reciters, the poetic they perform is unspoken, an echo on the edge of consciousness; to others, the poetic is a pattern sensed so clearly that they can articulate and parody it. To both kinds and to those between, their poetic is a heartbeat, an oral poetry, a structural formula most often assimilated and most frequently empowered unconsciously. Like Abou Ben Adhem's angel, this poetic is encountered in dreams or in the "becoming" between awake and asleep, asleep and awake, when dualities merge and are no more, and the present actualizes life by fashioning it into ancient forms.

That the oral formula, like Anglo-Saxon verse, can have any number of unstressed syllables per line allows the poet a great deal of flexibility. Ada Holyoak Fowler frequently uses lines with very few unstressed sylla-bles to create a powerful effect with her words hammering "clean to the bone" (121). Alida Connolly uses unusually long lines with many un-stressed syllables to express and share her joyous appreciation of "All the songs which were played, waltzed, fox-trotted, and one-stepped to," (80) to evoke the graceful movement and motion of dance. Poets use patterns to tell the stories they wish to tell and to convey the emotions they wish to convey. Changes in the pattern or tone are used to indicate changes in meaning. Poets internalize the oral formula by hearing and seeing it performed. Poets learn the form's conventions and commonplaces in the same way. In the same manner, poets learn that the Anglo-American oral formula is appropriate for expressing emotions.

Sometimes they do not use what they have learned until an occasion and a need occur years later. In the stillness of a storm or the solitude of an automobile or the freedom between states of being, they hear new worlds, joys, and woes shaped by old structures—oral formulaic composition built upon traditional Anglo-American structural formulas and attendant phrasal and imagery patterns. They hear. They assert consciousness. On scraps of paper with flashlight pens they create that which they have heard; they read their creations to family and friends; by their creation and by their reading they affirm life, and love, and all of that; by their affirmation of life, of love, of all of that a poet-reciter is born.

Reciters recite because it is a socially accepted way of entertaining and performing, taught by example and by schools as desirable and useful. Reciters recite because in so doing they keep alive the memory of parents and grandparents. Reciters recite because it is a good way to put kids to bed or keep them from destroying each other on long car trips. Poets write as grief work. Poets write because there is a socially valued role for poems written for events such as golden wedding anniversaries. Reciters recite both poems and stories they have written and poems and stories they have adopted because it is a way they have learned to express inexpressible emotions—a way of expressing and exorcising "some sort of ah-h-h-h-h," a way of coming to terms with life and love and all of that. Reciters recite and poets write for recitation because that which they create and that which they adopt and adapt alike embody their values and beliefs while fulfilling their expectations and their emotional needs. Reciters speak their lives and cultures as they speak their lines.

The same summer I recorded Van N. Holyoak and Horace Crandell, I also recorded Billy Simon. He sang a number of Western songs and contributed the two recitations he had learned from Bud Ogle. When I had recorded everything I knew that he performed and was ready to end the session, he stepped up to the microphone one last time and began the introduction to a poem he said he wished to use to conclude his performance.

153 *Sharlot Hall's Poem*

Billy Simon: Now, we've gone through all this rigmarole of songs and recitations and stuff, and I never did consider myself any good afoot, and to kinda put a lid on this thing to finish off with, I was reminded of a little piece of poetry that Sharlot Hall wrote. She was a great character, and everybody thought the world of Sharlot Hall, but this little one thing that she wrote is kind of stuck in my mind, and it's sorta like a prayer, and it goes like this.

A long, long train of horsemen,
Yet never a hoof beat sounds,
And never a dust bird rises
From the trampled sporting grounds.

Abreast in marshal order,
They wheel and swing to place,
But their forms are thin and misty,
And a shadow dims each face.

A pale and still battalion,
In Stetsons, chaps, and spurs,
And they still bow to the grandstands,
But the picture swims and blurs.

The picture swims and blurs, and Billy is gone, and Van is gone, and Uncle Horace is gone, and Grandpa Whiting is gone, and so shall the other performers be gone, too, in the fullness of their times, in the twinkling of an eye, in the shedding of a tear; yet by their recorded recitation performances built upon and reflective of their lives, their loves, and all of that, these my precious friends, my cherished memories, have become your precious friends, your cherished memories—still they bow to the grandstands.

And now my story's done.

Collection Notes

These notes are designed to give information about the authors and sources of the items whose performances are recorded and transcribed in the book and about the items themselves and their collection.

For recitations which are well known as folktales, tale type and/or motif numbers are given which refer to the systems employed in Ernest W. Baughman, *Type and Motif-Index of the Folktales of England and North America,* Antti Aarne and Stith Thompson, *The Types of the Folktale,* and Stith Thompson, *Motif-Index of Folk Literature*—the standard indices of narrative elements found in American folk tradition. Folklorists use type and motif numbers to annotate folktales in order to demonstrate their existence and distribution within tradition. Baughman's numbers are cited first, and Aarne-Thompson and Thompson numbers are used if Baughman does not list parallel material. Type and motif numbers are not given, however, for recitations which have not been frequently reported as folktales.

Since many of the items come from the borderline between popular and folk culture as they are usually defined, information about some is somewhat sketchy and simply not available for others. Unless noted otherwise, all recordings were made by Keith and/or Kathy Cunningham, and all transcriptions were done by Keith Cunningham.

Oh, I'll Tell You a Story

1. It is appropriate that "Lasca" is the first recitation in the book; this poem by the English playwright and journalist Frank Desprez (1853-1916) was for many years one of the most popular and widely known recitations in the American West. It is one of the most thoroughly researched of Western recitation texts. Its wide dissemination is reflected in its publication in *Montana Live-Stock Journal* in 1888 and its release on at least six commercial records between 1909 and 1922, including one version recorded by the great cowboy film star William S. Hart. The pioneering folklorist John Lomax reported in his autobiography that he learned the poem as a recitation in 1887 and performed it at an annual meeting of the Modern Language Association a few years thereafter. (If his ground-breaking collections of cowboy ballads had included recitations as well as songs, they would certainly be better known among folklorists today.) This performance was recorded at Northern Arizona University in Flagstaff, Arizona, July 3, 1971.

2. All three of Van's stories about his father have independent existences as folktales. The first, "Switching the Babies," was included in an episode in Owen Wister's *The Virginian.* The second is a part of the folklore of many Mormon families in the West, and the third has been frequently collected in Europe and America. Tale type 1920B, "I have not time to lie," applies here.

"Rodeo Judge" was one of Van's favorites. He included it in the collection of his poems he prepared and gave to his friends. It provides a fascinating view of the small local rodeos which are so much a part of the American West. Recorded July 3, 1971, at Northern Arizona University.

Mostly for Entertainment

3. The popular performer Cal Stewart, who billed himself as "the talking machine story teller," recorded thousands of recitations during the 1890s and the early decades of the twentieth century. His "Uncle Josh Weathersby" recordings were particularly popular, and a number of them have survived in traditional oral performance in the American West. Jim Lawson was featured in many of Stewart's recitations. The episode of Jim getting his wooden leg stuck in a knothole in a board sidewalk was a recurring joke featured in many of the individual records. Joe retained Stewart's trademark laugh, which he always employed at the beginning of his records and stage performances as a part of his Uncle Josh recitation. We have three recordings of Joe performing "The Revival Meeting at Punkin Center," and his introduction and text are very much the same on all three. This version was recorded at his home in Orderville, Utah, November 26, 1987, by his grandson.

4. "A Song of the Beach" is an item that was once used in vaudeville and burlesque shows, and was also printed in numerous jokebook anthologies. Dialect has long been a major source of American folk humor and is a major source of entertainment in the recitation as well. The central character and speaker of "A Son of the Beach" is an example of the worldwide "wise fool" tradition. Elda's closing comment, "Now, I want to tell you about my quilting," shows that she viewed recitation as one of her arts. Recorded at her home in St. Johns, Arizona, July 11, 1987.

5. Joe Bolander's "The Blue Hen Chicken" is another example of the many prose recitations in dialect. Joe's history of how he came to learn the recitation is extremely interesting. Recorded at his home in Orderville, Utah, November 26, 1987, by his grandson.

6. Milo Wiltbank, described by his cousin Alida Connolly as "just a big old cowboy," is the best known of the St. Johns, Arizona, popular poets because he was a regular guest on a Phoenix television program in the late 1960s and early 1970s. Uncle Horace's performance of "Trapper Bill" was recorded at a session at Northern Arizona University August 5, 1975, and was included on the documentary record *Uncle Horace's Recitations.*

7. Loosely narrative texts utilizing the same pun found in "Let Us Spray" as a punch line are most often encountered as jokes. Joe Bolander, however, used his tale for a change of pace or transition between longer items during his recitation performance. Recorded at Joe's home in Orderville, Utah, November 26, 1987, by his grandson.

8. E.Z. Nielsen's "Uncle Josh Gets a Letter from Home" is another of Cal Stewart's Uncle Josh recitations and, like Joe Bolander's (3), was learned by its present performer from a recording. This performance was recorded in St. Johns, Arizona, June 3, 1988.

9. Uncle Horace's "My Last Request," recorded at Northern Arizona University August 4, 1975, and included on the record *Uncle Horace's Recitations,* is an excellent example of the many dialect recitations that were once popular in the American West.

10. Recorded in St. Johns, Arizona, June 3, 1988, E. Z.'s "Coonskin Huntin' down in Moonshine Holler" is another prose, dialect recitation text that was learned from a recording originally. It is a version of a well known international folktale.

11. "When Melindy Sings," recorded at Northern Arizona University August 4, 1975, and included on Uncle Horace's recitation album, is a version of "When Malindy Sings" written by the well-known American popular poet Paul L. Dunbar (1872-1906) and published in 1903. The speaker is presented with great sympathy.

12.   Recorded in St. Johns, Arizona, June 3, 1988. "That Wedding Scaremony" is another reminder of the popularity of dialect recitations.

13.   "Are you Growing Older?" was recorded at Anona Heap's St. Johns, Arizona, home July 11, 1988, and may very well be too close to home. That, of course, is what makes it funny.

14.   The similarities in theme and plot and dialect between Uncle Horace's "The Jewish Wedding," recorded at Northern Arizona University August 5, 1975, and "That Wedding Scaremony" (12) are striking.

15.   Katy G. Lee's poem "The Joke," which she learned from her father, was recorded June 3, 1988, in St. Johns, Arizona, and is another recitation making fun of a group (in this case the English) in terms of popular stereotypes.

16.   Grant E. Brown was recorded by Carolyn Nielsen at his home in Eagar, Arizona, July 18, 1988. This recitation, "A Preacher Preaching About the Bible," has been collected in Illinois and Missouri as well as in Arizona.

17.   Recorded in St. Johns, Arizona, August 11, 1988, "The Christmas Villain," described by its author LaVelle Whiting DeSpain as "a kind of a reading," demonstrates the often close link between recitation and folk drama.

18.   Grant E. Brown's "Setting a Hen," recorded July 11, 1988, at his home in Eagar, Arizona, by Carolyn Nielsen, is clearly related to Joe Bolander's "The Blue Hen Chicken," and they probably have a common source. Katrina and Socrey were characters in a whole series of popular recitation texts.

19.   LaVelle Whiting DeSpain's "Good Morning, Dr. Martin" is a dramatic prose recitation she wrote for performance by a member of her family. Recorded at her home in St. Johns, Arizona, August 11, l988.

Mostly for Children

20.   "Oh, I'll Tell You a Story" is the recitation equivalent of the type of folktale know as an "endless tale." The idea is that the teller repeats the text over and over until the audience begs for mercy. The recitation was recorded at LaVelle's home in St. Johns, Arizona, August 11, 1988.

21.   Newspaper columnist and popular poet Eugene Field (1850-1895) is the author of the classic poem "The Sugar Plum Tree," which is frequently performed for children. It is interesting to note that Uncle Horace was quite sure he had heard Van Holyoak recite the poem, but Van had no memory of ever having done so. This performance was recorded at Northern Arizona University August 4, 1975, and included on the record *Uncle Horace's Recitations.*

22.   "Put My Little Shoes Away" is very well known as a folksong, and was written in 1873 by Samuel N. Mitchell and Charles E. Pratt. Madeline Collins's recitation version, contributed by her to the Northern Arizona Folklore Archive March 11, 1979, is a reminder that one performer's song is often another performer's recitation.

23.   How varied are the recitations used to put kids to sleep! Robert Service (1874-1958) was identified by Van as the author of "Big Wicked Bill," and Kristi's version was collected in Clay Springs, Arizona, November 30, 1987. The poem is one of the few recitations she has learned and performs that was not written by her grandfather Van. She associates it with him, and she loves the story.

24.   James Whitcomb Riley (1849-1916) was a journalist and popular poet who made more money from his writings than any other literary figure of his day—not bad for a period that included Mark Twain! Alice's performance, recorded in her home in Austin, Texas, November 28, 1987, is a reminder of the important fact that the dialects of recitations were sight dialects indicated imprecisely in print by spelling and often altered in performance. "Little Orphant Annie" was written by Riley to represent an Indiana Hoosier dialect. The language of Alice's version bears the stamp of both Kentucky, where she learned it from her grandmother, and Texas, where she has lived most of her life.

25.   Ralph Rogers's "Irish Washer Woman," recorded at his home in Clay Springs, Arizona, December 19, 1987, is an example of a poem usually performed as a song being used for a recitation. "Irish Washer Woman" in fact is most often reported today as a tune without words, so this recitation performance preserves a set of words that are, by and large, unknown at the present time.

26.   One of the folklore forms most sought after by American folklorists has been the long European folktales called *Marchen* in international folklore scholarship. Few of these stories have been reported from America and almost none outside of the Southern Mountain folk region. Elda Brown's "Willy and the Giants" is another version of the highly prized "Jack Tales." What is interesting beyond the rarity of the story is that her version is fixed text. From her memory of her father's telling, Elda fashioned and then memorized the version she created. Recorded at her home in St. Johns, Arizona, by a family member February 26, 1974.

1640 III, "Lucky Hunter"; K1082.1, "Missile thrown among enemy causes them to fight one another"; K771, "Unicorn tricked into running horn into tree"; K731, "Wild boar captured in church"; 1088, "Eating contests"; and K81.1, "Deceptive eating contest."

27.   Grant E. Brown's "Companion Poems" were recorded at his home in Eagar, Arizona, by Carolyn Nielsen July 18, 1988. They may have no redeeming value whatsoever, but they sure are fun, and kids love the playful anarchy they present.

28.   "The Bee Sting," recorded in St. Johns, Arizona, July 11, 1988, as performed by its author, is Alida's most popular recitation among the adults and children who are her usual audience.

29.   Alice's "Raggedy Man" was written by James Whitcomb Riley. The Raggedy Man was a character in several of his most popular poems. Recorded at Alice's home in Austin, Texas, November 28, 1987.

30.   Margaret Witt's performance of "Essay on the Frog," recorded at her home in Clay Springs, Arizona, May 14, 1988, is a thoroughly delightful piece of nonsense.

31.   "Big Klaus and Little Klaus," like Elda Brown's "Willy and the Giants" (26), is another European *Marchen* and traces to the same source as Grandpa Whiting. It has also become a fixed text recitation in its transmission. Recorded at LaVelle's home in St. Johns, Arizona, August 11, 1988.

1535, "The Rich and the Poor Peasant"; K1571.1, "Trickster as sham magician makes adulteress produce hidden food for her husband"; K114.1.1, "Alleged oracular horse-hide sold": K443.1, "Hidden paramour buys freedom from discoverer": K941.1, "Cows killed for their hides when large price is reported by trickster": K940.2, "Man betrayed into killing his wife or grandmother": and K842, "Dupe persuaded to take prisoner's place in a sack and killed."

32.   Joe Bolander's "The Good Old Days," which he attributes to Ruth Shook, is widely known and appreciated as an antidote to the romantic views of the past espoused by many other recitations. Recorded at his home in Orderville, Utah, by his grandson November 26, 1987.

33.   Grant E. Brown's "A Teacher's Tools" is a description of recitation performance and includes several short recitation items. My wife's father in Illinois said that the difference between a duck was that one of his legs ain't alike: version and variation. Recorded at Grant's home in Eagar, Arizona, July 18, 1988, by Carolyn Nielsen.

34.   Parodies of the familiar "Mary Had a Little Lamb" nursery rhyme are among the most frequently reported Anglo-American folk verses. This parody reflects the fact that rural Arizona was predominantly Democratic in politics in the 1930s. Recorded at Van's home in Clay Springs, Arizona, March 13, 1980.

35.   "Ooey Gooey Was a Worm" is a widely distributed children's rhyme. Kristi's nose wrinkling is beautiful to behold. Recorded at Clay Springs, Arizona, November 30, 1987.

36.   Ada remembers that "There Were Two Bums" was one of the most successful recitations Van taught Kristi to perform; it upset a lot of people! Recorded at Clay Springs, Arizona, November 30, 1987.

37.   Arthur Godfrey used to perform a "Mary, Mary, Quite Contrary" which was very similar to this version recorded at Clay Springs, Arizona, November 30, 1987.

38.   Unlike the "Mary Had a Little Lamb" taught to Van by his father, this version, which he taught Kristi, reflects the fact that rural Arizona was predominantly Republican in politics in the 1960s. Recorded at Clay Springs, Arizona, November 30, 1987.

39.   "I'm a Cute Little Girl," recorded at Clay Springs, Arizona, November 30, 1987, is remembered as being very successful at embarrassing parents and delighting grandpa.

40.   Recorded at Clay Springs, Arizona, November 30, 1987, "I Love Myself" was accompanied by gestures that Kristi remembers her grandpa teaching her as a part of its performance.

41.   "Fuzzy Wuzzy" is known all across America. Recorded November 30, 1987, at Clay Springs, Arizona.

42.   The story that Kristi tells as a part of her performance of "Where's the World's Best Grandpa?" was recorded at Clay Springs, Arizona, November 30, 1987, and has become fixed text; she incorporated the question and answer in the narrative every time she told us about them.

43.   "Questions and Answers," recorded November 30, 1987, at Clay Springs, Arizona, includes Kristi's description of Van's part in its performance and is an example of the link between folk drama and recitations.

44.   Kristi's statement that she wishes to teach her recitations to her cousins because she feels they will give them a part of their grandpa shows that for her, too, recitations concern life and love, and all of that. Recorded at Clay Springs, Arizona, November 30, 1987.

45.   "Garbage Truck Monster" was written by Jane Morton and published in the March 1988 issue of *The Friend*. It was recorded by Debbie Holyoak at her home in Clay Springs, Arizona, May 5, 1989.

46.   Recorded at Joe Holyoak's home in Clay Springs, Arizona, on December 19, 1987, "If I Was a Blossom" is a poem he wrote for his children.

47. "A Smile" is a version of "Let Us Smile" written by Wilbur D. Nesbit (1871-1927). Ralph Rogers's version was recorded at his home in Clay Springs, Arizona, on December 19, 1987. Although he reported that it was taught to him as a song rather than as a recitation, the original version was published as a poem without music.

48. Grant E. Brown's performance of "A Lime Tong, Tong Ago" was recorded by Carolyn Nielsen at his home in Eagar, Arizona, July 18, 1988. I don't know how long it took him to learn it, but I know it took me a lime tong, indeed, to transcribe it.

49. LaVelle's "The Day Mother Saved Our Bacon" recorded at her home in St. Johns, Arizona, on August 11, 1988, is the key to the mystery of Anglo-American folk verse. That's how they did it.

50. Alice's "The Tree Deedle" is, she is careful to make clear, another fixed form recitation, although in other performances it could be a non-fixed form tale. "Deedle" is an archaic dialect term for devil.

About Adventure

51. Joe Bolander's "High Chin Bob" is a version of the poem "The Glory Trail" written in 1908 by Charles Badger Clark, Jr. (1883-1957) and first published in 1911 in *The Pacific Monthly* in Portland, Oregon. His poem passed into tradition, became a folksong, and is best known in that form. Joe's performance, recorded at his home in Orderville, Utah, October 6, 1988, is particularly interesting because he learned only the first and last verses and uses a prose transition of his own composition between them.

52. Van's version of "Lasca" is both an example of his humor and of how performers re-create their texts. As he explained, his version is the original poem by Frank Desprez, which was the indirect source for Uncle Horace's performance (1). It was recorded in Van's home in Clay Springs, Arizona, March 12, 1980.

53. "Coffee," recorded in Clay Springs, Arizona, November 30, 1987, is performed by Kristi as a tribute to her grandfather. It was one of the poems he included in the pamphlet of poetry he prepared using the pseudonym "the Poverty Flats Poet" and distributed to family and friends.

54. "Lazy Horse" is another one of Van's poems that Kristi memorized and recites. Her performance was recorded in her home in Clay Springs, Arizona, November 30, 1987.

55. Billy Simon's performance of "Airtights" was recorded at his home in Prescott, Arizona, May 3, 1971. It suggests that toasts may well have once been as common in Anglo-American folklore as they are yet today in the folklore of the British Isles.

56. "Jake Neal," recorded from the performance of its author, Delbert D. Lambson, at St. Johns, Arizona, June 3, 1988, was not a eulogy when it was written because Jake was still alive, but it is very much in the tradition of narrative obituary verse often noted by folklorists.

57. Delbert D. Lambson's "Sweet Freedom," performance recorded June 3, 1988, in St. Johns, Arizona, is a remarkable poem both because of the anti-trapping sentiment it expresses and because of its unusual and complex poetic structure.

58. Horace Crandell's "Sheridan, Twenty Miles Away," recorded at Northern Arizona University August 5, 1975, is a version of the poem "Sheridan's Ride" written by Thomas Buchanan Read (1822-1872). Read was during his lifetime considered the artistic equal of his friend Henry Wadsworth Longfellow and was equally admired as the painter of the popular picture "Sheridan's Ride."

59. Billy the Kid has been the subject of many well-known folk, popular, and even belletristic poems and songs. Tex Bonnet's "Billy the Kid," recorded at his home in Winnemucca, Nevada, October 16, 1979, is not any of them.

60. Madeline Collins's recitation "The Irishman's Lament," which she contributed to the Northern Arizona University Folklore Archive March 11, 1979, is a song she says her father used to recite.

61. "Casey at the Bat," by Ernest Lawrence Thayer (1863-1940), was first published in 1888 and was performed as a recitation by its author at a Harvard University class reunion in 1895. It was popularized as a recitation by the well-known performer De Wolf Hopper. Wilford J. Shumway's version, recorded at his office in St. Johns, Arizona, on September 4, 1989, includes a very interesting introduction and conclusion describing performance.

62. Uncle Horace's "The Cremation of Sam McGee," recorded at Northern Arizona University August 5, 1975, is a version of the poem published under the same title by Robert Service (1874-1958) and written in 1906. The poem is one of the most popular recitation items all across America.

63. Van's comment about "The Hermit of Shark Tooth Shoals," recorded at his home in Clay Springs, Arizona, March 13, 1980—that it is based on Service and his style, maybe—is absolutely right, probably. The poem is almost a parody of Service's internal rhyme, and the characters, too, seem to be exaggerated caricatures. Service, however, wrote and published a number of similar self-parodies in the 1950s.

64. Van was correct when he introduced his performance of "Abdul A-bul-bul A-mir," recorded at his home in Clay Springs, Arizona, on March 13, 1980, with the comment that lots of people recite or sing it.

This song is generally credited to William Percy French (1854-1920), who supposedly composed it for a college smoking concert at Trinity College, Dublin, in 1876. According to the French family tradition, it was first published in 1877. While this account is commonly accepted, it is problematic. No 1877 edition has ever been located; the earliest known copy is one published in 1886 by John Blockley under the title "Abdul, the Bulbul Ameer." The Blockley version was attributed to "Ali Baba," with no reference to French. This suggests that Blockley considered the song to be in public domain. French did not copyright the song either, so he may also have considered it in public domain and have merely arranged an already existing anonymous song that he was later credited for writing. The earliest printed reference to French as the composer-lyricist is a copy of the 1906 song "The Darlin' Girl from Clare," where it is noted that French also wrote "Abdallah Bulbul Ameer." It is frequently collected in the American West both as a song and a recitation.

65. J. Milton Hayes (1884-1940) in 1911 wrote the best known and most parodied of all British recitations, "The Green Eye of the Little Yellow God," and presented it to the public on the Bransby Williams Sunday Night Show. It was an immediate success and is still widely performed in Britain. Van's version, recorded in Clay Springs, Arizona, March 13, 1980, is very similar to the British original, and I wish he had remembered where and how he had learned it.

About Love

66. LaVelle's poem "A Young Girl's Prayer," which was recorded at her home in St. Johns, Arizona, August 11, 1988, is very well known and widely distributed in the area.

67. Grant was right; this poem, recorded by Carolyn Nielsen at his home in Eagar, Arizona, on July 18, 1988, is not "The Old Maid's Prayer." It is, however, similar, and it is interesting that the two are linked in his mind.

68. Van's "My Life History," recorded at his home in Clay Springs, Arizona, March 13, 1980, was an item he frequently performed, and it was included on his Rounder label LP record album *Tioga Jim*.

69. Don Jackson's "A Shack in the Mountains," recorded in his home in Clay Springs, Arizona, December 19, 1987, was learned from him by Van, who used the title "My Buddy" and included his version on a Rounder label LP record album sampler.

70. "The Face on the Barroom Floor" is one of the best-known American recitations, and its present-day popularity is at least partially due to a superb dramatic performance (with rinky-tink piano) recorded by Tex Ritter on the Capitol album *Blood on the Saddle*. Grant's version, recorded by Carolyn Nielsen at his home in Eagar, Arizona, July 18, 1988, retains the drama without the piano. The poem was written by Hugh Antoine D'Arcy (1853-1925) and was one of the poems Robert Service reported having learned and recited while he was living in the Yukon.

71. "Socrates Snooks" was written by Fitz Hugh Ludlow (1836-1870), a leading local color writer of the period whose reputation at one point exceeded that of Mark Twain. He is remembered today, if at all, for his first book, *The Hasheesh Eater*, which seems in many ways to have been after the manner of De Quincey's *Confessions of an English Opium-Eater*. In his own time, his humorous recitations were his most appreciated work. All of his biographies stress that his first marriage ended unhappily; perhaps "Socrates Snooks" is autobiographical. Don Jackson's version was recorded in Clay Springs, Arizona, on December 19, 1987.

72. Don Jackson's version of "Brought Back" was recorded in his home in Clay Springs, Arizona, on December 19, 1987. The poem was written by John F. Nicholls, an extremely popular recitation author at the turn of the century who is almost completely unknown today.

73. Grant E. Brown's "A Chinese Poem" is unusual in that it uses multicultural conventions of writing and printing as a major source of its humor. The performance was recorded at his home in Eagar, Arizona, by Carolyn Nielsen on July 18, 1988.

74. LaVelle's "Once Upon a Time," recorded in her home in St. Johns, Arizona, on August 11, 1988, includes an explanation in the introduction so that the poem is intelligible to a wider audience.

75. Horace Crandell considered "My Mother-in-Law" an extension of "Young Jacob Strauss" (88). The poem was also written by Charles Follen Adams (1842-1918) in a German sight dialect commonly called "scrapple English" and identified with the Pennsylvania Dutch emigrants. Uncle Horace's version was recorded at Northern Arizona University on August 5, 1975.

76. "Betty and the Bear" was frequently anthologized as recently as the 1920s and 1930s, but always as an anonymous poem. It was included in *Poems Teachers Ask for*, and the title says a lot. The Northern Arizona University Folklore Archive has several other versions collected from oral tradition in the West. This version was recorded at Joe Bolander's home in Orderville, Utah, on September 3, 1988.

77. Ada's "William and Mary" is an example of a poem written as a present. Her reading was recorded at her home in Clay Springs, Arizona, November 30, 1987.

78. "Lady, Queen of My Heart," by LaVelle Whiting DeSpain, indicates another link between recitation and song. Her reading and description of performance were recorded at her home in St. Johns, Arizona, on August 11, 1988.

79. "Hands" was recorded August 11, 1988, in St. Johns, Arizona, in the home of LaVelle Whiting DeSpain, who wrote the poem. It is in the tradition of special poems written for wedding anniversaries and is reminiscent of the song "These Hands," which is often sung at funerals in the area.

80. Alida's "Anona's Golden Wedding Day," recorded at Anona's home in St. Johns, Arizona, on July 11, 1988, is an example of a poem written for an anniversary.

81. Joe identifies Owen Sanders of Hurricane, Utah, as the author of "Let the Damn Grass Grow." Joe's performance of the poignant poem was recorded at his home in Orderville, Utah, by his grandson on November 26, 1987.

82. Anona included this poem from Lorenzo Brown's journals in a play about his life but performed the poem separately as a recitation. It was recorded at her home in St. Johns, Arizona, on July 11, 1988.

83. Alida's "Building for Life Eternal," recorded in St. Johns, Arizona, on July 11, 1988, employs carpentry images as an extended trope.

About Children

84. Delbert D. Lambson's "A Grandson's Love," recorded in St. Johns, Arizona, on June 3, 1988, is a description of the emotions called forth by being a grandfather.

85. "Drifted Out to Sea" was written by Rose Hartwick Thorpe (1850-1939), best remembered as the author of the immortal "Curfew Must Not Ring Tonight," which was one of Queen Victoria's favorite poems and is extremely well known both in the form she admired and in parodies. Margaret's version, which she calls "The Ocean Voyage," was recorded May 14, 1988, at her home in Clay Springs, Arizona.

86. "Quick As a Telephone" is notable for its Victorian English and by the fact that it is one of the few serious prose recitations included in the Northern Arizona University Folklore Archive. Margaret Witt's performance was recorded at her home in Clay Springs, Arizona, on May 14, 1988.

87. Margaret's versions of "A Child's Prayer," recorded May 14, 1988, at her home in Clay Springs, Arizona, is almost Shakespearean in the way it uses the prattling of a child to speak great truths.

88. "My Young Jacob Strauss" is another of the Charles Follen Adams's cycle of poems like "My Mother-in-Law" (75) written in "scrapple English." It was recorded at Northern Arizona University on August 4, 1975.

89. Ralph Rogers's version of "Freckles" was recorded as a recitation at his home in Clay Springs, Arizona on December 19, 1987. His performance of the same poem as a song was included on an Arizona Friends of Folklore label LP documentary record album.

90.   Joe's "Dad Book, Number One," recorded in his home in Clay Springs, Arizona, on December 19, 1987, recounts his response to Vandee's having a serious allergy reaction to a medication given to her at a hospital.

91.   "The Moon Shines Brighter" is another poem Joe wrote. His performance of it was recorded at his home in Clay Springs, Arizona, on December 19, 1987.

92.   Sam Walter Foss (1858-1911), author of "The Auctioneer's Gift," was another extremely popular, successful poet of his time largely forgotten today. Margaret Witt calls her version "The Auction," and her performance was recorded at her home in Clay Springs, Arizona, on May 14, 1988.

93.   Anona Heap's "To Ramah and My Father" is an autobiographical account of her years at Ramah, New Mexico. She performs all three versions she has written, and her choice of which to perform is based on her audience. All three are fixed text.

94.   Alida's "Busy Little Mother," recorded in St. Johns, Arizona, on July 11, 1988, is in the popular literary tradition of advice from an older to a younger person.

95.   "Memories of Vernon," written by Alida Connolly and recorded in St. Johns, Arizona, on July 11, 1988, is interesting because of the ethnographic detail it includes.

About Home and Place

96.   "Home" was written by Edgar A. Guest (1881-1959), who is said to have written more than 11,000 poems and was one of the most successful twentieth century writers of frequently recited poetry. Guest originally published the poem under the title "A Heap o' Living'" in 1916. Anona's version of "Home" was recorded at her home in St. Johns, Arizona, on July 11, 1988.

97.   LaVelle was recorded reading her poem "At Grandma's House" at her home in St. Johns, Arizona, on August 11, 1988. It is interesting that it describes the family's Christmas program and refers to "Big Klaus and Little Klaus" (31) as told by the family's grandfather.

98.   A survey by *Reader's Digest* in the 1940s reported that according to their readers Sam Walter Foss's poem "House by the Side of the Road" was the best known, best loved poem in America. Delbert's narrative recorded in St. Johns, Arizona, on June 3, 1988, adds meaning to the poem.

99.   According to Horace Crandell's comment, the poem "Are the Hills Still Green?," which was recorded at Northern Arizona University on August 5, 1975, is of relatively recent composition.

100.   Margaret Witt's version of "Putting the Town on the Map," recorded at her home in Clay Springs, Arizona, on May 14, 1988, is a fascinating echo of a time in the American West when every town expected and desired to become a metropolis.

101.   Jerome, Arizona, is one of the West's most famous ghost towns. It was a mining center that in 1929 had a population of 15,000. When the price of copper fell on the world market, mining became unprofitable, and the mining company at Jerome was dissolved in 1938. Because of the picturesque quality of the town with its old homes, stores, and churches perched precariously on steep slopes, the town has been reborn as a tourist attraction and art colony. Alida's poem "Jerome," recorded at St. Johns, Arizona, on July 11, 1988, humorously captures the romance of the town.

102. Nutrioso, Arizona, elevation 8,000 feet, is a beautiful and historic community located in tall pine country. "Our Fair Nutrioso," recorded in performance in St. Johns, Arizona, on July 11, 1988, by Alida Connolly, captures some of the appeal of the town.

103. Alida's poem "St. Johns," recorded at St. Johns, Arizona, July 11, 1988, is a lovely idealized description of American small town life.

104. Wilford J. Shumway was insistent that the poem "St. Johns' Pioneers," recorded in his office in St. Johns, Arizona, September 4, 1989, be described as something he changed to fit the area and its history. The poem was published in the St. Johns' centennial history.

105. Delbert's "This Was a Harsh and Barren Land," recorded in St. Johns, Arizona, on June 3, 1988, describes a typical Western experience of establishing a community in a difficult land.

106. "Dixie" was written by Charles L. Walker about 1870, and according to tradition, was first sung in a concert attended by George A. Smith (for whom the town of St. George, Utah, was named) and Brigham Young. It vividly describes the hardships of settling this desert land in southern Utah, which has average precipitation each year of just over six inches. The poem was once widely known and performed as a folksong with the title of "St. George and the Drag-on" and was collected in this form as recently as 1960. It is included in this form on a Library of Congress documentary LP album *Songs of the Mormons and Songs of the West.* Mormon folksinging, however, seems to have almost completely passed out of existence as a tradition in the American West, and Joe's recitation, recorded by his grandson on November 26, 1987, at his home in Orderville, Utah, thus preserves a set of words that otherwise might no longer be performed.

107. Joe's version of this poem, which he acknowledges is known by the titles "Once I Lived in Cottonwood," "The Red Hills of November," and "I Was Called to Dixie," was recorded by his grandson at his home in Orderville, Utah, on November 26, 1987. He performs it with "Dixie" (106) as a thematically related unit, and his prose introduction, aside, and conclusion are a consistent part of his performance. The poem, like "Dixie," was once widely distributed as a Mormon folksong. The original poem was written by George Hicks. Joe's comment that George Hicks "got in Dutch" with church leaders over his song echoes a widespread Mormon oral tradition. It was first published in a Salt Lake magazine in 1870.

108. Kristi Hodge's "Arizona," recorded at her home in Clay Springs, Arizona, on Nov. 30, 1987, is a reflection of the link between public schools and writing poetry for recitation. Yes, Arizona did get a pro team, and no (I asked), she had never read Tennyson's "Tintern Abbey."

109. Madeline Collins contributed her version of "Fair California" to the Northern Arizona University Folklore Archive on March 11, 1979. She attributes the poem to Marie K. Stokes.

110. "When the Frost Is on the Pumpkin" was included in a fifty page book *The Old Swimmin' Hole and 'Leven More Poems* James Whitcomb Riley (1849-1916) published in 1883. It proved to be one of his most popular and enduring poems. Uncle Horace's performance was recorded August 4, 1975, at Northern Arizona University and was included on the LP record album *Uncle Horace's Recitation.*

111. Joe's version of "Bacon" was recorded by his grandson at his home in Orderville, Utah, on November 26, 1987. The poem was written by Badger Clark and published in 1915 in the first edition of *Sun and Saddle Leather,* a collection of his poetry.

112. Milo Wiltbank's poem "Winds!" describes the major element in northern Arizona weather. Anona Heap's version was recorded at her home in St. Johns, Arizona, on July 11, 1988.

113. Badger Clark's "Jeff Hart" was published in the 1920 edition of his book *Sun and Saddle Leather.* Joe's version and artful introduction were recorded at his home in Orderville, Utah, on October 6, 1988.

114. Delbert's introduction to "His Guiding Hand," recorded as a part of his performance in St. Johns, Arizona, on June 3, 1988, adds greatly to the power of the poem.

115. Johnny Cash wrote "The Stars and Stripes" and performed it on several network television programs celebrating the anniversaries of major events in American history during the 1970s and 1980s, but Delbert, whose performance was recorded in St. Johns, Arizona, on June 3, 1988, had acquired the poem indirectly and was unaware of its author. Tradition lives.

About Mothers, Fathers, Sons, and Daughters

116. Stanley Shumway's "Recompense," recorded at his home in St. Johns, Arizona, on September 4, 1989, is sophisticated poetry both in theme and form. He provided copies of all of his poems included in the book as well as reading them, and the stanza divisions in these printed versions are his.

117. Van's "A Prayer for a Cowboy" was recorded at his home in Clay Springs, Arizona, on June 14, 1975. The poem was also read at his funeral.

118. Joe's "The Telephone Conversation," recorded at his home in Clay Springs, Arizona, on December 19, 1987, is a reflection of the ancient, widespread Euro-American belief that a person's last words are of particular significance and should be cherished.

119. Joe's poem "A Shadow," recorded at his home in Clay Springs, Arizona, on December 19, 1987, is remarkable for many reasons and particularly for the fact that the last stanza echoes the words his father wrote for his father (117).

120. Joe's comment in "Hello, Mr. Tombstone," recorded December 19, 1987, at his home in Clay Springs, Arizona, about "the record part" is one of the best reasons I've ever heard for collecting folklore.

121. Like her brother Joe, Ada Holyoak Fowler wrote poetry as a way of dealing with her father's death. Her "Farewell to Daddy" recorded at her home in Clay Springs, Arizona, on November 30, 1987, demonstrates her particularly effective use of short lines as a part of her craft.

122. Ada's "My Hill," recorded November 30, 1987, at her home in Clay Springs, Arizona, is another of her poems written for her father. Her explanation of the place of poetry in her life that she uses to conclude her performance is an important clue for us all.

123. Like her mother and uncle, Kristi turned to poetry to "get her feelings out" concerning her grandfather's death. Her performance of "Granddad" was recorded in Clay Springs, Arizona, on November 30, 1987.

124. Kristi does not like her poem "My Granddad," recorded November 30, 1987, in Clay Springs, Arizona, because, she explains, she "didn't really feel it." The first stanza echoes the poem Van wrote for his father (117), and the poem specifically mentions Van's skill at reciting.

125. Anona Heap's performance of "A Little Parable for Mothers" was recorded at her home in St. Johns, Arizona, on July 11, 1988. It is one of the few serious prose recitations in the Northern Arizona University Folklore Archive.

126. "End of a Perfect Day" is a song written by Carrie Jacobs Bond (1862-1946) in 1910. In spite of its unusually complex melody, it was an immediate popular success and continues to be sung at funerals to this day. One of her other major successes was the song "I Love You Truly," which was widely used at weddings for several decades. Anona Heap's version, recorded at her home in St. Johns, Arizona, on July 11, 1988, as a recitation, is a reminder that the words to the song have frequently been published separately as a poem.

127. Alida's "You Ask Me Am I Sad," recorded in St. Johns, Arizona, on July 11, 1988, echoes and extends the imagery of the well-known popular funeral hymn "Beyond the Sunset."

128. "Happy Birthday, Billy," recorded as performed by its author Alida Connolly on July 11, 1988, in St. Johns, Arizona, is in some ways a western "Little Boy Blue."

129. Mormon belief is reflected in LaVelle's "I Like to Think in That Far Land," recorded in her home in St. Johns, Arizona, on August 11, 1988, but the sentiments are universal.

130. LaVelle wrote "To My Dad" for her father and presented it to him. This performance was recorded August 11, 1988, in St. Johns, Arizona. She, like Joe Bolander, includes explanatory prose asides as a part of her performance.

131. "To Helen," recorded at St. Johns, Arizona, on August 11, 1988, is a poem LaVelle wrote for her sister.

132. Tex Bonnet was never able to recite a complete version of "That Silver Haired Daddy of Mine," a popular country and western song that he attributed to Gene Autry, without crying because it reminded him so much of his father. This performance was recorded at his home in Winnemucca, Nevada, on October 16, 1979.

About All of That

133. Margaret Witt's version of "The Old Plantation Mule," recorded at her home in Clay Springs, Arizona, on May 14, 1988, is sermonic.

134. Stanley Shumway's poem "Life," recorded at his home in St. Johns, Arizona, on September 4, 1989, is unusual in its form. It is important to note that stressing the last syllable of "eternity" to rhyme with "me" is a common convention of Western oral performance tradition.

135. The fact that questions unanswered remain in Stanley Shumway's "Storm Tossed," recorded on September 4, 1989, in his home in St. Johns, Arizona, echoes the ambiguity and tension that are the hallmarks of belletristic poetry.

136. Stanley Shumway's description of recitation instruction at Arizona State Teachers College is a fascinating conclusion to his personal poem "My Symphony" recorded September 4, 1989, in St. Johns, Arizona.

137.   Joe Holyoak said "The Snow," recorded at his home in Clay Springs, Arizona, on December 19, 1987, didn't start out to be a poem with theology, but it ended up getting that way.

138.   "Silver Jack" has a long and varied history as both a lumberjack and a cowboy ballad. Van's version, recorded as a recitation at his home in Clay Springs, Arizona, on March 13, 1980, probably derives from the version he read in one of the Lomax collections of cowboy songs, but it still is clearly his own.

139.   Many writers have commented on the Western cowboy's natural religion; "The Cowboy's Prayer," written by Badger Clark for his mother and published in his book *Sun and Saddle Leather* in 1915, is a powerful statement of this theology. Joe's version was recorded at his home in Orderville, Utah, on October 6, 1988.

140.   Billy's version of "She Was a Woman Long and Thin," recorded at Northern Arizona University on May 11, 1971, is similar in plot and theme to a number of Victorian poems.

141.   "Blue Eyes, Brown Eyes" is an assertion of selfhood very much in keeping with Western philosophy. Billy's version was recorded at Northern Arizona University on May 11, 1971.

142.   One of the major hits of the British music halls in 1936 was the poem "The Touch of the Master's Hand," written by Myra Brooks Welch and Ernest Longstaffe. The recitation was adapted to America by changing references to money from British currency to American currency, and the recitation quickly passed into tradition in the United States. Reflective of the fact that Leon was a professional entertainer for many years, his version with his band is extremely polished and dramatic. The introduction he wrote following the basic rhythm and rhyme of the original makes the version contributed by him on a cassette recording on June 9, 1988, uniquely his.

143.   Sam Walter Foss copyrighted "The Volunteer Organist" in 1892. The very next year, the Glenroy Brothers, popular entertainers whose performances mixed boxing and recitation, copyrighted it as a song. Uncle Horace's version was recorded at Northern Arizona University of August 5, 1975, and was included on his LP album of recitation performances.

144.   "Where Is My Wandering Boy Tonight?" was composed by the Reverend Robert Lowry (1826-1899), who also wrote "Shall We Gather at the River?" and the tune of "I Need Thee Every Hour." The song became extremely well known because it was included in a popular drama, "The Old Homestead." Uncle Horace's version, which was included on his documentary record album, was recorded at Northern Arizona University on August 5, 1975.

145.   LaVelle's "'Twas a Few Weeks Before Christmas" is a seasonal poem with a moral and was recorded on August 11, 1988, at her home in St. Johns, Arizona.

146.   Madeline Collins contributed her version of "Lady Yardley's Guest" to the Northern Arizona University Folklore Archive on December 7, 1978.

147.   James Henry Leigh Hunt (1784-1859) was an early champion of Keats and Shelley and is at least partially responsible for their successes. During his lifetime he was best known as a critic and journalist, but his poems "Abou Ben Adhem" (1834) and "Jenny Kissed Me" (1844) have survived in recitation tradition long after his familiar essays have been forgotten. Ralph Rogers's version of "Abou Ben Adhem," recorded at his home in Clay Springs, Arizona, on December 19, 1987, is a remarkable example of truncation. His text omits much of the original, yet retains its essential plot and theme.

148.   Stanley Shumway's "Not Enough," recorded at his home in St. Johns, Arizona, on September 4, 1989, reflects the emphasis on civic and religious responsibility basic to his life.

149.   "Homecoming," by Alida Connolly, recorded in St. Johns, Arizona, on July 11, 1988, is the poem she wishes to have read at her funeral.

150.   "This Is My Creed," by Alida Connolly, was recorded July 11, 1988, in St. Johns, Arizona. The final line, "a race well done," is an interesting variation of the familiar "a race well run."

151.   Like Oliver Wendell Holmes's "The Last Leaf," Alida's "The Harvest of Leaves" uses the seasonal cycles of a deciduous tree as a metaphor for life. This performance was recorded July 11, 1988, in St. Johns, Arizona.

152.   Tex Bonnet recorded a version of the song "Don't Fence Me In" written by Cole Porter for a Broadway musical the same day he performed this version with the same name as a recitation, October 16, 1979, in Winnemucca, Nevada. His recitation is not the same as the Cole Porter song although they share an image and a theme.

And I'll Tell You Another

153.   Billy attributed this poem to Sharlot Hall (1870-1943), a pioneer Arizona poet who traveled the state by horse and wagon gathering material for her writing and sharing her poems with the people she met. Billy's version was recorded at Northern Arizona University, May 11, 1971.

Index of Authors and Performers

Italic numerals refer to recitation numbers. Others indicate page numbers.

Index of Titles and First Lines

Numerals refer to recitation numbers.
Titles are in italics, and first lines are in ordinary roman type.